MERIDIAN

Crossing Aesthetics

Werner Hamacher

& David E. Wellbery

Editors

Translated by
Rodney Livingstone

Stanford
University
Press

Stanford
California
1999

SOUND FIGURES

Theodor W. Adorno

Assistance for the translation was provided by Inter Nationes, Bonn.

Sound Figures was originally published in German as *Klangfiguren*.
The present translation follows the text in Theodor W. Adorno,
Musikalische Schriften I–III, vol. 16 of *Gesammelte Schriften*,
ed. Rolf Tiedemann, © 1978, Suhrkamp Verlag Frankfurt am Main.

The translation of "Bourgeois Opera" is a revised version of
the one by David J. Levin in *Opera Through Other Eyes*,
ed. Levin (Stanford, Calif.: Stanford University Press, 1994).

Contents

Translator's Acknowledgment

I should like to take the opportunity to acknowledge the generous assistance of Dr. Rick Graebner of the Music Department of Southampton University, who read through the entire manuscript and made countless suggestions and improvements, as well as contributing a number of footnotes.

R.L.

SOUND FIGURES

§ Some Ideas on the Sociology of Music

The creation of a sociology of music in terms of accepted scientific conventions would mean defining its scope, dividing it up into specific branches, reporting on the problems it tackles, the theories it develops, and any results it produces, and integrating all these, as far as is possible, into a coherent system. This would be to treat it as one branch of sociology among others. It would then be organized into subordinate disciplines, which would at best be assembled under one roof, a single "frame of reference." But society is both an umbrella concept that subsumes every more specialized subsystem within itself and something that manifests itself as a totality in each of its branches. It cannot be conceived, therefore, as either a general collection of more or less unconnected facts or a supreme logical category to be arrived at by a progressive process of generalization. Instead it is a process; it produces both itself and its subordinate parts, welding them together into a totality, in Hegel's sense of the term. The only knowledge of society worthy of the name is one that would grasp both that totality and its parts through the process of critical analysis. For this reason it appears more profitable to think in terms of models of musical sociology than to aspire to an overview of the subject and its methods. Such an overview can all too easily exhaust itself in self-important gestures, making a virtue of its incorruptible objectivity as a way of compensating for its failure to shed light on its material. Let us abandon the separation of method from subject matter. Method is not something to be applied to an object in a fixed, unvarying manner. Instead, method should adapt itself to its object and legitimate itself by the light it sheds on it. The individual fields of research should be treated not as neatly coordinated with, or subordinated to, each other, but in terms of their dynamic interrelationships. Even the plausible distinction between the spheres of production, reproduction, and consumption should be thought of as a social product in need of explanation rather than simple acceptance.

So conceived, a sociology of music has a dual relationship to its object: an internal and an external dimension. Any social meaning inherent in music is not identical with that music's place and function in society. The two do not even need to be in harmony with each other, and indeed nowadays are often in conflict. Great music of integrity, once the essence of a genuine consciousness, can degenerate into ideology and even into a socially necessary illusion. Even Beethoven's most authentic compositions, works notable, in Hegel's phrase, for the unfolding of truth, have been debased into cultural commodities by the music industry. They supply consumers with prestige and even with emotions that they do not themselves possess but to which their nature cannot remain immune. Music in its present state is defined by contradictions such as that between the social content of a work and the context in which it is received by the public. As a manifestation of objective spirit it finds itself situated in society and functions within it. It plays its role not just in the life of mankind, but also in the economic process, as a commodity. At the same time it is essentially social in itself. Society has been inscribed in its very meaning and its categories, and the task of a sociology of music is to decipher them. This compels it to acquire an understanding of music that encompasses the most minute technical details. It can only transcend the disastrously superficial reduction of products of the intellect to social circumstances if it locates the social dimension in their autonomous form and perceives it as aesthetic content. Sociological concepts that are imposed on music from outside, without being able to demonstrate their credentials in strictly musical terms, remain devoid of force. The social meaning of musical phenomena is inseparable from their truth or untruth, their success or their failure, their contradictory nature or their inner coherence. The social theory of music implies its critique.

This means that the sociology of music deals with music as ideology, but not only as ideology. Music only becomes ideological when it is objectively untrue or when its nature contradicts its function. The fact that music is fundamentally nonconceptual—it does not directly proclaim any teachings nor can it be reduced to any unambiguous assertions—may seem to imply that it is free of ideology. We may refute this, however, by pointing to the use made of music by politicians and other authorities who regard it as a cohesive social force, as something capable of creating the illusion of immediate community within a reified and alienated society. This was the fate of music under fascism, and this is how it is manipulated in totalitarian countries today, and even in nontotalitarian ones with their "national and youth music" movements, their cult of social bonding [*Bindungen*] and collectivity as such, and the integration of the individual into busy communal activities. The rationalized world, which is actually still the irrational world, disguises its true nature by cultivating the realm of the unconscious. This means that the sociology of music must maintain its vigilance so as to prevent the social legitimacy of music from being confused with its social function, that is, with its impact and popular appeal in society as it is actually constituted. It must not allow itself to be forced by its own definition onto the side of music as a social force. Its critical role increases in importance as musical activities of the most varied kinds are made increasingly subservient to unexplained trends and needs—mainly those of domination.

But music is not just ideology in the sense of being a clear tool of domination. It is also a manifestation of false consciousness, a way of trivializing conflict and producing spurious reconciliations. Traditionally, the novels of a writer like Gustav Freytag were labeled ideological, and in the same way we may think of much music of the so-called heyday of liberalism as ideological—even including some very famous works, such as those of Tchaikovsky—because of their use of the symphonic form, for example. Instead of working through the conflicts contained in their own premises, such works are content to place those conflicts on view, superficially, decoratively, but so as to obtain the maximum effect. They operate with stereotypes much like the black-and-white characters of the conventional novel. There is a complete failure to perceive the relationship between the whole and the parts as an interactive, even conflictual process of production. In fact the effectiveness of such pieces—the possibility of easy listening—is based on that refusal to work things through and that smoothing out of contradictions, which thus become reduced to mere components of a reified form that is inflated by simple contrasts. The popularity of such pieces is founded on reducing to a sensuous plane something that could be justified only in intellectual terms.

At every point here the true problem of the sociology of music is one of mediation. The nonconceptual nature of music deprives us of the kind of evidence for our insights that in the case of traditional literature appears to be legitimated by its contents. Hence assertions about the intrinsic ideological character of music are constantly in danger of being reduced to mere analogies. The only remedy here is a technical and physiognomical analysis that describes formal features as elements of an organized musical meaning (or that points to the absence of such meaning) and goes on to infer social significance from those features. The task is to articulate the social meaning of the formal constituents of music—its logic, in short. How to learn or practice this is something that is scarcely capable of abstract formulation. Attempts to achieve it tend to be arbitrary and to be justified only through internal consistency and the ability to shed light on music's individual features. The crucial task facing a sociology of music—the task of socially decoding music itself—resists the kind of positivistic verification of tangible realities of the sort provided by data about musical consumption or the description of musical organizations, but which shies away from analysis of the music itself. The precondition of a productive sociology of music is to understand the language of music. This goes far beyond anything available to the sociologist concerned merely with applying his own categories to music, but also far beyond anything communicated by the official and ossified musical culture of the conservatories or university musicology. The future of the sociology of music will depend essentially on the refinement and reflexive powers of the methods of analyzing music itself and their relation to the intellectual substance that can be realized in art only by virtue of the technical categories at work in it.

Taken globally, the function of music in society is mainly to act as a diversion. Questions such as whether Mr. X plays Beethoven's G Major Piano Concerto better than Mr. Y, or whether the voice of the young tenor has been put under too much of a strain, have scarcely anything to do with the substance and meaning of music. But it all contributes to the creation of the cultural veil, the concern with spirit degraded to the level of "education," which prevents countless listeners from obtaining any perception of more essential realities. The neutralization of music through its reduction to matters of cultural activity and cultural chitchat would itself be a rewarding subject of investigation by a sociology of music, as long as it refused to collude in that neutralizing process. But to attempt to combat that neutralization by simply invoking the living power of music to affect people, without realizing the extent to which music depends on society as a whole, is to capitulate to ideology even more abjectly. Music is especially prone to that capitulation because its nonconceptual nature encourages its listeners to think of themselves as feeling subjects, to give their thoughts free rein, and to think whatever ideas happen to come into their heads. Music functions as a kind of wish fulfillment and vicarious gratification, but unlike film it does not really get caught in the act. This gratification extends from dozing off—the promotion of a condition that largely precludes any rational or critical behavior—to the cult of passion, the philosophical irrationalism that has been so intimately linked with repressive and violent social tendencies ever since the nineteenth century. Music makes its own contribution to the "ideology of the unconscious," even though this frequently conflicts with its own form and meaning. Impotent and deluded in the face of the progressive freezing of the world under the pressures of rationalization, it provides solace, it "warms the heart"; on the other hand—as in Wagner—it may even go so far as to justify the persistent irrationality of the world as a whole.

It was Max Weber, the author of what up to now has been the most comprehensive and ambitious attempt at a sociology of music (it can now be found as an appendix to the new edition of *Wirtschaft und Gesellschaft*), who first identified "rationalization" as the crucial concept for the sociology of music. In so doing, his richly documented argument struck a blow against the irrationalism that prevails in the current view of music, albeit without really making much of a dent in the bourgeois religion of music. There can be no doubt that the history of music exhibits a progressive process of rationalization. Its different stages are the Guidonian reforms, the introduction of mensural notation, the invention of continuo and of equal temperament, and finally, the trend to integral musical construction, which has advanced irresistibly since the time of Bach and has now reached an extreme. But rationalization—which is inseparable from the historical process of the bourgeoisification of music—represents only one of the social features of music, just as rationality itself, Enlightenment, is no more than one aspect of the history of a society that is still developing in an irrational and "natural" manner even today. Within the global development in which music shared in the progressive emergence of rationality, music at the same time always remained the voice of all who fell by the wayside or were sacrificed on the altar of the rational. This defines the central social contradiction of music, and by the same token it also formulates the tension that has driven musical productivity hitherto. By virtue of its basic material, music is the art in which the prerational, mimetic impulses ineluctably find their voice, even as they enter into a pact with the processes leading to the progressive domination of matter and nature. This is the material to which music owes its ability to transcend the business of mere self-preservation, an ability that led Schopenhauer to define it as the immediate objectification of the will and to place it at the apex of the hierarchy of the arts. If anywhere, it is in music that art rises above the mere repetition of what just happens anyway. At the same time, however, this material fits it for the constant reproduction of stupidity. The very element that raises music above ideology is also what brings it closest to it. As a carefully cultivated preserve of the irrational in the midst of the rationalized universe, music becomes negativity pure and simple, as this is rationally planned, produced, and administered by the Culture Industry. This irrationality has been calculated down to the nth degree, and its sole effect is to ensure that people are kept in line. As such, it constitutes a parody of the protest against the dominance of the concept of classification, a protest of which music is uniquely capable when, as with all the great composers since Monteverdi, it subjects itself to the discipline of the rational. Only by virtue of such rationality can it transcend rationality.

In such phenomena as the socially manipulated irrationality of music we see expressed the much larger reality of the primacy of production. Sociological research that would prefer to avoid the problems of analyzing production and to confine itself to questions of distribution or consumption remains imprisoned in the mechanisms of the market and hence gives its sanction to the primacy of the commodity character of music, even though to investigate this quality should be one of the foremost tasks of a sociology of music. Empirical studies that take audience responses as their starting point, on the assumption that they constitute the ultimate, secure foundation for scientific data, lose validity because they fail to see these responses for what they have become, that is to say, as functions of production. And incidentally, we must note that what used to be thought of as artistic production has now been replaced by a production process organized and controlled on the pattern of industrial processes, a change that has affected the entire realm of music for the consumer. Furthermore, the difficulties of nailing down the social effects of music are scarcely smaller than those involved in discovering the meaning of their intrinsic social content. In the end, all that can be determined is the opinions of interviewees about music and their relationship to it. These opinions, however, have been preformed by social mechanisms such as propaganda and the selection of material on offer, and hence remain inconclusive in themselves. What respondents think of as their relationship to music, especially in the form in which they verbalize their experience, falls far short of what actually transpires subjectively—in terms of both individual and social psychology. If, for example, they claim that what attracts them to a piece of music is its melody or rhythm, they will normally have only a very hazy idea of what those words entail. They will use those concepts to designate a vague, conventional meaning: in the case of rhythm, no more than the interaction of the formal beat with syncopated deviations from it; in the case of melody, the easily identified top part in eight-measure periods. The analysis of one's own musical experience is a problematic business for anyone who has not made a special study of music or who lacks exceptional ability and training in introspection. Moreover, reliable experimental methods that are intended to avoid such difficulties by relying on precise counting and measuring lead nowhere. Whether a listener's pulse quickens, and so forth, is an irrelevant abstraction in a discussion of his specific reaction to music he has heard. Consider research of the kind developed by Frank Stanton in the Princeton Radio Research Project. Here the attempt was made to discover indicators that register whether people have a positive or negative reaction to specific passages in a piece of music. Such a procedure is based on a view of listening that is both atomistic and overphysical. It conceives of reactions to music as the sum of sensory stimuli, a theory that itself stands in need of scrutiny. The primitive nature of such experimental methods rides roughshod over the complexities involved in our responses to even the most primitive pieces of music. The preoccupation with precision becomes a fetish that conceals from the investigator the irrelevance of his conclusions. This is not to assert that such laboratory techniques are wholly devoid of scientific value; in many ways they fit their victims like a glove. They may have a use in establishing quantitative estimates of social attitudes toward music; but even these will be useful only if the sociologist confronts listeners with the meaning of what they are reacting to and the objective social conditions of such reactions.

A further consideration is that the concept of production should not be hypostatized, nor should it be simply equated with the social production of goods in general. If a special sphere of musical production has developed and made itself independent of reproduction and consumption, this must be regarded as itself the consequence of a social process, specifically, the process of bourgeoisification. It should be analyzed in connection with such categories as the autonomy of the subject, on the one hand, and of the commodity and its value, on the other. The salient point is that it was above all thanks to the social division of labor that the production of music came to diverge from its other aspects. This is what made the great music of the last 350 years possible—a fact overlooked by naive sociological observers who would like to revoke that autonomy in the sphere of production in deference to the idol of musical immediacy. Musical production is not "fundamental" in the same sense that the production of food is fundamental to the sustenance of society. It does not emerge until much later. Historically, however, it has acquired an importance that a contemporary sociology of music cannot ignore. At the same time, features of production such as the autonomy of expressive need and above all of the objective logic of the composition must be distinguished from the laws governing the production of commodities for the marketplace that have played a role throughout the entire bourgeois epoch and whose influence secretly affects even the most sublime aesthetic moments. The tension between these two elements is one of the most crucial features of musical production. They were not only in opposition to each other but also mediated by each other in the sense that over considerable periods of time the autonomy of a piece of music was honored by society in the name of the purity of art and the rights of the individual. Even the freedom of music from social purposes has been boosted by society itself. Only in our day, when the entire culture of music appears increasingly to have been taken over by administration, does that freedom seem to have been abrogated, in the same way that the internal laws governing the development of music seem to have turned against its own inner freedom. But even the individualism of high bourgeois music is not to be taken literally. It cannot be constructed on the model of private property, as if great composers could create music as they wished by virtue of their unique psychology. As with every productive artist, the composer "owns" far less of his own composition than can be imagined by outsiders, who still think in terms of the creative genius. The greater a piece of music, the more the composer acts as its executor, as someone who complies with what the work requires of him. Hans Sachs's assertion in *Die Meis-*

tersinger that the composer makes the rule and then follows it reveals the dawning awareness of this truth and also of the "nominalism" of modernism, which is no longer faced with the demands of any substantial artistic order. But even a rule someone has proposed for himself seems to be only that. In reality it reflects the objective stage reached by the language and the forms of music. Both are socially mediated. The path leading to their inner core is at the same time the only path leading to the discovery of their social significance. The composer's subjectivity is not something added on to these objective conditions and desiderata. It proves its worth precisely because it elevates his own impulse, which of course cannot be imagined out of existence, and merges it with that social objectivity. This means not only that he is tied to the objective social preconditions of production, but that his own achievement is itself social, even though it is the most subjective thing about him, a kind of logical synthesis of his own nature. The compositional subject is no individual thing, but a collective one. All music, however individual it may be in stylistic terms, possesses an inalienable collective substance: every sound says "we."

This collective substance, however, is only rarely that of a specific class or group. Attempts to reduce music to its social origins have something dogmatic about them. Neither a composer's origins nor his life history, nor even the impact of his music on a particular social stratum, yields any compelling sociological insights. The gestural language of Chopin's music is aristocratic—in a sense that would have to be specified concretely. Its popularity, however, stems precisely from this aristocratic manner. We may say that it transforms the ordinary citizen, who aspires to hear himself in its mellifluous melancholy, into a gentleman. Music that is alive today is bourgeois in its entirety; prebourgeois music is played only out of historical interest. And the claim of the Eastern bloc that what they produce emanates from socialism is refuted by the music itself, which simply warms up late Romantic, philistine clichés and sedulously avoids everything that threatens to deviate from conformist consumer needs. But by the same token, music also reflects the trends and contradictions of bourgeois society as a totality. The idea of a dynamic unity, a totality, in traditional great music was nothing but the idea of society itself. The reflection of social activity—which means ultimately the production process—lies fused with the utopian idea of "free human beings" united in solidarity. To this day the insoluble contradiction implicit in all great music is that of the general and the particular—and the greatness of the music depends on whether it gives formal shape to this contradiction and renders it visible, instead of concealing it behind a harmonious façade. The essence of that contradiction lies in the fact that the interests of the individual and those of humanity point in different directions. Music transcends society by enabling this contradiction to find expression and at the same time by reconciling the irreconcilable in an anticipatory image. But ever since the middle of the nineteenth century, ever since *Tristan*, the more profoundly it has devoted itself to this cause, the more it has become alienated from any understanding with existing society. If music on its own initiative makes itself into something desired, something socially useful, something by which human beings may profit, then, by the light of its own truth content, it betrays those human beings. Its relationship to exchange value is, like that of all the arts in our day, dialectical through and through.

If ascribing works of music to particular social interests and tendencies is a dubious practice, it remains true nevertheless that specific social characteristics can be read off from traditional music. No one is likely to fail to register the somewhat forced echoes of a secure bourgeois background in Mendelssohn. No less obvious is the aura of the more progressive, upper middle class in Richard Strauss. His intuitionist *élan vital* with its hostility toward the pedantry of any well-honed musical logic, coupled with a certain brutality, a residue of vulgarity, is not dissimilar to the expansionist outlook of the German industrial bourgeoisie. Freedom from stuffy narrow-mindedness is combined with imperialist ruthlessness. Compelling though such characterizations are—and they are probably of greater value than the more accurate data collected by musical statisticians—it is no easy task to justify them according to the criteria laid down by the established sciences. It is at this point that the sociology of music must combine its talent for an empathetic understanding of music with the ability to distance itself from the artistic phenomenon so as to make it socially transparent. A physiognomical eye for the social significance of the formal languages of art is an indispensable element of the sociology of music. It may base itself on the canonical rule that all musical forms, all the materials and elements of the language of music, were once contents. They bear witness to social processes, and their social meanings must be brought to life again by the persistent observer. He should not confine himself to the social origins of these elements, their connection with song and dance, for example, but must focus on the forces that have transformed elements that were substantive, social, and functional in origin into compositional and formal features and that have developed them further.

These forces are complex. On the one hand, they relate to the quasi-autonomous, internal development of music, much as the history of philosophy consists of a more or less self-contained body of problems. This is the side of the history of music that comes closest to intellectual history [*Geistesgeschichte*]. It differs from the latter only in that it is concerned not just with a subjective "understanding" of the composer's intentions, but also with the objective technical aspects of music. Like Leibniz's monads, the autonomous development of music is "windowless," yet at the same time it reflects the entire universe, simply by virtue of its own logic. Thus the integrated mode of composition that grows out of demands for ever greater inner coherence reflects the tendencies of bourgeois society to achieve an ever greater integration because music's underlying dominant categories are identical with those of the bourgeois mind, even though it is not always possible to demonstrate the impact of external social forces on them. On the other hand—and from this point of view the history of music is at variance with intellectual history—the internal development of music, whose social implications have to be uncovered in each particular instance, is anything but self-contained. Music develops in accordance with its own internal laws, which are secretly those of society. But again, it can also be moved and deflected directly by social force fields. To that extent it does not exhibit a seamless stylistic progression, a continuum. The *style galant* of the early eighteenth century, which displaced Bach and the stage of mastery of the language of music he had achieved, is to be explained not with reference to the logical development of music but in terms of the consumer, the needs of a bourgeois clientele. In the same way, Hector Berlioz's innovations are largely unconnected with solving the problems thrown up by Beethoven. They are far more readily explained by the emergence of industrial techniques unrelated to music, but which led to a radically different view of technique from those of classical composition. In Berlioz and the composers who directly followed him, Liszt and, later on, Richard Strauss, the achievements of Viennese classicism are ignored, much as the latter had ignored those of Bach. Such ruptures are just as much a part of the sociology of music as the continuities, and the study of the relationship between the two would not be the least important aspect of the subject. In general it is through such ruptures, such discontinuities, rather than directly, that the main social tendencies governing music come to prevail. This rules out a straightforward, linear account of musical development. Such an account could in any case refer only to the stage reached in the rational mastery of the musical material, and not to the musical quality of the compositions themselves. The quality of the works is of course inseparable from that degree of formal mastery, but is by no means identical with it. Moreover, even that increase in formal mastery advances in a spiral movement that can be comprehended only by a knowledge that is also aware of what has been sacrificed or left by the wayside. For such a conception of the history of music, antinomies, unavoidable contradictions, play a crucial part in the process of fermentation of social knowledge. The technical inconsistencies in a composer of such supreme grasp of form as Richard Wagner proclaim the social impossibility of what he wanted to achieve: a work of art that would provide bourgeois society with a cultic unity. They reveal the untruth of the objective substance of his works and thereby their ideological nature. The reduction of successful, great music to its social origins is as dubious as the reduction of any truth. However, any failure that does not arise simply from defects of talent but is perceived to have a necessity of its own does point to social causation. Moreover, the concept of talent is not one that a sociology of music can afford to leave unexplored, as if it were a natural given. The different epochs and forms of society nurture the talents that are appropriate to them, including the critical talents. At the present time, music is characterized by attempts at integration that are being taken to extremes and are overshadowed by the process of reification. Such attempts do not follow simply from the present state of musical technique and the procedures developed by Schoenberg's Viennese school. They also harmonize with the administered world that they unconsciously mimic and, indeed, through the process of defining it, transcend. The criterion of the social truth of music today is the extent to which it enters into opposition to the society from which it springs and in which it has its being—in short, the extent to which it becomes "critical," however indirectly. That was possible in certain epochs without disrupting the process of social communication. An instance is the age which people are now pleased to describe as that of the emerging bourgeoisie. The Ninth Symphony could proclaim the unity of what fashion had strictly separated, and could still find an audience. Since then a direct correlation has emerged between the social isolation of music and the seriousness of its objective social content, even though isolation as such may be purely solipsistic and hence no guarantee of social content on its own.

The sociological interpretation of music is the better grounded, the higher the quality of the music. It becomes dubious in the case of simpler, more regressive, or worthless music. It is harder to see why one hit song should stand higher in public esteem than another than to distinguish between the social significance of public reactions to different works by Beethoven. The analytical procedures developed by the Radio Research Project were applied to light music in America, and their analysis of this music as the product of a monopolistic market hit the nail on the head. Nevertheless, the most banal piece of light music is still the most mysterious as to its social existence and impact. To these mysteries belong the question asked by the Viennese theoretician Erwin Ratz, who inquired how it can be said that a piece of music is vulgar and indeed what the social and aesthetic meaning of banality can be said to be in general. The answer to such questions implies that we can answer the opposite question too: How can it be possible for music to rise above the realm of mere being, to which of course it owes its very existence? It would be important to investigate the social implications of the division of music into serious and light. This division has become institutionalized and established by categories, such as that of popular music, that now stand rigidly opposed to each other as fixed entities. This division corresponds to the distinction between high and low art established in antiquity, a distinction that proves nothing less than the failure of all cultures that have ever existed hitherto. Now of course the Culture Industry is preparing to take over the whole of music. Even music that is different can survive economically and hence socially only under the wing of the Culture Industry it detests—one of the most flagrant contradictions in the social situation of music. No doubt, thanks to such trends as the increasing sophistication of jazz, this centralized control will enable lowbrow music to be brought up to the standard of the latest technological developments, much as happens in the cinema in the case of its cruder, barbaric elements. At the same time, music is reduced by the dominant bureaucracies to the level of the commodity production that lies concealed behind the wishes of the consumer. And because those wishes are manipulated and reproduced they tend to converge with those of the bureaucracy. As a branch of leisure-time activity, music comes to resemble the very things it opposes, even though it only derives its meaning from that opposition: that is its sociological prognosis. The self-contradiction in which it is caught up gives the lie to the coming integration of production, reproduction, and consumption. The unity of contemporary music culture under the patronage of the Culture Industry is one of total self-alienation. The intolerance of the Culture Industry toward everything that does not bear its stamp has become so all-embracing that this alienation has ceased to be visible to the consumer. What has been achieved is a false reconciliation. What should be close at hand, the "consciousness of suffering," becomes unbearably alien. The most alien thing of all, however, the process that hammers the machinery into men's consciousness and has ceased to contain anything that is human, invades them body and soul and appears to be the nearest and dearest thing of all.

§ Bourgeois Opera

To focus our thoughts about contemporary theater on opera is certainly not justifiable in terms of opera's immediate relevance. Not only has the crisis of opera been well known and persistent in Germany for thirty years (that is, since the time of the great economic crisis), not only have opera's place and function become questionable in society today, but beyond this, and quite apart from its reception, opera has come to seem peripheral and a matter of indifference, an impression that is combated only by somewhat forced attempts at innovation. Indeed, it is hardly a coincidence that these attempts at innovation usually get stuck halfway, especially as far as music itself is concerned. If we are to speak of opera at all we should rather do so because in more respects than one it marks a prototype of the theatrical—indeed, a prototype of precisely those elements that have been profoundly undermined today. There are aspects of the collapse of opera that belong to the most fundamental level of the stage. We experience these perhaps most drastically in opera's relation to costume. Costume is essential to opera: in contrast to a play, an opera without costume would be a paradox. If the gestures of singers—which they often bring along as if straight from the prop room—are themselves already part of their costume, then their voices are entirely put on—donned, as it were, by natural human beings as soon as they step upon the operatic stage. The American expression "cloak-and-dagger," the idea of a scene in which two lovers sing to each other while murderers lurk left and right behind pillars, eccentrically expresses something of the matter itself: that aura of disguise, of miming, which attracts the child to the theater—not because the child wants to see a work of art, but because it wants to confirm its own pleasure in dissimulation. The closer opera gets to a parody of itself, the closer it is to its own most particular element.

This may explain why some of the most authentic operas, like *Der Freischütz*, but also like *The Magic Flute* and *Il trovatore*, have their true home in the children's matinee and embarrass the adult, who imagines himself too sensible for them, simply because he no longer understands their pictorial language. Traces of this element of opera cling to every great drama, and the act of theater performance becomes unbalanced when those traces fall victim to intellectualization, like the last memory of the green wagon. However, the imperative of intellectualization cannot be suspended by calling for a return to naïveté. The Director's speech in the "Prelude in the Theater" was such a call, and that is why Goethe subjects it to irony. *Faust* balances on the narrow ridge traversing the naive and the intellectual and articulates its own consciousness of that. In the most powerful works of the human spirit that have been bequeathed to the theater, works like *Hamlet*, we can perceive that operatic quality, like a trace of *Simon Boccanegra*, and if it were erased, the truth content of the tragedy of individuation and alienation would remain impotent.

Opera is governed by the element of illusion [*Schein*], in the sense of Benjamin's aesthetics, where it is positioned in contrast to the element of play [*Spiel*]. The use of the term *Spieloper* for a special genre attests precisely to the primacy of illusion, in that it emphasizes an element that otherwise recedes. Opera has reached the state of crisis because the genre cannot dispense with illusion without surrendering itself, and yet it must want to do so. Opera runs head on into the aesthetic limits of demystification [*Versachlichung*]. For instance, if a producer—made wise or weary by innumerable backstage jokes—were to present a *Lohengrin* in which the swan is replaced by a beam of light, the premise of the entire work would be attacked to such an extent as to be rendered pointless. If the animal of fable can no longer be tolerated, this implies a rebellion against the plot's horizon of imagination, and the abstract swan only serves to underscore this. A child who attends a *Freischütz* and finds the Wolf's Glen reduced to nature symbolism is right to feel cheated out of the best part. Demystified opera inevitably threatens to degenerate into an arts and crafts affair, where stylization threatens to substitute for the disintegrating style. Modernity, which does not really intervene in the matter, becomes mere packaging, becomes modernism—but despite all this, the operatic stage director finds himself forced again and again into all sorts of desperate maneuvers.

The limits of demystification reveal themselves even more drastically in the production than in the mise-en-scène. When the demystification of opera began more than sixty years ago, the "cloak-and-dagger" principle was, in all innocence, fervently maintained in the name of realism: *Cavalleria* and *Pagliacci* can tell us a thing or two in this regard. But even new music, in which opera is self-reflexive, has failed to clear that hurdle. Not only has Schoenberg as an operatic composer remained within the realm of expressive opera and thus of *musica ficta*, of illusion, both in aesthetic terms and in terms of his relationship to the text; but with artistic finesse and the subtlest touch, Alban Berg—to this day, the only composer in the new century whose inspiration was primarily operatic—has sustained the world of illusion as an operatic essence distanced from empirical reality. In *Wozzeck*, the monological isolation of the half-crazed hero affords a medium of dreamlike displacement in which the drama of the setting sun and the imaginary conspiracy of the Freemasons play into one another. *Lulu* is modeled on the circus, in accordance with Wedekind's sense that something of opera resided there, namely a consciousness of the muteness of the spoken word, and Lulu's coloratura soprano has to perform a vocal ballet that prevents any identification of the events with the everyday, which of course makes the performance eminently more difficult. Incidentally, in his most productive stage works, *Renard* and *L'histoire du soldat*, Stravinsky—who with good reason avoided opera and finally sought to master it through simple stylistic imitation—likewise had recourse to the circus, probably under the influence of the cubist painters. This was very much in the spirit of Wedekind, for whom the circus was "corporeal"—that is, an art form removed from the spell of expression—and yet entirely detached from empirical reality. It is when opera seeks an identification with that reality, when it seeks a solid representation of some so-called social problem—as in Max Brand's *Maschinist Hopkins*—that it falls victim to helpless and corny symbolizing.

The limits of the demystification of opera revealed themselves perhaps most drastically when an archenemy of Romanticism like Brecht—a man who once said of a concert performance of Hindemith's *Cardillac*, "That is *Tannhäuser!*"—took an interest in opera. He and Kurt Weill used theatrical techniques to inquire whether music was supposed to be "cold" toward the theater or whether it was supposed to "warm up" stage events, and they decided in favor of the latter. In works like *The Threepenny Opera* they left expression in its place, albeit as shredded and parodic expression—and this was presumably the main reason for its broad popular success. This was one of the last successful works of musical theater that was avant-garde, at least on the level of drama.

But to call opera an entirely Romantic genre would be to miss the essence of both opera and the Romantic, especially since its history reflected all the different facets of style subsumed under such terms as "classical" and "Romantic." Even Wagnerian music-drama, which music history situates in late Romanticism, is full of anti-Romantic strains, among which the technological perhaps assumes primacy. It would be appropriate to think of opera as the specifically bourgeois genre that, in the midst of, and with the methods appropriate to, a world bereft of magic, paradoxically endeavors to preserve the magical element of art. This thesis concerning the bourgeois nature of opera sounds provocative for more than one reason. For ever since Prospero laid down his magic staff, ever since Don Quixote encountered truths in windmills, the overall aesthetic tendency of the bourgeois era has of course been the opposite, that of disillusionment. But the positivist tendency of bourgeois art—if we can call it that—never ruled pure and unchallenged. Just as aesthetic magic itself bears something of enlightenment within itself, in that it renounces the claim to unmediated truth and sanctions illusion as a special realm, so bourgeois art—in order to be at all possible as art—has once again brought magic to the fore even while transforming it. Opera was particularly suitable for this process, since music enhances the very existence against which it strikes. Other genres, too, have arisen out of ostentation (the archetype of all operatic illusion) and in the context of the bourgeoisification of art: according to recent theories, even the cathedral arose thus. In his study "Egoism and Freedom Movements," Max Horkheimer has demonstrated the significant role of pomp for all bourgeois ideology, and in this we might perhaps see a secularization of, or a substitute for, cultic, ritualistic display. Secular ostentation—the material representation, as it were, of the irrational power and greatness of the very class that imposed the ban on irrationality itself—has been essential to opera from a very early stage of its development right up to Richard Strauss: in opera, costume can scarcely be separated from ostentation.

There are also historical grounds for ascribing opera to the bourgeoisie rather than to feudal or courtly culture, with which it has been linked by convention. Fullness of sound and choral masses alone point toward an incomparably wider circle than the aristocratic one, which asserted its claim to the privilege of the proscenium but left the stalls, the actual auditorium of opera, to the bourgeoisie. We might indeed ask whether in a strict sense there has ever been a feudal or aristocratic art at all. Did not the feudal lords, who despised all menial work, always cause art to be created by members of the bourgeoisie? And has not the Hegelian master/ slave dialectic always prevailed in art, with the consequence that whoever works on the object is also granted control over it, so that bourgeois artists working for the high and mighty prefer nevertheless to address their equals rather than their patrons? The depiction of feudal relations, as they have been portrayed in works of art since Homeric times, already presupposes that these relations are no longer accepted at face value, but instead have in a certain sense become problematic to themselves. Feudal lords rarely think in "restorationist" terms; instead, from Plato to de Maistre, they never look for anything other than autonomous, rationally speculating subjects who seek explanations for an already past state of things. Similarly, feudal lords, in the form of kings and heroes, are the subject matter of older art, and so they cannot shape that matter at a distance from themselves: Volker, lord of Alzey, is Hagen's friend, but he is not Hagen.

In any case, the origins of opera have an element of rational assertion [*Setzung*] and construction—indeed, of abrupt discontinuity—that would be extremely difficult to reconcile with conceptions of feudal traditionalism. Like late technological genres such as film, opera owes its existence to a decision that invokes historical parallels—the revitalizing of ancient tragedy—but that, apart from the very rudimentary madrigal-opera, fits into no historical continuity. According to an essay written by Hanns Gutman some thirty years ago, opera was invented by literati, namely a Florentine circle of connoisseurs, writers, and musicians of an ascetic and reformist bent toward the end of the sixteenth century. The genre first blossomed in the Republic of Venice, that is, under the social conditions of an evolved bourgeoisie, and the first great opera composers—Monteverdi, Cavalli, Cesti—belong there; it is hardly coincidental that the German vogue for opera developed in the Hanseatic city of Hamburg, thanks to Reinhard Keiser. The actual courtly phase of opera, the late seventeenth and the eighteenth centuries, the world of maestros, prima donnas, and castrati which grew out of the Neapolitan school, already marks the late phase of absolutism in which the general emancipation of the bourgeoisie was so far advanced that opera hardly isolated itself from the bourgeoisie. It was around this time that the bourgeoisie also forced its way onto the musical stage, into the plot of the intermezzo.

Opera shares with film not just the suddenness of its invention but also many of its functions, among them the presentation to the masses of the body of inherited common knowledge, as well as the massiveness of the means, employed teleologically in the material of opera as in film, which lent opera—at least opera since the middle of the nineteenth century, if not earlier—a similarity to the modern Culture Industry. Meyerbeer had already tackled religious wars and historical state events, personalizing them and thereby neutralizing them, in that nothing of the substance of the conflicts was left; thus the Catholics and Huguenots of the St. Bartholomew's Day massacre are admired side by side, as in a wax museum. Out of this tradition film, particularly technicolor film, in turn shaped its canon. It is, by the way, astounding how early some of the worst abominations of today's Culture Industry announced themselves in opera, at the precise point where the naive person, in looking to the past, expects to find something like the pure autonomy of the genre. In this sense, the text of *Der Freischütz* is already an "adaptation," like those prepared in Hollywood, while the "scriptwriter," Kind, has rerouted the tragic conclusion of the novella of romantic destiny upon which the opera is based into a "happy ending," presumably in deference to the Biedermeier audience, which was already anxiously keeping watch to ensure that the heroes end up married. Even the Wagnerian Humperdinck—although saturated in the defamation of all things commercial by the founders of Bayreuth—turned the tales of the Brothers Grimm into consumer products by making sure that the parents of Hansel and Gretel no longer cast the children out as in the fairy tale, since respect for the devoted father in the late nineteenth century must be preserved at all costs. Such examples demonstrate how deeply opera as a consumer product is entangled in calculations regarding the public—in this sense, too, it is related to film. We cannot allow ourselves to disregard this, as if it were a mere superficiality in the notion of aesthetic autonomy. According to its own logic, dramatic form implies the audience. While we are justified in speaking of poems as such or music as such, to speak of the stage as such is an absurdity.

But the logic of opera has been bound to myth ever since the experiments of the Florentines, even throughout the course of its progressive secularization. This relationship to myth, however, does not imply simply the imitation of mythic interconnections by musical ones—to think of it in such terms was perhaps Wagner's undoing. Rather, in opera, music intervenes in and transforms fate's blind, inescapable ties to nature (as they are represented in Western myths), and the audience is called upon as a witness, if not indeed as a court of appeal. This intervention is itself anticipated in one of the great Greek myths, that of Orpheus, who with music softens the terrible reign of Pluto, to whom he lost Eurydice, only to fall prey once again to the very fate he had just escaped because of his inability to break the spell and to tear his gaze away from that infernal realm. The first authentic opera, Monteverdi's *Orfeo*, took just this as its subject matter; the Gluckian reform went back to Orpheus as the archetype of opera, and it is hardly too much to claim that all opera is Orpheus—a claim that is denied only by Wagnerian music-drama.

The operas that most purely satisfy the requirements of the genre almost always correct myth through music, and thus the statement that opera partakes of the Enlightenment as a total societal movement has an even greater claim to validity than that it partakes of myth. Nowhere is this more evident than with *The Magic Flute*—in which magic weds Freemasonry, rendering the natural powers of fire and water powerless before the sounds of the flute, and in which the spell of the always-same is dissolved. Sarastro's sphere rises out of the realm of the Mothers with its ambiguous interlocking of right and wrong. He knows nothing of the vengeance that Nietzsche, the mythologist and man of the Enlightenment, hoped to eliminate, declaring that redemption from it was his highest goal. In similar vein the fanfare of *Fidelio* consummates almost ritualistically the moment of protest that breaks open the eternal hell of the prison cell and puts an end to the rule of force. This interlocking of myth and Enlightenment defines the bourgeois essence of opera: namely, the combination of imprisonment in a blind and unself-conscious system with the idea of freedom, which arises in its midst. The metaphysics of opera cannot be simply separated from this social dimension. Metaphysics is absolutely not an unchanging realm to be grasped by looking out through the barred windows of the historical; it is the glimmer—albeit a powerless glimmer—of light which falls into the prison itself. The more powerful it becomes, the deeper its ideas embed themselves in history; the more ideological it becomes, the more abstractly it stands opposed to history. Opera, hardly infected by philosophy, has remained more truly philosophical than drama, which contaminated its metaphysical content with conceptual contents. For just that reason, drama lost its metaphysical content, and sacrificed the philosophy it objectively intended to the specific philosophical themes, which it directly addressed.

The unity of truth content and historical content can be graphically demonstrated in those operas whose texts—or, as they are more properly called, libretti—have fallen into disrepute ever since Wagner's criticism: those operas, that is, of the nineteenth century. We can hardly deny the conventionality, the outlandishness, and the manifold silliness of these texts, nor can we deny their affinity to the marketplace, the commodity character that in fact made them into placeholders for the as-yet-unborn cinema. At the same time, we can also hardly fail to recognize that libretti—which are of course not literature but the stimuli of music—contain an antimythological, Enlightenment element, exactly in proportion to that secularized mythical stratum. Paradoxically, libretti contain that element by virtue of their deference toward the self-glorifying and already imperialistically greedy bourgeoisie. In operas like *Il trovatore* or *La forza del destino* this antimythological, Enlightenment element is contained in the way in which the idea of subjection to destiny is taken to the verge of farce. The form of the antimythological in the libretti of the nineteenth century is, however, exogamy, just as on the other hand, and quite logically, Wagner, who surrendered opera to myth as prey, shifted incest to the center of the opera ritual. Already in Mozart's *Seraglio* the voice of humanity (of course, at this point and for the moment, it is merely a *speaking* voice) is that of the exotic tyrant who holds the European couple in custody, in order, like Thoas, to allow them to depart in peace. Since then opera has shown an endless love for those who are of foreign blood or are otherwise "outside." Halévy's *La Juive*, Meyerbeer's *L'Africaine*, *La dame aux camélias* in Verdi's version, and the Egyptian princess Aida, Delibes's *Lakmé*, as well as the slew of gypsies, culminating in *Il trovatore* and *Carmen*: all ostracized or outsiders, around whom passions explode and come into conflict with the established order.

In comparison with this ritual of attempted escape, Wagner, the enemy of convention, remained far more conventional than the librettists whom he despised: with Wotan's primeval wisdom that "everything is according to its kind," he strengthened the dominance of bourgeois society and blocked that escape; indeed, he propagated a biological stew at the very point where sinning brothers and sisters seemingly shock the audience seated in the stalls. The transfiguration of that which is simply according to its kind, which is simply there, into a mystery, that metaphysics, which he wrongly considered far superior to the state spectacles of grand opera, is precisely related to the fact that in Wagner, for the first time, the bourgeois imagination disavows the impulse toward escape and resigns itself to a situation that Wagner himself conceived as worthy of death. In the nineteenth century, the bourgeois yearning for freedom had successfully escaped into the representative spectacle of opera, just as it had escaped into the great novel, whose complexion opera so frequently recalls. Wagner, in whose works myth triumphs over freedom, was the first who on this point showed himself to be quite submissive in his unrealistic music-dramas to the demands of the resigned and cold bourgeois realism. And only in the era of fully fledged imperialism, with Puccini's *Butterfly*, is the exogamy motif built back into the motif of the abandoned girl, but without the navy officer—whose marriage is racially pure—ever being seriously drawn to the Japanese lady. It is precisely because opera, as a bourgeois vacation spot, allowed itself so little involvement in the social conflicts of the nineteenth century that it was able to mirror so crassly the developing tendencies of bourgeois society itself. It is the seal of authenticity in Alban Berg's oeuvre that in his second opera, *Lulu*, simply by following the instinct for play and the operatic sense of costume, he once again chose exogamy and escape as operatic material. The girl without a father and mother is irresistible; everyone who steps into her circle wants to up and leave with her, like Don José with the gypsy. All are overtaken by the vengeance of existing reality, and in the end revenge engulfs the picture of beauty herself, who is different and who, in going under, celebrates the greatest victory of all. In opera, the bourgeois [*der Bürger*] transcends into a human being.

The opera texts offer merely a hint of all this. What is decisive is the relation of the music to the text, or rather—since the opera text has long been what the film script in Hollywood admits to being, namely, a "vehicle"—to the stage and those performing on it. The contradiction between real, live people who speak as in drama, on the one hand, and the medium of singing, on the other, which they make use of in the process, is well known. Again and again—in Florentine monody, the Gluckian reform, the Wagnerian *Sprechgesang*—attempts have been made to get around that contradiction, or to alleviate it, and thus to promote the pure, unbroken, undialectical closure of operatic form. But the contradiction is far too deeply embedded in the form itself to be resolved through half measures like the recitative, which surely has its place in the form as a means to create contrast. If there is any meaning to opera at all, if it is more than a mere agglomerate—and surely we must be allowed to assume this, as far as the great examples of the genre are concerned—then that meaning is to be sought in contradiction itself, rather than in vainly seeking to do away with contradiction in the name of an all too seamless aesthetic unity, the kind that flourishes drearily under the name "symbolic."

In the process we are reminded of the definition Lukács offered forty years ago of a complementary art form—the novel. According to Lukács, the novel asks, in the middle of a disenchanted world: How can life acquire essential meaning? But the answer to that is also sought whenever a live person on a stage starts to sing. The singer's voice seeks to catch something of the reflection of meaning for life itself. Indeed, therein lies the specifically ideological element of opera, its affirmative element. The heroes of Attic tragedy, from which opera is separated by a historical and philosophical chasm, had no need to sing. Through the impact of the tragic process on the omnipresent myth, the meaning—the emancipation of the human subject from its mere place in nature—revealed itself directly. It would not have occurred to anyone to confuse the heroes of the tragic stage with empirical people, since of course what takes place in them and through them is nothing other than the representation of the birth of Man himself.

Opera, in contrast, shaped to an equal extent by Christianity and modern rationality, has from its very inception had to do with empirical people, namely, with those who are reduced to their mere natural essence. This accounts for its peculiar costume-quality: mortals are disguised as heroes or gods, and this disguise is similar in function to their singing. Through song they are exalted and transfigured. The process becomes specifically ideological in that it represents the transfiguration of everyday existence; something that merely *is* presents itself as if its simple being were already greater, as if social orders—as mirrored in operatic convention—were identical with the order of the absolute or the world of ideas. This original ideological essence [*Urwesen*] of opera, which is its besetting sin [*Unwesen*], can be observed in decadent extremes, as in the comic affectations of singers who fetishize their voices as if they truly *were* the gift of God, as the cliché would have it. Surely, the true reason for the sense of disillusionment referred to as "the crisis of opera" is that this ideological element became unbearable, that the presentation of the meaningless as meaningful has become a mockery in a world in which the mere fact of existence, the web of sheer delusion, threatens to swallow people up.

But opera is no more confined to this ideological element than is aesthetic semblance in general. The latter is both: the gilding of what already exists and the reflection of that which would be otherwise; the surrogate for the happiness that is refused to people and the promise of true happiness. The gesture of dramatic characters singing covers up the fact that, even though they are already stylized, they have as little reason to sing as they have opportunity. But in their song there resounds something of the hope for reconciliation with nature: singing, the utopia of prosaic existence, is at the same time also the memory of the prelinguistic, undivided state of Creation, such as rings out at the loveliest moment in Wagner's Ring poem, in the words of the forest bird. Opera's song is the language of passion: not just the exaggerating stylization of existence but also an expression of the truth that nature prevails in man against all convention and mediation, an evocation of pure immediacy. Ever since the invention of figured bass and opera, there has been a doctrine of musical affect, and opera is in its element wherever it gives itself over breathlessly to passion. In this "giving itself over to nature" lies its elective affinity with both myth and the modern successor to the epic, the novel. But passion, which thus finds expression, is appeased insofar as sung passion comes flooding back like an echo, and insofar as the sound of the immediate is reflected, rising above the mediations of the hardened life. And thus the constrained existence of those who sing in the opera is appeased as well, so that they appear unconstrained. That is why opera is no simple copy of myth but its rectification in the medium of music, which is both an element of nature and the refraction of nature through the intellect. In opera, song allows free rein to that which, as passion, incorporates people into the context of nature. At the same time, in song, people experience themselves as nature, which their prejudice against nature resists, and it is thanks to this that the mythic element—that is, passion—is appeased. Their freedom does not lie in the intellect, which high-handedly raises itself above creation. Instead, as music, intellect becomes similar to nature and, on the strength of that similarity, discards its lordly essence.

The genre celebrates this process in the singing of people, who as people are—and must be—ashamed to sing. Opera fulfills itself perhaps most completely where it sacrifices its claim to soul and expression and employs artificial language. The coloratura is no mere form of outward exaggeration, but an extreme in which the idea of opera emerges most purely. Nowhere did Wagner come closer to that extreme than in the role of the forest bird. Berg was inspired by the genius of opera when he wrote the role of Lulu, the destructive force of nature with which his opera becomes reconciled, as a coloratura, without, however, committing himself in the least thereby to reproducing phases of opera that are lost beyond recall.

That Berg could not complete the instrumentation of the work says something about the genre. Opera has been in a precarious situation since the moment when high bourgeois society, which supported it in its fully developed form, ceased to exist. The inner convulsion of the genre and its lack of resonance go together, although the question of which is cause and which effect is not easily determined. Opera was founded on so many conventions that it resounds into a vacuum as soon as these conventions cease to be underwritten by tradition. At once barbaric and precocious, the newcomer who has not learned as a child to be bowled over by opera and to respect its outrageous requirements will feel contempt for it, while the intellectually advanced public has almost ceased to be able to respond immediately or spontaneously to a limited stock of works, which have long since been relegated to the living-room treasure chests of the petty bourgeoisie, like Raphael's paintings, worn out by countless reproductions. However, the growing intrinsic difficulties of the genre—primarily the repression of inner tension, which can be seen in contemporary artistic practice in its entirety—have thus far prevented opera from gaining new relevance through production. In fact, opera corresponds in great measure to the museum, including the latter's positive function, which is to promote the survival of things at risk from being overwhelmed by silence. Taken together, what happens on the operatic stage is for the most part like a museum of bygone images and gestures, to which a retrospective need clings.

This is matched by that type of operatic audience that always wants to hear the same thing and suffers the unfamiliar with hostility or, even worse, with apathy, since, alas, it is condemned to it by its subscription tickets. The state of opera is not to be envied amid an administered humanity, which, regardless of political system, no longer concerns itself with liberation, escape, and reconciliation, as in the opera of the early bourgeoisie, but instead desperately stops up its ears to the sound of humanity in order to be able to survive—happy, contented, and resigned—while caught up in the wheels of industry. At one time, the bourgeoisie was the standard-bearer both of the critique of mythology and of the idea of the ultimate reestablishment of nature; today that critique and the longed-for idea have become equally foreign to it, and the bourgeoisie has reconciled itself as much to its own alienation as to the semblance of inevitability which envelops it—a second mythology. As long as this state of mind and the harsher conditions that dictate it persist, opera can expect little.

This would perhaps change if opera could succeed in freeing itself from its ideological essence with its transfiguration of mere existence, and if it could instead give prominence to that other essence, reconciliatory and antimythological. But can we have the one, the so-called positive, without the other, the negative? The limit of any demystification of the theater through principles of construction is living people, on whom the stage still depends. If theater dispenses with private psychology or the fraud of human immediacy, then it is threatened by prefabricated slogans, by an overarching intention arbitrarily imposed on empirical experience, which would become bearable only if we were to omit from empirical existence everything from which it, in turn, derives its certainty and force. This impasse is hardly resolved by simply dismissing what was disliked by labeling it Romantic—an asceticism that then often leads to the path of least resistance, namely, a regressive, simplistic compositional practice. Consider, for example, the technique of demystifying opera by stringing together thinly motivic materials without development and with stereotypical rhythmic displacements—borrowed from Stravinsky, and consistently inferior to his own mastery; even today, the antidramatic music for musical drama exudes so much monotony and boredom that we may wonder why the composers themselves do not rebel, Stravinsky included. In the movement toward a nonideological, unpretentious method of operatic composition, we can at least demand that the subtlety and complexity of the compositional process be preserved in its entirety and the superstitious belief in origins be abandoned.

Music ought to be composed with a hammer, just as Nietzsche wanted to philosophize with a hammer; but that means testing the soundness of the structure, listening with a critical ear for hollow points, not smashing it in two and confusing the jagged remains with avant-garde art because of their similarity with bombed-out cities. Today, the worn-out notion of a musical economics of scarcity—a prosaism that exempts itself from taxing the imagination and credits its own self-satisfaction with overcoming that which is not—has become as clichéd as the conventions of the court theater. This has not led to the unchallenged survival of the preserved magic of theater as a special sphere seeking to escape from film. But the richer, the more diverse, the more full of contrasts, the more intricate the construction of theatrical works becomes, the sooner the works will acquire a share—through such artistic and, so to speak, windowless rectitude—in a meaning which no longer needs to culminate in a message as the cliché requires. Only if the entire panoply of musical techniques could combine with a subject worthy of humanity to awaken something of that tension between the musical and the theatrical media—an effect that is totally lacking in the theater today—only then could opera once again recapture the power of its great historical moment.

§ New Music, Interpretation, Audience

Whoever listens to a lot of new music, particularly works that he knows well, will not lightly abandon his view that very many performances are incomprehensible, for all the sympathy he may feel for the players who have embarked upon a thankless task—incomprehensible not just to the layman, who does not expect anything else, and almost wants things that way, but specifically to anyone who is familiar with the music and who identifies with it. It often sounds in reality much as the indignant Philistine expects it to: chaotic, ugly, and meaningless. This experience is well captured by Alban Berg's macabre joke that he could very well imagine what the performance had been like after reading a review of it by Korngold Sr., the archenemy of new music. But the belief in the incomprehensibility of new music is so well established, among audiences and also many performers, that hardly anyone bothers to ask whether this incomprehensibility is an aspect of the works themselves or of their performance. The performers themselves are frequently not in a position to judge the quality of their own playing, thanks to the pressure (not necessarily unavoidable) of their commitments. I have myself been present at a concert where an excellent conductor who had grown up in the responsible tradition of new music caught my doubtful look after the performance of an admittedly very difficult work and remarked apologetically, "One more rehearsal and it would have gone like a Haydn symphony." Going over it again afterward in my mind, I was unable to perceive the decisive combination of the theme with its diminution and augmentation at one of the most important points in the work. If the meaning of the musical events is not made real in performance, no listener deserves a rebuke if he dismisses the piece as meaningless, if the performance is all he has heard.

"It would have gone like a Haydn symphony"—in other words, it would have worked, the whole orchestra would have been together at every movement of the conductor's baton, nothing would have got out of line. Performers, and conductors in the first instance, always have a double task: they have to master the apparatus that translates the score into sound, and they must reveal the musical meaning, the connections between the musical events. Chronologically, the first task mainly comes before the second, though in reality the two can scarcely be separated. But in line with the universally dominant trend to substitute means for ends, and probably because of the prevailing mood of despair among professionals about ever managing to reach the second stage, performers are usually satisfied if everything "goes all right," as the phrase would have it—in other words, if there are no wrong notes, there are no mistakes, and the general façade of sound more or less holds up. It is nevertheless a delusion to imagine that in the case of new music a certain measure of meaning could be established of its own accord. It is possible for everything to be in working order in terms of the notes, which are not inspected too closely, and for the result still to be absurd. The quality of the performance does not mean that there will be more or less musical meaning; rather, there will be a qualitative rupture: if the meaning is not wholly realized, if every aspect of the work is not related to it and bearing its stamp, then, in critical cases, all will be lost.

To make this more concrete: ever since Richard Wagner introduced the concept of "divided melody"—that is, orchestrating in such a way that a melodic line was split up into different successive colors that, as it were, modeled the course it took—truly differentiated compositions have increasingly dispensed with an uninterrupted melodic line over long stretches. On the one hand, the procedure developed by Viennese classicism of making the chief events leap from one voice to the next has been developed ever more radically; on the other, the individual melodies have dissolved into increasingly subtle values. The problem this presents for performance is to reunite those elements that have been separated in terms of orchestral color—particularly, to bridge the leaps from one instrument or instrumental group to the next. In traditional music, thanks to the scaffolding of universally known chord progressions, the central thread that went through the entire movement could be followed reasonably easily, although even Mozart and Beethoven set the performer tasks that are far more demanding than the naive ear can imagine. Today, however, the central thread has become a question purely of interpretation. If, let us say, a long drawn-out theme opens with English horn figures, which gradually expand and whose top note is then taken over by a trumpet, the unity of the melodic shape will be completely destroyed unless at the critical moment the sounds of horn and trumpet merge so that, despite the difference in timbre, the trumpet is heard as the immediate continuation of the English horn. If that is not achieved—and how much effort, how many rehearsals, are needed to establish the central thread and solve all such problems?—the meaning of the entire melody can be lost in the fourth measure of a theme, and the listener starts to lose his bearings and sense that the course of the music is a matter of chance, something for which he blames the composition. Complex modern pieces, however, may be said without exaggeration to consist of innumerable such instances; they scarcely contain a single note that does not throw up questions, and frequently a strenuous effort of immersion is needed to discover the right solution, let alone to realize it in terms of actual performance.

No less severe are the problems posed by the new multivoiced music, or for that matter the truly polyphonic pieces of Bach. When independent voices are heard simultaneously, it becomes increasingly important to differentiate between them until they are palpably distinct. Schoenberg was so conscious of the problem that he began relatively early to introduce markings for principal and secondary parts, in order to make clear what was in the foreground; what was also essential, but of lesser significance; and what really belonged in the background. But unless the orchestration is idiot-proof, in other words, has anticipated the possibility of misinterpretation and has allowed for it—Mahler was the unsurpassed master in this respect—such markings are not very useful. In complicated passages especially, like those I have in mind here, all the performers become very nervous if they are not absolutely sure of themselves. And nervous playing always means playing too loud, and despite every precautionary measure there is the constant threat that everything will degenerate into that porridge of muffled mezzo forte sound in which subtleties of voice texture are obliterated.

But these difficulties extend to the simplest things as well—to the production of individual melodies by individual instruments like the violins or the clarinet. Again and again one discovers that, in new music, such melodies do not have the space to breathe that they would have if sung by a human voice. The inadequacy stretches from primitive errors in phrasing to quite minor flaws: insensitivity to accents, lack of dynamic flexibility, over-rigidity in following the time while disregarding musical sense, coarsening of the ritardandi. The effect is comparable to reading aloud in a foreign language with a correct accent but without understanding the meaning of the words: the listeners will understand no more than the reader himself. Such flaws may be minute—though they are the most dangerous in the performance of new music—but they can be described precisely by the true interpreter. In ordinary practice, however, musicians tend to observe or ignore these details as matters of natural musical judgment, and under the cover of their faith in this gift nonsensical practices proliferate.

Nor is the treatment of tempo any better off. Schoenberg and Berg used to talk about "tempi for first performances"; they recommended that unfamiliar works be played rather slowly so as to make it easier for the listener to pick up the huge quantity of information that is conveyed simultaneously and successively—and also, no doubt, to make it easier for the conductor to obtain an acoustic overview and smooth the rough edges in performance. The superstitious faith in functionality, in the course of events, and the deep fear of losing the listener's attention and boring him as soon as his attention is not held by the virtuoso handling of the tempi constantly lead conductors to take the music at full speed, though the players are no more able to follow than is the audience: in their haste, all the outlines become blurred.

Conversely, however, even the "first-performance tempi" do not guarantee the delivery of musical meaning. On another occasion I heard a very difficult work played by an ensemble of young, enthusiastic musicians endlessly concerned about the music. From fear that some note or other might come to harm, they played so slowly and cautiously that nothing was left of the vivacity of the outer movements that essentially give the piece its character, and the whole performance left the audience as perplexed as if the piece had been played in a tearing hurry: a case of infidelity as a result of excessive fidelity. Nowadays, no doubt, we have to start out with the right tempi; the difficulty, however, is not to achieve the right tempo as such, but to make sure that even with a quick tempo everything in the composition finds itself clearly articulated in the performance: diversity in unity. But how many performers today understand something that occurs in music often enough, namely, that there are very fast melodies—very fast and yet still melodies.

Lastly, average performances of new music neglect the sensuous quality of the sound. It is undoubtedly true that in advanced modern performances color is no longer an isolated attraction, an end in itself, but is functionally determined, as a means for realizing the musical structure through listening. But that means neither indifference to the sound nor submission to the listener's stereotypical belief that new music sounds awful and that's how it's supposed to be. As long as its authentic works distance themselves from the sonic wallowing of the late Romantics, and as long as they continue to refuse to comply with the demands for the sugary harmonies that have long since found their home in Hollywood film scores, they will have no need to renounce sonority as a mediating link between the essence of the music and its external form. If the authentic works are performed faithfully and in an appropriate manner, they will also sound good in a higher sense. For even sensuous sonority is not an isolated thing—it appears so only to the atomistic listening of an audience trained to enjoy the saccharine. Instead its beauty depends on the structure of the music. If the sonorities are transparently related to that structure, and if the musical meaning shines through every color, then the overall sound will be at home with itself. Anyone who has ever heard Berg's *Lulu* Suite played by eminent musicians from the Romance countries, such as Sanzogno, will be aware that in great music magical sound is rarely just stuck on from outside and that instead we are hearing the composition manifesting itself—that, in short, what is truly functional is the suprafunctional. Berg once alluded to this when, explaining the ideal of musical functionality, he said that in a proper table the glue does not stink and the nails do not stick out. The commonly heard interpretations that do not achieve the union of internal and external tend to content themselves with mere unruliness, and so reinforce the general prejudice. When they fail to achieve an integral music totality the overall façade of sound is fragmented—for which they then maliciously claim credit.

Of course, if the distinction between traditional and new music is not as absolute as a cultural industry that divides music into sectors would have us believe, then all the difficulties of performance must be looked for in traditional music as well. For there, too, performances today are in the vast majority of cases senseless. It is precisely the familiarity with new music that allows us to see this retrospectively. But with the conventional repertoire—the constantly shrinking number of works that every so-called musical person knows by heart—this passes unnoticed. The quality of the known, or perhaps even more, the older idiom of tonality, carries one comfortably over all the ruptures and contradictions. Its more or less typical, established vocabulary creates something like a context of meaning, even where the true meaning, the way in which the structure of the whole is imprinted on every detail, is not achieved in the performance. In the case of new music, however, the internal is turned inside out and in effect the structure is converted into the focal core of the music, thus ruling out the use of formal supports to buttress the course of events. In consequence, whereas in ordinary performances of Beethoven chaos lurks just beneath a smooth surface, here it becomes immediately apparent. If in new music the overall meaning is destroyed by omissions of the kind described here, the upshot is the gibberish that is noticed in performances of traditional music only by the person who already understands it. For that reason, both the performance and the understanding of traditional music may be found to be more difficult than in the case of new music; but only new music has helped to make us aware of the situation and to make us more conscious of the idea of true interpretation.

With regard to more than a few interpreters of new music, problematic performances can be blamed on faulty understanding. The contradictions in the relations between productive musical forces and society also have a bearing on the relation between interpretation and composition. The interpreters find themselves left in the lurch by their musical training, particularly when it comes to understanding the new works that have significance. Their profession makes them more immediately dependent on success than is the case with composers, and also more dependent on contact with the public, whose mental attitudes they often adjust to unconsciously. This is why their own musicality, however specialized they may be, often lags behind the development of music itself. Even in the case of such important musicians as Furtwängler or Casals, one encountered the most indescribable misjudgments about new music in general and about the qualities of specific works in particular. Because of their need to consider the impact on audiences, self-righteous, traditionalist interpreters cling to the outworn notion of the musician who is supposed to be in close touch with his audience and who lets himself be

guided by intuition, adding nothing of himself but his own temperament. Whatever does not fit in with this approach is worthless. What is
forgotten here is that although musical qualities are the precondition of
worthwhile music-making of every kind, they only prove their worth by
being sublimated and preserved through awareness of the compositional
structure. Instead of that—even the greatest names can easily be included
here—one rarely finds more than the combination of pleasing sound,
brio, and, at best, rhythmic accuracy. Many no doubt suspect that something is amiss in such music, but they react by projecting their own inse-
curity onto the music they ought to understand but do not, and that is
why they then blame it for being intellectual. The task of the interpreter
should be to act as the advocate of new music to the public, unless he
wishes to be reduced to the status of a museum attendant. Nevertheless, it
is all too easy for him to slip into the role of defending the public against
the new music.

But misinterpretations are by no means the monopoly of ignoramuses
or the unruly. More important is the nature of the operation in which
everyone is caught up and, above all, the lack of rehearsal time. Pieces
that could be decently performed only after a minimum of twenty rehearsals are whipped through in two or three. For all the objections to be
made to Toscanini, it was he who put an end to this practice, and for all
his musical limitations, this was an achievement for which we are indebted to his immense authority. Anyone who lacks such authority has
normally to bow to the weight of financial considerations. The social
progress that has turned practicing musicians into protected trade-union
members whose every minute is precious becomes the obstacle to artistic
progress because it prevents that expansiveness that calls for the lavish use
of time, much as great architecture calls for the lavish use of space.

The consequences of all this can scarcely be exaggerated: the musical
performance that ought to resolve the tension between public and work
in a fruitful way instead deepens the chasm between them. This chasm
indeed is barely perceived as such anymore, but has become frozen into
an ideology. People are happy to see incomprehensibility confirmed by
incomprehensible performances, while the expert onto whose shoulders
they like to shift the responsibility is no more able to understand the
nonsense he hears than the indignant subscriber. It is a very serious question whether the plethora of concerts devoted to new music that suffer
from such defects do not do more harm than good despite the best ef-

forts of the musicians involved. It is not for nothing that the most responsible people of all tend to embargo the performance of their own works, or those entrusted to them, rather than encourage a performance. I know of a long-playing record of one of the most important contemporary operas that was bought by many enthusiasts and people of good will, and whose conductor is one of the faithful supporters of new music, but which renders the musical events unrecognizable over long stretches. This only encourages a shrug of the shoulders or a hypocritical enthusiasm for something about which enthusiasm is impossible because it has at best no more than a tenuous connection with the work being presented. The only mystery is that the conductor concerned did not block the release of the record. At the same time, one hesitates to utter such objections out loud, for fear of providing indolent and reactionary dullards with the pretext to avoid new music on the grounds that prevailing conditions rule out adequate performances, and to stick to Tchaikovsky with a good conscience, whereas in reality judgments on the internal tensions and legitimacy of any artistic practice have always been made possible only by the relation to current—and advanced—production. If performers, who are the very people who mediate between new music and musical life in its broader sense, were to refuse to participate, the upshot would only be to help neutralize new art and turn it into the cultural property of experts, thereby increasing the general indifference toward it. Even though productive artists must refrain from casting amorous glances at the public, they cannot remain wholly indifferent to a complete lack of resonance. Art would scarcely make itself more serious and substantial if it gave way at the outset and renounced any attempt to reach nonspecialists and combat their resistance. For that would mean capitulating to society as it is and making a home in a special niche within the general division of labor, even though it is the task of art to point the way beyond that division if it wishes to retain the integrity of its own meaning.

Purists may talk of compromises with conformity if they wish, and reject such concerns about performance as cowardly pandering to audiences. Such purism is no more than a self-indulgent refusal to grapple with a real problem. In the first place, a piece of music is not just the score; it needs a genuine performance, just as, in its turn, the sound itself stands in need of the score. A feeling of indifference toward interpretation is also indifference toward the original work. But segregating new music as a realm separate from the public—the most obvious manifestation of this is the institution of the Third Program—also has its questionable side. Indispensable though such segregation may be on occasion to protect artistic progress from the rage of the monolithic majority, Third Programs, art cinemas, and the like, by avoiding conflict, reserving works for experts, and ensuring that nothing happens, in fact guarantee only that nothing further does happen. The advanced and esoteric nature of the works themselves always contains a dig at the public. If that dig is softened, the music starts to lose some of its tension; the wallpaper patterns and the neat arithmetical calculations that threaten to take the sting out of the aesthetic avant-garde inevitably entail the abandonment of the dialectical interaction with the audience. That dialectic ought to consist not in an accommodation to the audience's prejudices but its opposite. When, in *Die Meistersinger*, Wagner's Hans Sachs demands that the masters should submit their rules to the judgment of the people, this idea undoubtedly embodies something of that healthy commonsense attitude that threatens to make short work of intellectuals and other deviationists, but it also contains the dawning awareness that an esotericism fueled by an obsession with technique jeopardizes the very cause it promotes. Little speaks so much in favor of Brecht as the fact that he ignored the frontier between integrity and success that had been so long sanctioned by the industry, and that his extreme theory of art (one of his closest friends once called it "barbaric futurism") was able to intervene in established culture instead of shutting itself off in a special reserve. The split between art and society is socially dictated, but even people who bow to what they think of as fate nevertheless submit to the dictates of society. Modern painting has contrived to assert itself in a hostile society through its own ruse of reason, namely by exploiting the market value of its products. New music could do the same by exploiting musical performance. For the true suggestive power of a performance is identical with the realization of musical meaning.

But only the radio could help to bring this about. Snobbishness toward the mass media is idiotic. Only by changing the function of the mass media can the intellectual monopoly of the Culture Industry be broken; it cannot be accomplished by retreating into social impotence. Today the radio alone can provide a shelter for new music, separate as it is from the market, and can take up its cause, which is that of human beings, in its battle against human beings. In the same way, radio can guarantee performances in which the music is truly realized. The most important factor here would be to ensure adequate rehearsal time—which would have to be a multiple of the time available today. It is well known what difficulties broadcasters have in their ceaseless search for pieces to fill the programs. Would it not be more meaningful to divert some of the time available and use it for rehearsals, like the legendary ones for Schoenberg's Chamber Symphony No. 1 after the First World War in the Viennese Association for Private Musical Performances, which was never "performed" officially? Such rehearsals need not be lost to the listeners. On the contrary, the rehearsals themselves should be broadcast. Every improvement in the representation of musical meaning redounds to the benefit of the listener. The seriousness and rigor with which the performer lays bare the overall meaning of the work brings home to the listener a sense of the seriousness and rigor of the composition, and helps to destroy the prejudice that it is arbitrary and chaotic, that it does not much matter whether a note sounds one way or another. Moreover, in listening to spa orchestras and similarly inadequate organizations, one can see in the gaps and cracks of the ramshackle performances the inner truth of the compositions glimmering through, and in the process one can get to know the works much as a little girl gets to know her doll by slitting it open. This educational function of the faulty and imperfect should be exploited in the interests of greater understanding by allowing the listener to hear how the orchestra improves to the point of perfection. Furthermore, such performances should not be confined just to orchestras, where rough edges are unavoidable, even given unlimited time and the greatest mastery—after all, good orchestral works already have allowances for such rough edges built into the process of composition. The same attention should be given to chamber music, which should be minutely rehearsed down to the very last note, and here too the rehearsals should be broadcast. The precondition here would be that the most important radio stations sign up the best ensembles, especially the best string quartets, on a long-term basis. The repertoire should by no means be limited to modern works; such rehearsals would be of equal benefit to traditional music.

In this way it might be possible to overcome the apathy of the listening masses toward new music, and to put a stop to people slipping into the primitive sects formed by those who are no longer satisfied by traditional musical life yet have no grasp of the new. For this, however, it would be necessary to strengthen the autonomy of the radio so as to fend off the organized pressure exerted by the very same popular taste that it must change if it is to fulfill its obligations toward the public. For the public at large is always better, even nowadays, than those few who appeal to popular taste with the intention of thwarting the emergence of music worthy of human beings.

§ The Mastery of the Maestro

Thirty years ago Toscanini brought the ensemble of La Scala, Milan, to Berlin for a guest performance. The impact by far surpassed anything that had been experienced in the theater up to that time. Toscanini's performance fell in the brief period between the economic stabilization and the renewed crisis. So favored, it became the occasion for what the newspaper jargon of the period termed a social event, a spectacle of eerie splendor surrounded by the hectic aura created by the sense that not much time was left. Moreover, the event left a lasting impression on musicians and everyone with a serious interest in music. Toscanini's performances, particularly those of Italian operas, displayed a precision that went far beyond anything seen in the German-speaking world. He set a standard for orchestral precision that became the benchmark for the future, especially in America, where he took charge of the orchestra of NBC, one of the largest radio companies. There he created a style of conducting that has in the meantime become second nature. Furthermore, Toscanini paved the way for an approach to musical interpretation that can be roughly summed up with the term "matter-of-factness" [*Sachlichkeit*], even though as a man firmly rooted in the nineteenth century he may have had little in common with the movement that became known as the *Neue Sachlichkeit*. A certain kind of methodicalness, clarity, and lucidity characterized his performances, for all his élan and brio. There was nothing vague about him, but equally, there was no obvious sign of expressive idiosyncrasy. He was the true antipope to Furtwängler, a Settembrini of music, just as in his convictions, above all in his hostility to fascism, he displayed an admirable integrity and civic courage by taking up the cudgels on behalf of rational humanity. At the same time, his matter-of-factness was not boring and was free from parsimonious asceticism. His performances flashed and sparkled, as if polished with chrome. The cogs of the machine fit perfectly into one another with a satisfying hum, conjuring up the sense of inexorable necessity. Every resistance on the part of the musical material, every threat from the adventitious or the unforeseen, seemed to have been circumvented, and the self-confident temperament of the Italian theatrical tradition seemed to carry all before it. As the ideal maestro, he personified more than that concept; he seemed to embody the ideal of mastery itself. He introduced the element of rationality into the art of conducting, the "streamlining" that began to establish itself in Europe in the early 1930s, both in the forms of manufactured objects and in the structure of social and economic organizations. In short, he not only did away with the tradition that Gustav Mahler had denounced as sloppiness [*Schlamperei*] some twenty years earlier, but he unerringly discovered the style of the times as well. It elevated him from the status of Italian celebrity to the master monopolist of orchestras.

This gives some idea of his historical significance as a conductor. It coincided with a critical point in time when music began to turn against the distortions of late Romanticism. This recoil against the great personality with his desire to fascinate—a phenomenon which at that moment had begun to migrate from music into politics—together, of course, with the first signs of an allergic reaction to expressiveness as such, was combined with a sense of aesthetic responsibility that was grounded in turn in a conscious awareness of the constructed nature of great music. It placed a higher value on an idea of music-making that was appropriate to the musical meaning than on the arbitrary projection of subjective impulses onto the notes of the score. Tendencies of this kind were beginning to make themselves felt everywhere, most obviously in Vienna, which witnessed Schoenberg's attempts at structure-driven performance immediately after the First War. But they could also be seen in the circle around Stravinsky, as well as in the young Hindemith, in a style based on machinelike impassivity and hostility to expression. Even though he was much older, Toscanini seemed to have arrived at similar results, although in his case they derived from his work on his own material, the orchestra. He not only lent such changes the authority of his name, but he also translated them into the practical realities of official musical life. Official music at the time displayed an even greater resistance to compositional innovation than it does today, if that is conceivable. His energetic attempts to reform orchestral playing were facilitated by the wealth of musical institutions at the time, and in particular by the opportunities for unlimited rehearsing. As a conducting virtuoso famed for his accuracy and lightness of touch, he made a fanatical onslaught on virtuosity itself and so provided members of the younger generation with a confirmation of their own ideas. At the same time, he won over the older generation and the culturally conservative public by his devotion to the tradition, which he subjected to an unremitting purification. The result was ideal performances of the kind that, apart from Mahler, had not been experienced since the great days of Bayreuth. Anyone opposed to the dreadful state of music could only welcome the abrasiveness of Toscanini's intentions and learn from him; many took over what were for the time the unusually quick tempi that Toscanini preferred, sometimes without concerning himself overmuch about their justification.

However, indispensable though Toscanini's reforms were, the context in which they operated gradually changed. We have long since come to see the price of unconstrained and cheerful matter-of-factness and streamlined functionality in the realm of production—that is, composition; and as everywhere, the sphere of reproduction is dependent on production. This is not to assert that there could ever be a revival of the Romantic manner that Toscanini made appear so dubious. It is not to suggest that a conductor should once again play the first notes of the Fifth Symphony slower than the rest so as to impress the audience with the dignity of Fate. But matter-of-fact performance does demand that the whole essence of the music should be articulated with all its implications, its formal wealth and its latent sensuousness, rather than being submerged beneath a shiny, unbroken texture that leaves the listener to infer what is going on beneath the surface, even as the overprominent façade prevents him from apprehending it. Espressivo and rubato have long since ceased to be the danger; the present threat is a straightforward functionality on the model of organization and administration. These are procedures that for all their matter-of-factness fail to do the matter justice; instead they centralize it, putting it on the leash and finally breaking it. These questions are not matters of stylistic fashion and changes in artistic attitudes; they concern the works themselves. Today the question that could be asked of Toscanini is whether his matter-of-factness was sufficiently matter-of-fact; whether the work has been the real beneficiary of his assiduous devotion, or whether this devotion has only created an ostentatiously self-regarding apparatus for controlling the music. It may well turn out that Toscanini's individual limitations are really those of the historical tendency in music that is personified by his name. In the meantime he has been promoted to the ranks of the grand old men whose patriarchal authority has assumed a kind of vicarious function within the anonymous hierarchy of the administered world—that of "personalization"—to which the impotent consciousness of countless admirers desperately clings. People believe in Toscanini so as to have something to believe in, and this belief is the symptom of a mental state that is as much an obstacle to independent judgment in artistic matters as it is elsewhere. To doubt Toscanini seems blasphemous, whereas in reality it is blasphemous to be willing to turn him into a god. Matter-of-fact ideas about the prophet of musical matter-of-factness will do little to modify this reverential stance, but they may shed some light on the phenomenon of authoritarian attitudes today, attitudes that have also taken root in art.

For my own part, doubts of a purely musical nature about Toscanini began to arise in my own mind long before it was possible to make connections of this sort. I am reminded of a radio broadcast of a performance of the Seventh Symphony [of Beethoven] in Salzburg in the summer of 1934 that I listened to among a rapt circle of hotel guests in Madonna di Campiglio. Everything seemed incomparably less powerful when insulated from the suggestive ambience of the opera house or concert hall. On the one hand, it suffered from an absence of internal tension—as if with the first note everything had been decided in advance, as with a gramophone record, instead of gradually coming into being. It was as if the interpretation had already turned into its mechanical transmission. Then again, in the Allegretto it seemed old-fashioned and ignored Beethoven's unambiguous performance directions. Subsequent performances in New York where I was present confirmed these impressions. I particularly recollect one evening when I listened to another radio broadcast at home, this time with a musically very competent friend, and we compared Toscanini's tempi in the Ninth Symphony with Beethoven's metronome markings. Today, we are well provided with Toscanini recordings on long-playing records and this enables us to listen as often as we wish and to compare his performances as totalities and in detail, and to translate our overall impressions into more or less precise findings.

Toscanini's strange programming policy was always striking: his dislike of advanced contemporary music no less than his faulty sense of compositional quality. He never scrupled to perform the works of third-rate Italian confrères, and even today one of the long-playing records still in circulation contains an old-fashioned kitschy waltz, "Les patineurs," with the comment that it was one of his favorite compositions. Since even the most hardened Toscanini snob would scarcely feel tempted to rush to its defense, one is left with the opposite supposition: that he chose it out of naïveté. Now, the taste of musicians is of course often uncertain, since it may be overconcerned with immediate effects. We should also remind ourselves that the division of musical taste into high and low is specifically German and alien to the Latin peoples. They have no word for kitsch. Until recently, moreover, they made no rigorous distinction between music's autonomous and social functions, and in general they did not take their art with the dogged seriousness typical of us [Germans]. But once Toscanini had projected himself as the champion of great music, he tacitly committed himself to distinguishing between it and commodity art. For otherwise his commitment to authentic performance would itself degenerate into mere earnestness. Finally, the absence of any living relationship with contemporary production seems incompatible with his ideals as a performer. For performance always derives its ideas and its strength from the most advanced music and all decisively new trends in interpretation draw their sustenance from the latest developments in composing. The drive for matter-of-factness with which Toscanini identified loses its force if it is not measured against the principles of construction governing composition in the present age. In reality, his kind of matter-of-factness springs from a different source from that of modern composers. His reaction against chance and superfluous events is that of the animal trainer: nothing should go awry. His perfectionism is rooted in his intimate feeling for the needs of the apparatus of the orchestra. Here his control is total. The idea of shaping it to the needs of the composition was secondary. His prime aim was to ensure that everything functions, fits together, and works smoothly as never before, without being disturbed even by the conductor. This dedication to the apparatus for its own sake involves Toscanini's conducting in one element that later emerged in composition too, with disastrous effects, namely, the privileging of means over ends, fetishism. Under Toscanini's gaze music is reified into a prefabricated product. By eliminating the errors stemming from technical tensions, he also does away with the latent tensions beneath the surface of the composition. Everything appears clear and distinct, down to the last note, as if it could all be packaged in a germ-free container and taken home. Instead of the interpreted work we are given a cast in synthetic wrapping. The unity Toscanini achieves and which exercises such a powerful attraction initially ignores the resistances in the music. It unwinds mechanically, most obviously perhaps at the beginning of the first movement of Brahms's Fourth Symphony, where the decorated and varied repetition of the main theme is beaten through without nuance as far as the start of the first climax. The mechanical impression is heightened by the rigid downbeat accents in this repetition. The unity in performance, as in the composition of highly articulated music itself, is successful only where it is wrested from the diversity of conflicting impulses, where it is simultaneously process and result. In Toscanini, however, it is preestablished, an a priori; it lacks the element of suffering that is essential if it is to become a true unity. No doubt the tempi are often— but by no means always—brisk and modern, in contrast to the overlong Romantic tempi. But modern tempi on their own do not suffice. What is decisive is what happens within them, and whether they are able to gather in the harvest of articulated and differentiated sound. But this harvest is denied to Toscanini. Doubtless under his baton the second subject of the first movement of Beethoven's First Symphony is played more quickly and unsentimentally than was possible in the bad old tradition, but especially after the modulation into the minor he completely loses his grip on accentuation and articulation, and a briskly cheerful movement for its own sake becomes the price of a rapidity that is anything but magic. A piece like the scherzo from Mendelssohn's *Midsummer Night's Dream* is simply reeled off without any articulation. Much of it is of course admirable: the virtuosity of the wind section, the series of syncopated accents linking them up into a new rhythm, a new breathlessness hitherto not noticed in this work. But it has lost all its gloss. A shrewd and incorruptible musician of Latin origins to whom I gave the record as a present in the pre-Hitler period remarked that it was brilliant but that it sounded as if the Italian goats had devoured the German forest.

As a compensation for the lack of shaping and articulation that results from this mechanical reeling-off process we discover in Toscanini an unexpected subjective element. Either the Italian music master whips up the orchestra and indiscriminately scatters Verdi-like *stretti* over the music in search of applause; or, with a striking absence of taste, he yields to a primitive love of sound for its own sake, lingers on the so-called purple patches, relishes them sensuously, regardless of the damage done to the formal context that he otherwise is so eager to respect. In this manner the master of rigor goes halfway to meet the culinary needs of the devotees of pop music. The first movement of Brahms's Fourth Symphony is full of salient structures. In an extraordinarily lyrical eight-bar passage in B major a wind antecedent contrasts with a consequent on the strings. The latter naturally has a richer sound than the cooler wind antecedent. However, Toscanini hurls himself with such enthusiasm onto the strings that the consequent ceases to be heard as the half-theme, the response, that it is in Brahms's work. Instead, thanks to its exaggerated and oversweet tone, it is turned into the main event and reduces the exposition of the theme to a secondary issue, thereby throwing the entire formal pattern out of kilter. More subtle formal categories are alien to Toscanini's music-making. That Brahms theme is followed by a passage which, like a number of comparable passages in Schubert, fades away—dozes off, as it were. There is no trace of this in Toscanini. Everything is drawn on as if by a thread, it all operates on the same plane; he does not distinguish between different degrees of presence.

Above all else, the supremacy of control means that Toscanini refuses to follow the music to any place where it cannot be kept in check. He is incapable of allowing the music a free rein. In the slow movement of the Brahms Fourth Symphony, just before the end, there is an inexpressibly moving, transcendent melody for solo clarinet. Its formal meaning is that for a few seconds it suspends the onward progress of the movement. Furtwängler—to whose Brahms's Fourth all sorts of objections can be made—played this passage with the greatest intensity. In Toscanini, nothing happens apart from the regulation ritardando. Or again, in the coda of the first movement of Beethoven's Ninth, where the horn picks up that passage from the main theme particularly elaborated in the development, a moment of unforgettable color is lifted out from the whole texture. Toscanini just hurries straight on past it. Not even the color of the horn makes itself felt properly; the relative autonomy that defines every authentic musical episode is flattened out. Something similar occurs in the overture to *Die Meistersinger*, a piece that, oddly enough, Toscanini gets completely wrong. The brief, highly modulatory passage that leads into the middle section is followed by the *Abgesang* theme of the Prize Song in 4/4 time and transposed into E major, in a magnificent piece of harmony, with a depth that uncovers an unsuspected dark warmth. Anyone who wants to understand *Die Meistersinger* must have responded to this at some point. Here, too, Toscanini just rushes on past, as if he did not want to lose the thread but had to move on at all costs, whereas the unity of music as rich in finely carved detail as *Die Meistersinger* actually demands that one should lose one's way; indeed, it is based on a process of losing one's way and finding it once more, rather than on a simple identity of everything with itself. But in Toscanini's entire approach to the overture to *Die Meistersinger* we miss that sense of excess, of unrestrained luxuriating, which is essential to the meaning of the piece, not some external trapping. In terms of technique the fault doubtless lies in Toscanini's habit of focusing on the melodies in the upper parts at the expense of the harmonic counterpointing that is actually essential to Wagner. The middle voices are of no importance in his eyes. He never wastes his time on anything but the prominent principal event. But the true interpretation of music calls for the ability to throw something away in order to gain even more, the paradox being that one should not throw oneself away in the process—but paradoxes of this kind are ignored by Toscanini.

He is unable to linger. Behind his confident manner lurks the anxiety that if he relinquishes control for a single second, the listener might tire of the show and flee. This is an institutionalized box office ideal detached from people, which mistakenly sees in itself an unwavering capacity for inspiring the audience. It frustrates any of the dialectic between the parts and the whole that operates in great music and that is realized only in great interpretations. Instead we have an abstract conception of the whole right from the start, almost like the sketch for a painting, which then is, as it were, painted in with a volume of sound whose momentary sensuous splendor overwhelms the listener's ears such that the details are stripped of their own proper impulses. Toscanini's musicality is in a way hostile to time, visual. The bare form of the whole is adorned with isolated stimuli that shape it for the kind of atomistic listening associated more readily with the Culture Industry. The streamlining of the orchestral machinery and the atomization into merely sensuous details may be meticulously joined together, but even so the music remains disjointed in reality; the detail never strives of its own accord to grow into the totality. Instead there are climaxes that have been plotted in advance and planned according to overall dynamic shape rather than developed from specific motivic impulses. They are then followed by moments of release in which the resolution of the tensions in the piece are replaced by sheer volumes of sound. The greater the musical tension, the more crass the discrepancy: for instance, at the end of the development in the first movement of the Ninth Symphony where the main theme reenters, drum crescendi, unspecified by Beethoven, are introduced within the fortissimo. This is particularly evident in the *Missa Solemnis*, which sometimes lends itself to such manipulations. We are given a sustained monumentality that obviously has not the faintest understanding of the spiritual depths of the work. On occasion the sound is intensified where, at moments of extreme dynamic contrast, a pianissimo following on from a fortissimo is not even audible. The ideal of clarity that seduces him into such extremes collapses into its opposite. If the sound engineer is to blame for this effect, Toscanini should have blocked the release of the record.

Such observations may appear pedantic on their own, but they give an insight into a central fact about Toscanini's music-making. His fidelity and perfectionism turn against themselves, not just in the vague sense that they are incompatible with the so-called spirit of the works, but to the point where they come into very palpable conflict with the works themselves. For example, Toscanini's tempi frequently do not coincide with Beethoven's metronome markings. His idea of strictness is indeed alien to the capricious interpretations of old-fashioned "star" conductors. But even so, it takes its cue far more readily from the overall appearance of the sound than from the substance that is supposed to become manifest. As soon as tensions between the two musical elements make themselves felt, as is constantly the case in highly organized music, Toscanini's matter-of-factness leads him to react "realistically," that is to say, in tune with the wants and needs of the machinery. The exposition of Beethoven's Ninth contains a passage where a thirty-second-note passage dissipates itself across the whole texture. In his unmistakable desire to polemicize against the Romantic tradition, Toscanini plays the entire movement faster than Beethoven's marking. Even if we concede his right to do this, his style of treating the entire piece in a way that prevents us from even becoming conscious of its length would oblige him to keep strictly to his chosen tempo. Once he has resolved to be Toscanini, he has to stick to it. But the thirty-second-note passage cannot really be played at that speed, and so he instantly abandons his principle and, adapting himself to what the orchestral apparatus allows, slackens the pace. Musicians retell a joke of the pianist Moritz Rosenthal. When Rosenthal first heard Paderewski play and was asked for his opinion, he replied, "He is certainly an excellent pianist; but he is no Paderewski." In the same way, the admirable Toscanini lacks the very qualities that have been ascribed to him and that have helped to create the myth. His perfectionism, like every pleasure taken in functionality for its own sake, goes hand in hand with regression. In difficult situations he opts for caution; in easy ones, or whenever he fears the music might slip from his grasp, he gallops off as if he were in the circus.

It might be said that I would object, whatever Toscanini did. If he just keeps beating out the time, I shall accuse him of a failure to differentiate; if he deviates from his own norm, I accuse him of acting capriciously. We might reply that the treatment of details should necessarily conform to the pattern established by Toscanini himself; if in general he respects the tempo to the point of mechanical punctiliousness, he cannot slacken the reins just because it is technically more convenient, but ought instead to look for possibilities of variation within the chosen tempo. However, the central criticism to be made of him is not his basic choice of and slavish adherence to wrong tempi, but his inability to articulate the music on the basis of his own assumptions. The meaning of that thirty-second-note passage—and such details are very well suited for airing differences of opinion, that is to say, they enable us to reach definitive judgments about the quality of a performance—is, as I have indicated, that of a take-off, of intensified movement. If the basic beat is pulled up short at this point, the figure turns into its opposite and we find a slowing down rather than an intensified flow. Toscanini's pliancy toward the apparatus strikes a blow at the meaning of the music.

For a conductor of Toscanini's claims Beethoven would surely be the appropriate measuring rod, but there he is found wanting. His basic view of the first movement of the Ninth, and incidentally also of the *Eroica*, fails to hit the mark. His eagerness to de-Wagnerize the movement leads him to forget the most obvious things, namely Beethoven's own performance direction: Allegro, ma non troppo, un poco maestoso. There is no sign of majesty here, nor any sense of the main theme producing itself out of a few errant sparks. Instead, with the very first note everything is equally strongly marked, equally definitive. Instead of the theme acting as the product of the motives from which it springs—a thoroughly dynamic interrelationship—it turns into a mere juxtaposition, an addition.

We are presented with something ready-made, not developed. If the music loses its depths, its atmosphere should not be explained in terms of Latinate *limpidezza*, an explanation that has been used to excess in Germany ever since Nietzsche first proposed it; nor as an instance of incorruptible fidelity to the work itself. It is based rather on a technical defect, that is to say, on a lack of matter-of-factness, on Toscanini's inability to develop the introductory motivic fragments into a great theme, and to articulate this as a process. There is no need for poetic talk about atmosphere, but simply to do justice to the objective process of composition. The atmosphere of the work would then have made its appearance without further ado.

Enthusiastic journalists have testified to the demonic obsessiveness of Toscanini's indefatigable rehearsals and his Reinhardt-like domination of the orchestra. But however full of temperament he may have been, musically he was a demon without the demonic. The dimension of depth, which musically has its precise technical locus in the intersection of present and nonpresent elements in the unfolding of the music, shrivels up, to be replaced by pure abstract presence. If Toscanini arrives at the principal theme of the Ninth without really undergoing any process, then, as a punishment, that theme somehow eludes his grasp. Its melodic shape, that of falling intervals, is buried beneath the weight of the expansive sound, which attempts to achieve what should have resulted from demonstrating the motivic interconnections. This lack of definition infects what follows. In the upshot, the second subject, which is built out of short, alternating entries and which contrasts structurally with the principal theme, falls into the background, thanks to Toscanini's efforts to hold all the phrasing together. The vitality of the individual entries is stifled, and this destroys the character of the entire theme, which is then stripped of the three-dimensional spatial quality that alone would have enabled it to survive lyrically in the gigantic shadow of the principal theme. This effect is even more pronounced in the return of the second subject in the recapitulation than in the exposition.

We have to ask whether Toscanini really had any understanding of phrasing at all, or whether his focus on coherent sound-surfaces had not caused his instinct for any breath of musical life to wither. He stifles it just where it should start to sing. And it is this impulse that diminishes the very clarity that a matter-of-fact approach to music-making ought above all to promote. The neurotic obsession with smoothing the transitions between musical figures ends up grinding them down to such an extent that they become almost indistinguishable from one another. Let us take the case of a principal theme of an orchestral movement, reduced to a chamber music setting. If in such a passage, in which a whole century was needed to grasp fully the implications of the Ninth Symphony, the theme now recurs piano in the development, Toscanini turns out to be quite out of his depth and unable to make any sense of it musically. The undefined, tentative nature of the passage can be meaningful only if the material it vaguely calls to mind were previously presented in an authoritative manner.

In contrast to his treatment of Beethoven, Toscanini's interpretations of Wagner often refute the idea that southerners will find music based on Nordic mythology alien. Here the theatrical conductor triumphs over the musician: the mis-en-scène that presides over the Wagnerian *Gesamtkunstwerk* is the same that governs his approach to conducting. The pleasure he takes in excerpts from Wagner without the vocal parts reminds one annoyingly of potpourris, and even though Wagner, as a tactical concession, gave his blessing to such excerpts, we cannot offer this in mitigation. Nevertheless, Toscanini's recording of Siegfried's Rhine journey has something magnificent about it, even though the preceding scene, which is also included, is falsely described as a prologue and has been badly mutilated by cuts. The unity of precision and the instinct for sonorities, Toscanini's forte, are absolutely appropriate here. His version of the *Tristan* prelude, too, can appeal at least to the authority of Wagner's emphatic views on slow tempi in the essay on conducting, and his willingness to adopt extremely slow tempi is rewarded by an expression of desire, of unrequited yearning, that is foreign to the normal theatrical and musical practice that moderates the work and tones it down.

But wherever music is truly transcendent, wherever it speaks as the voice of mankind, Toscanini's interpretation falls silent. Almost nowhere in the Beethoven symphonies is the sound of humanity more compelling than in the trio of the Allegretto of the Seventh. Under Toscanini's baton, however, it just flows by as on a conveyor belt, as if the music scarcely ventured to raise its eyes anymore. And if music really may no longer do that, Toscanini is all too willing to serve as the executor of the historical trend. Or take the moment just before the trio in the Scherzo of the same symphony. All of a sudden, the orchestral unison hangs suspended in the air, like a signal, as the folk song–like theme comes to an end. With Toscanini this becomes a sustained beat, a hasty motive with its hasty continuation, nothing more. It is necessary only to compare such passages with the Wagner recordings, or even with Toscanini's recordings of Italian music, in order to become aware of the *splendeur et misère* of the maestro.

As is well known, the Seventh Symphony was described by Wagner as the apotheosis of dance. But Toscanini is himself the apotheosis, the ultimate consummation of what is fundamentally a preintellectual, preartistic type: namely, the theatrical conductor who in his struggle with the machine neither tires nor succumbs but bends it to his will, though at the price of coming to resemble it. He embodies the Platonic Idea of the regimental band leader. As a phenomenon, Toscanini and the effect he has had join forces with the dominant tendency to regression. Wagner has given us a good-humored, if arrogant, account of the old-time German conductors of the nineteenth century, claiming that they were really just time-beaters who were incapable of liberating the music. Old Wilhelm Riehl has left descriptions of some of these men. It almost seems as if Toscanini's elegant mastery had come full circle and brought conducting back to that unliberated, homely, preliberal standpoint; as if his critique of Romantic interpretations had not led to the realization of a higher form of music, combining rigor and meaning, but rather had split it down the middle, separating it into mere rigor, on the one hand, and its correlate, sheer sensual gloss, on the other. But this is achieved as a substitute for translating musical meaning into the realm of sound, or into what Hegel, speaking of beauty in general, called the sensuous manifestation of the Idea. It is precisely this, the suggestive reinstatement of a merely presubjective standpoint by a self-willed subject, that appeals to listeners. In their eyes the maestro is both a substitute for a *Führer*-personality and -religion and the expression of the victory of technique and administration over music. They feel safe in Toscanini's hands, as they too are now the objects of music administration. They imagine that their enthusiasm provides proof of their own cultivation. But to my mind they resemble some youths I once saw in Florence who had been driven by their teacher out of the Pitti Palace and onto the square in front. Having done their duty by culture, and with evident relief, they crowded around a giant Cadillac, which they regarded with the deep feelings of reverence that their teacher had probably tried in vain to evoke in them inside the palazzo. For all his subjective integrity, for all his supreme craftsmanship, Toscanini's efforts wreak havoc because they are confined to craftsmanship. They transform music into a force that impresses because it goes like clockwork, but is inwardly empty. By coming to embody the objective spirit of the age in such an effective way, and by refusing to go beyond that identification, he shows himself to be in collusion with what he imagines himself to oppose so bravely and uncompromisingly. He became one of the people who used their art to ratify the supremacy of the existing world over any alternatives, over utopian possibility. The story is told that he was once shown a contemporary score. It contained a pizzicato note marked both crescendo and decrescendo. Toscanini is said to have written *"stupido"* in the margin. As an expert, his reaction was to show up the composer's stupidity, which in his view consisted in demanding that a plucked note should grow louder or softer even though the performer ceases to control it once it has been played. In so doing he placed a higher value on the empirical, the practical, on pigheaded reality than on the ingenuity that might find ways of arousing the life in such a note. Ingenuity challenges the conductor to discover the ways and means of achieving this, and it would still be in the right even if such means could not be found. Toscanini called this *"stupido,"* but the worldly wisdom he displayed in so doing is stupidity in the first degree, technocratic hostility to the spirit.

§ The Prehistory of Serial Music

The current objection to the new principles of musical form that go by the name of twelve-tone technique, serial composition, or serial music accuses them of being arbitrarily imposed, external to the composition. As such they only appear to organize what happens concretely in the music, but fail to permeate it from within. Music of this type, so the criticism runs, breaks apart into an abstract order that is not perceptible as such, on the one, and a chaos for the receptive ear, on the other. It is not disputed that such music exists, just as bad new music in general exists. There was just as much bad traditional music, too, held together on the surface by its tonal organization without structure and individual event ever truly coalescing. But this is no truer of new music, as a whole, than it was of music in the past. Today, the unquestioned authority of the works of Schoenberg, Berg, and Webern testifies to the meaningful union of formal principles and musical surfaces. That authority alone precludes the possibility that the formal principles informing their works might be arbitrary. When Schoenberg once spoke of his invention of twelve-tone technique, Eduard Steuermann rightly countered that he had not invented it, he had discovered it. What he thus takes away from the illusion of something created from nothing is compensated for by the realization that the new procedures are contained in the nature of music itself and have been extrapolated from it, rather than imposed on it from outside. Furthermore, the customary objection is based on a distinction between natural elements of music and merely manufactured, arbitrary ones, a distinction that is in itself arbitrary. While claims are made on behalf of a natural music that is damaged by the composer's intellectual intervention, the truth is that this so-called natural music itself contains an element of rationalization: musical nature is always a second nature. At every stage of its history, the relationship between the material and the spiritual, the preexisting data and the composer's intervention, between form and the to-be-formed, is renewed; both are being constantly redefined. The serial principle, too, was not introduced into music by chance, but is the product of a historical development, until, in Hegel's famous simile, it cast off the seed leaf beneath which it had ripened and stood revealed as something qualitatively new.

Its origins are to be sought in traditional music, above all, that of free atonality, which seems to be opposed to it, thanks to its emancipation from all reference systems. To spell out the stages of this development is not to provide new music with a certificate of its ancestry; nor is it to prove that the principles governing it have always existed and hence cannot be all bad, or to clear away the initial strangeness that is part of its essence and without which it evaporates. Instead, proof of its origins will result in a better understanding of its objective necessity. It can be shown that the novel principles were not pulled out of the air, as many of its advocates would like to think, because traditional music had reached an impasse; rather, they bring to the surface what was already latent in the emancipation of music from the limits of traditional systems.

It is customary to derive twelve-tone technique from the principle of the variation.[1] But this leaves the concept of variation too undifferentiated. It contains a dynamic that is bound up with both the subjective tendency and the tendency toward integration in the history of modern music. The older variation was more or less the paraphrase of a theme that was thought to be unchangeable. As late as Schubert we still frequently find this type of variation. Beethoven rebelled against such rigidity, which treated the theme as an alien, untouchable thing, as contrasted with the subjective will to shape. By emphasizing the distinction between individ-

---

1. This treatise on the prehistory of serial composition, like the essays "The Function of Counterpoint in New Music," "Criteria of New Music," and "Music and Technique" (pp. 123–44, 145–96, and 197–214 in this volume, respectively) is closely related to *Philosophie der neuen Musik* [trans. Anne G. Mitchell and Wesley V. Blomster as *The Philosophy of Modern Music* (New York: Continuum, 1973)—Trans.]. What is touched on there is further developed here, and dialectical motifs are elaborated. A knowledge of the older text is presupposed; no cross-referencing has been attempted.

ual variations or groups of variations and the original theme he also distanced himself increasingly from its original shape and hence transformed it structurally, from within, instead of just figuratively changing its outer appearance. In the late *Diabelli Variations*, where he goes furthest in the characterization of each individual variation, the link with the original theme has become as hidden as the row becomes in new music with the progress of the composition. The theme only functions to the extent that some element, dimension, or, in the contemporary jargon, parameter is taken up and retained, while everything else is varied or newly invented. However, all of that is kept within certain limits. On the one hand, each variation becomes a rounded and coherent whole that calls to mind and, as it were, respects the original shape of the equally self-contained theme. On the other hand, the original theme is left intact precisely because it remains a distant cause of those modifications, beyond all of them. Every conceivable characteristic has been derived from it, but the theme itself is not dissolved by their succession, and its own character is not affected by the further course of the composition. Thus the development of the technique of variation moved in the direction of serialism by going beyond the limits accepted by Beethoven.

As is well known, Schoenberg's approach is normally characterized in crude terms by saying that he subordinated Wagnerian and New German chromaticism to classical Brahmsian principles. But this account is in need of refinement if we wish properly to understand the origins of serialism: even in the principles of construction, there is more of New German music than has been realized hitherto. Berlioz, with whom the classical Beethoven tradition is broken off, is the first to make consistent use of the leitmotif, which before then had made only a desultory appearance. This was made possible by the need for characterization; and also by the need to make music better fit the idea of a pure process—guided at least in tendency by free association—than was permitted by the static, architectonic repetition of formal elements corresponding one to another. In addition, the leitmotif also has a form-creating function, however clumsy and rudimentary. By virtue of its own identity, its purpose is to hold together what threatened to collapse into chaos, once the traditional architecture of the sonata was no longer reconcilable with the poetic programs. In Berlioz, and then in the New German school up to Strauss, the leitmotifs are more indispensable as cement for the work as a whole than the themes or models of variations had ever been in Beethoven. The shortening of the more extended theme into a brief motive helps in this respect: because the theme becomes more mobile, easier to manipulate, it can make its appearance in a variety of situations and do its duty. But in the process it becomes much further removed from its original form than it was in Viennese classicism. Through its development it is superseded, fragmented. The fact that the *idée fixe* of the *Symphonie fantastique*, the allegory of the woman of his dreams, is distorted and debased in the last movement also has an absolute musical significance. Berlioz can still feel what he is doing to the traditional, static concept of the theme, including Beethoven's theme, but nevertheless ventures to do something unimaginable in Beethoven. As often occurs in the history of music, the element of distortion and caricature conceals the emergence of the new quality.

Then in Wagner, in the guise of the psychological variation, a development that had still been shocking in Berlioz became an unproblematic, self-explanatory, and fully worked out technique of composition, a stylistic principle. Nevertheless, what Berlioz had launched into the river of music went drifting on. In the latter parts of *The Ring*, in *Götterdämmerung* above all, Wagner found himself faced by the problem of reusing familiar, preexisting material, adding only a minimum of new motives as *The Ring* came to a close. But in the course of the dramatic progression, the musical characters were forced to change. In *Siegfried*, Siegfried's horn motive is a fanfare derived from the natural tones of the instrument. In *Götterdämmerung* this turns into a heavily armed theme, almost crushed beneath the weight of its armor, that is supposed to provide an allegory of the hero, in contrast to the child of nature. The theme is now harmonized, the rhythms are changed, and it is handed over to a powerful brass chorus, as far removed from the earlier fanfare as a man is from the childhood in which he can no longer recognize himself. Even today, we can still feel the violence with which Wagner manipulates the horn motive. Frequently, single themes are smashed and rewelded by the composer, much like Siegfried's sword after Siegfried's programmatic speech in the sword-forging scene. Thus this seemingly forced element in new music, an element identical with its ability to shock, has a long tradition. It begins in the moment when Beethoven's reconstruction of a musical ontology, the subjective justification of the objectivity of classical form, lost its authority for the contemporary stage of musical consciousness. The leitmotifs were authoritative in their identity, and yet, looked at from the perspective of the whole, they were radically changed against their own will and reduced to mere material. As such, they may be thought of as the first rows.

Like the symphonic poems that are actually typical of the New German school—expanded overtures—Schoenberg's earlier large instrumental works all had one movement: *Verklärte Nacht, Pelleas und Melisande*, the First Quartet, and the Chamber Symphony no. 1. As "symphonic poems," the underlying idea behind these single movements was to do away with the archaizing schemas of preordained interchangeable types, musical character-masks, distantly reminiscent of the suite, and replace them with the unity of subjective intentions. But that too always had its objective, form-creating side, the tendency to integrate, to unify the musical structure, here, in the simplest and most literal sense that a single internally organized movement took the place of a multiplicity of more or less unconnected movements. Strauss's later symphonic poems were already large symphonies in one large movement. Whereas in *Verklärte Nacht* and *Pelleas* Schoenberg followed the impulse to a single movement derived from program music—in other words, he adapted the form of the music to that of the underlying poem—from the First String Quartet on he shifted in the direction of constructivism. The link between the single movement and integral composition explains why his last instrumental works—the Piano Concerto, the String Trio, and the Phantasy for Violin and Piano—where in so many ways he takes up again the intentions of his early compositions, remind us of that tendency to compose in one movement. Likewise, recent compositions of the most varied kinds, none of which have anything in common with program music, are once again moving toward one movement. Examples are Steuermann's Piano Trio, Improvisation and Allegro for Violin and Piano, and Stockhausen's *Zeitmaße* and *Gruppen*. From the First String Quartet on, Schoenberg interpreted the New German ideal of a single movement as one of synthesizing constructivism, and he merged it with the developed thematic work of the tradition from Beethoven to Brahms—in other words, with the idea of contrasting, dialectical composition that had been reserved hitherto for works in several movements. Those great one-movement pieces from the so-called second phase, the First String Quartet, the First Chamber Symphony, and later on the Piano Concerto and String Trio, all have, like Strauss's *Ein Heldenleben* and *Sinfonia domestica*, a latent structure of a number of movements, just as, conversely, many of the pieces with several movements, such as the Second Quartet and the Second Chamber Symphony, can be regarded as one-movement works in disguise. The task was to construct the main sections of these one-movement works, their "movements," in such a way as to unify them. It could be solved by handling the themes in a manner that came very close to what Berlioz and the New Germans had done with the leitmotif. They both retain the identity of the theme while simultaneously modifying it. In this way the themes in the First Quartet go a long way toward fulfilling the serial principle. The model of the sub-ordinate theme from the great Allegro with which the First Quartet opens is brief enough to put us in mind of the leitmotif. Schoenberg's infallible instinct has already introduced it as a kind of "material," as something that can be treated serially, such that it initially appears as a first violin melody working like a real theme. This for its part is covered by that higher voice, purposefully, unobtrusively exposed. This subordinate theme is in fact treated in a serial manner. From it Schoenberg derives the theme of the subsequent main section following the great elaboration that cor-responds to a scherzo. Admittedly, the changes undergone here differ in important ways from the later serial technique. What is maintained is the rhythm and the general outline of the subordinate theme; but the char-acteristic interval, the minor ninth, with which it originally closes is lev-eled out in the scherzo, reduced to a mere octave, whereas in twelve-tone composition the intervals would be maintained and the rhythms changed. Despite this, what the two thematic shapes, taken together, have in com-mon with serial technique is that underlying both is a kind of "subcuta-neous" material—we are reminded of Schenker's *Urlinie* and in general of Beethoven—from which completely different characteristics are derived whose tone and expression take no notice of each other. In short, the prin-ciple of variation is removed from the surface and becomes part of the way the material is deployed, whereas the so-called individual variations come to represent quite new themes or motives. Variations are no longer com-posed on themes: composition becomes variation in general, without a static theme. The extent to which in the serial manner the treatment of a theme leaves its original form behind, in other words, the extent to which the theme becomes material, can be seen in the final section of the First Quartet, corresponding to the rondo, where the theme constitutes a sub-sidiary idea that has the same contours as the original subordinate theme but none of the rhythmic shape and not even the characteristic interval. It has now been transformed into fresh, carefree music-making, quite without its former tension, which has been completely resolved as it ran

its course. Such procedures, which are fully explicit in the very first movement, needed only to free themselves from tonal structures and relationships for Schoenberg to be left with the principle of serialism in his hands,
as the essential content of his treatment of thematic work.

The more unobtrusive a shape, the more suitable it is to become a row.
The main theme of the First Quartet, contrasting with the subordinate
theme by the way it is spun out as a lengthy melody, has as an accompaniment in its first three measures a bass voice ascending in seconds that
then, as is mainly the case in Schoenberg, is switched with the top voice
along the lines of a double counterpoint.[2] Schoenberg then uses this cello
counterpoint, quite in the spirit of the later rows, as a new theme in the
elaboration. The intervals are sustained, but the note values diminished
and the rhythm altered. The identity with the theme can scarcely be registered by the ear any longer, but it is transmitted as a unifying element
in the highly complex musical events.

The invisibility of this unifying element, a central feature of serialism as
opposed to thematic work, is not the belated consequence of a fixed technique. It points back to the compositional process itself. Schoenberg himself discusses it in the essay on twelve-tone technique that has now been
published in the volume *Style and Idea*. The Chamber Symphony op. 9
contains, within the complex of its first subject, two main themes, one
passionately ascending on the cello and the other—corresponding to the
traditional [contrasting] entry—a flowing theme on the violin in the opposite direction. Schoenberg writes that after completing the work he was
worried because the two had no connection with each other. He even
considered doing away with the continuation, but then decided to rely
on his original idea, and twenty years later discovered that the characteristic inflections of the second main theme were the inversion of the main
intervals of the first. In other words, the principle of thematic inversion
that had fallen into oblivion after Bach, and that is denounced by trivial
minds as overintellectual, turns out to have reasserted itself unconsciously,
under the compulsion of Schoenberg's intuitive sense of form. Now, the
way in which a work of art becomes what it is is irrelevant to the question of its quality. Only the work itself counts, not its origins. However,
the banal argument that thinks itself qualified to judge artistic matters by

---

2. See "The Function of Counterpoint in New Music" [pp. 123–44 in this volume—Trans.].

producing the question "Was this intentional?" can always be refuted if it is pointed out that what was held to be the calculated intention of the composer, or the despicable intellectualism of the critic, is grounded in reality in the depths of the form itself. In the same way something like a row lies hidden behind the two very different main ideas of the first thematic complex in the Chamber Symphony. And precisely in this case there are analogies with Beethoven, in the *Waldstein* Sonata, for example, where the line of the subordinate theme inverts that of the principal theme. Little heed was paid to such relationships in the traditional music of the nineteenth century. Scarcely anyone apart from the most important composers bothered to cultivate them. The overall coherence was guaranteed by tonality, or at least its semblance, which only the most advanced ear mistrusted. However, the harder the traditional guarantors of unity found it to cope with the threatened changes, the more we find elements of music that had been regarded as apocryphal ever since the end of the Middle Ages coming back into the focus of construction.

In the Second Quartet, Schoenberg returned to a plurality of movements, without abandoning the idea of a fully constructed unity for the work as a whole. This unity is realized by making the third movement, with its vocal part, an unusually authoritative sequence of variations that at the same time takes over the task of a great elaboration of the entire work, whereas in the first movement, the elaboration, ingenious and concise, is kept relatively short. The variation theme of the third movement accordingly appears as a model of elaboration that combines essential elements of the preceding movements. The main motive is the principal theme of the first movement rhythmically transformed according to serial practice; the additional counterpoint on the first violin is at once imitated by the cello, and is identical with the model of the second principal subject from the first movement; the middle motive on the viola is the faithfully rendered, likewise rhythmically varied second theme of the scherzo; the consequent of the theme, finally, is the last-exposed theme from the first movement in double augmentation. From this thematic mosaic a new theme arises, a basic set, as it were; what strikes the listener as rowlike about it is the monody, which is only interrupted in the first measures by two brief contrapuntal passages. This extraordinarily condensed piece, in which the variations seem not so much distinguished from one another as interwoven, is developed in such a way that the constituent elements of the theme are taken up and spun out separately. They are joined by a contrapuntal passage where the vocal part enters and cuts into the repetition of the consequent phrase of the theme. Virtually identically with twelve-tone music, there is scarcely a single "free" note in the entire movement; literally every one is thematic, that is, either an immediate constituent of one of the elements of the theme or visibly derived from it. When we come to the succeeding, last movement, the *Entrückung*, it is as if the indescribable tension of this movement had to be followed by a huge sigh of relief, for that movement, aside from its grand architecture, is largely athematic, albeit with thematic reminiscences, especially in the consequent of the variation theme. It is also the first piece of free atonality of Schoenberg's, without a key signature, despite the F# major conclusion.

The relationship of the great, highly thematic chamber works from Schoenberg's second phase to twelve-tone technique is very evident, and Schoenberg, who was now in full control of the new technique, took his cue from them, most clearly in the first movement of the Fourth Quartet. However, at first sight, free atonality appears to be the absolute antithesis of such an approach to form, with its attempt simply to leave the natural life of the sounds to the inner ear. But a closer scrutiny leads to the conclusion that during this phase the principles of construction he had acquired were now extended further. They are perhaps all the more effective, and approach even closer to the serial principle, because now, with the elimination of the vestiges of sonata form and the traditional elaboration, they no longer simply rest on the surface as they do in the first two quartets and the First Chamber Symphony. It would be a mistake to think that the works of this phase, Schoenberg's third, were as athematic as the score of *Erwartung*, the only composition on a larger scale that this concept fits. Composition after World War Two was essentially confronted with the task of recuperating from the free atonal period the prose element of music, now cleansed of all structural façades, which Schoenberg had sacrificed at the beginning of the twelve-tone period. In this process, the free compositional events wish to be organized into a structure; freedom and necessity are elevated in earnest to a state of identity. This conception, which surfaces in a variety of places, obtained an opening only because the formal principles of what Alois Hába called "the compositional style of freedom"—free atonality, in other words—had not been abandoned.

The Orchestral Pieces, op. 16, was the third work in free atonality, and had been preceded only by the George songs—which belonged to the traditional lieder genre, for all their harmonic emancipation—and the relatively simple Piano Pieces op. 11. Nevertheless, they already show a return to the thematic. Webern had been struck by this as early as his Schoenberg essay of 1912. He noted in addition to their loose, proselike structure that "the themes in these pieces too are quite brief, but are developed." In a number they are straightforward basic sets, though without concern for the entity value of the twelve-tone set, but freely invented, more like Schoenberg's procedure at the start of the twelve-tone phase in the Piano Pieces op. 23. In op. 16 he needed the thematic work in order to be able to integrate the highly polyphonic orchestral writing, whereas because of their relatively homophonic structure, the songs and piano pieces can still work without a built-in counterforce.

The organization of the first Orchestral Piece is very transparent, but given its spare dimensions it is overrich in motives. As is general in the phase of free atonality, the most powerful contrasts have been compressed into the tightest possible space. Nevertheless, the diverse materials are organized according to a strict economy. The main characters by no means form the basic material of the piece. Thus the first or, if you like, the principal theme (mm. 1–3, cello) is formed by the repetition of the three-note motive E-F-A, whose identity is concealed by the rhythmic treatment. This motive also recurs, diminished and inverted, in counterpoint, played as a principal theme on the deep woodwinds. It contains at the outset a further melisma, likewise on three notes, D-C#-G, that becomes very important for what follows (m. 1, double-bass clarinet and contrabassoon). The fourth measure, with which a completely unconnected consequent begins, seems quite new; in reality, however, it is derived from the first measure: the C#-D-F# on the horn in m. 4 is identical with the original motive [E-F-A], the Eb-Db-G on the clarinet (likewise m. 4) is closely related to the beginning of the counterpoint. From this arises likewise the A-G#-D on the horn and then the clarinet (m. 5) that supplies the rest of the consequent. A further novelty seems to appear in m. 4 after cue 1, but it too arises from the original motive. Its highly rhythmical inflections— E on the first oboe, F in the pizzicato first violins, Ab on the piccolo— correspond to the initial construct. The dyad C#-E, and then the tetrachord D-F-C#-E, however, is part of a harmonic complex that dominates the whole second section. Were it completed, it would be the hexachord of the D minor scale—D-F-A-C#-E-G; however, it is only ever heard split up into its different elements, never as a complete harmony. If the exposition is followed through in detail, it comes down to this complex.

Melodically, it is dominated by two motives, E-F-A—the principal motive—and D-C#-G—the beginning of the first contrapuntal passage.
Arranged in thirds and played simultaneously, these two basic sets together would yield the hexachord D-F-A-C#-E-G, which in fact forms
the harmonic basis of the entire piece. Hence, when Schoenberg wrote the
Orchestral Pieces fifty years ago, he had not only mastered the subtleties
of twelve-tone technique—changes in rhythm, augmentation, diminution, distribution of the melody among the different parts, inversions and
retrogrades; but in addition, even though he was composing in a completely free style, he anticipated what would subsequently prove to be the
most disconcerting feature of twelve-tone technique: the integration of
horizontals and verticals—in other words, the notion that successive notes
in the row can be collapsed into simultaneous sounds. What has been attributed to abstract calculus was in fact developed within a completely unregulated style that was simply obeying the requirements of the ear.

One of the two basic sets of the first Orchestral Piece, the sequence of
second and third, which, inverted and retrograded, can be rotated on its
own axis, is nearly identical with Mahler's almost exactly contemporane-
ous *Lied von der Erde*. Here it furnishes the quintessence of Chinese pen-
tatonicism, whose critical intervals are in fact seconds and thirds. Even in
Mahler, this motive is not given thematic importance, but instead functions as a stylistic principle, as a means of fusing the musical texture together, thus unobtrusively echoing the exotic tonal system that seemed
appropriate to the choice of texts: a kind of cement that unified the otherwise disparate musical events. Wagner had already used such bonding
techniques, which were different from succinct leitmotifs; they were evident above all in *Tristan*. Those cementing motives from the nineteenth
century, whose precise frontier is distinguished by the Wagnerian leitmotif—although the simplicity of Wagnerian leitmotifs sometimes makes
them very imprecise—point to a very essential aspect of serial technique,
namely the prefabrication of the material prior to the manifest composition. This method of construction likewise was discovered when, following the critique of the traditional forms and the traditional language of
music, it became apparent that overall coherence had to be strengthened,
and specifically at the points where previously the idiom had stepped in
and where, at the same time, the growth of differentiation—as if in accordance with the principles advanced around the same time by the sociologist Herbert Spencer—met up with its correlate, growing integration.

The latency principle itself is probably rooted in the desire to make sure that the labor involved in creating art, the production process, should be hidden from view, much like factory chimneys in bourgeois residential districts during the nineteenth century. Only as a belated and radical consequence of the New Objectivity, comparable to the principles of the Bauhaus, did it become acceptable for the methods by which music was produced to become visible in the music itself; only with Webern did rows and row-relations become directly thematic.

It might be objected that the Orchestral Pieces contain thematic work and that therefore their link with twelve-tone music comes as no surprise—even though at the time Schoenberg was himself very struck by the evidence of their serial character. But even in Schoenberg's atonal compositions there is quite unambiguous evidence of serial thinking that has little or nothing to do with thematic work in the usual sense. In order to achieve extremes of expressiveness, the first atonal Piano Pieces, op. 11, used extreme contrasts to form themes and thematic complexes. To increase the tension in the music Schoenberg abandons the usual mediations, which seem almost accidental when contrasted to the thematic centers. The new musical idiom is defined by those contrasts—as well as by the abrupt cessation of musical figures as soon as their impulse is exhausted, the refusal to spin things out in the traditional way. For Schoenberg's sense of form, however, his supersensitive feeling for the objective authority even of apparently unregulated expressive impulses, those contrasts threw up a problem right from the start. To put it as a paradox: Even the rejection of mediations itself required mediations if it was not to degenerate into pure randomness, into that chaos with which the short-winded listener all too readily reproaches Schoenberg.

A contrast like the one between the slow consequent of the main subject in the first piece, op. 11, and the following dissolution in thirty-seconds had not been attempted before in Western music. Schoenberg goes on to make sure the piece does not just fall to bits by drawing that dissolved figure in thirty-seconds retrospectively into the middle section, thus incorporating it into the form and preventing it from standing alone simply as a shock effect, external to the overall structure. Similar contrasts serve to crystallize the Piano Pieces op. 19, comprising six small works. In the fourth, with its hinted-at three-part structure, a middle section in ritardando is succeeded once again by a total dissolution. But because the dimensions of the piece have been reduced to a miniature, the composition is not able to catch up through any further unfolding, as in the earlier, more substantial op. 11, no. 1. Schoenberg finds himself compelled to unify quite disparate, unconnected, nonidentical material through a coup de main. To achieve this, he derives the beginning of the martellato figure of the final segment in a strict serial manner by diminution from the initial notes of the main subject. The complete contrast of the codalike ending is nothing but a variation of the beginning. At the same time, the shock of the coda comes as a total surprise.

In order, finally, to understand the particular nature of those predecessors of serial technique contained in *Pierrot lunaire*, it is necessary to recall the spirit of these "three-times-seven melodramas." They form one of the last works that Schoenberg composed before the great gap in his oeuvre that finally ended with the introduction of twelve-tone composition. They are a work of alienation. They even came from outside, having been composed in response to a commission, and we find in them the clear tendency to break out of expressionism and the desire to tackle the problem of objectivity through a renewed confrontation with preexisting types—much as in the very similar Serenade, op. 24. For the first time in a long while the work cites traditional forms: the waltz, passacaglia, lied, canon, chorale setting, and fugue. But with that incorruptible ontological tact, that sense of what is possible and impossible historically, which confirms Schoenberg's rank among the great composers, he never simply invoked these forms, unlike the neoclassicists. As might be suggested by the playful *Jugendstil* poems, a general irony sustains all its forms, penetrating deep into their framework. Even their objectivity seems to grow from within the glass walls of the solitary subject: Maeterlinck's *Herzgewächse*, which Schoenberg had set shortly before, could serve as the motto for the whole of *Pierrot*. Its objectivity is one that inhabits the realm of an objectless interior. This puts its imprint on the form as a whole. In this glass house the forms are not "brought to life," as the saying goes, but created from the material structure and the process of composition: for this reason they remain the property of the subject. The "let's pretend" quality of this objectivity, its playful character, is imparted to the process of composition. The latter has something inauthentic, playful about it, worlds away from the literal-minded earnestness of expressionist protocols: its themes are scarcely themes anymore as such, but are peculiarly stunted and condensed. This playfulness manifests itself also as a kind of insatiable inventiveness. The fact that *Pierrot* does not rely simply on the objectivity of inauthentically recurring forms and that these have to be propped up from inside, from the purely immanent mode of construction, forms the basis of its lavishly artificial structure.

The section of *Pierrot* most famous for its artistry is *Mondfleck*; its polyphony scarcely needs to be fully apprehended. The lunatic overdetermined nature of every note serves, rather, a poetic intention: it symbolizes the vicious circle represented by the image of Pierrot vainly rubbing away at a white moonbeam on his black coat "until the dawn." Absolute musical events from the phase of free atonality joined forces here with an explicit literary intention to precipitate the twelve-tone technique. The double canon of the two winds and two strings is Schoenberg's first strictly retrograde composition, the first exacting, specific use of the retrograde technique in a composition. That canon is accompanied by a fugue on the piano. However, its theme and the canonic chief subject on the clarinet behave exactly like two completely different rhythmic versions of the same row: both utilize identical notes. This indescribably polyphonic and complex piece is, therefore, built out of the identical basic material, if we ignore the second canon, the one played on violin and cello, which is essentially no more than an accompaniment. But it is no twelve-tone composition, if only because the initial row does not yet conform to the twelve-tone rule. The more complex the music becomes, and the more diverse, the greater the need there is for it to be integrated: the more diversity, the more unity. It is this relationship alone which gives twelve-tone music its raison d'être. It came into being at that moment when what seemed to be no more than a melodramatic trick in *Mondfleck* became an unobtrusive and natural premise in all composition, except that now it would no longer tolerate any accompaniment external to it. But if Schoenberg jokingly observed of *Mondfleck*, parodying the old rule in counterpoint, that he allowed consonance only when it was prepared and unaccented, he nevertheless provided thereby the formulation for one of those allergies from which the rules of twelve-tone technique followed.

The demonstration of how deeply rooted twelve-tone technique is in its own prehistory, both of the nineteenth century and of Schoenberg himself, should not be allowed to diminish the rupture represented by the first serial compositions, Schoenberg's opp. 23 and 24. The concept of dialectics is precisely relevant to Schoenberg in the sense that everything had really always been present, yet at the same time, everything was completely new. With the codifying of all the formal principles that emerged blind, as it were, from his compositions, the entire climate of composition changed, just as it had changed once before, with the first Piano Pieces, when Schoenberg abandoned tonality—which then resurfaced in the chamber music works of the second period, when it surrounded the substance of those works like an ethereal cloak. There can be no doubt that much of the corpus of formal principles that had hitherto come to maturity within music was then sacrificed to the codification and rationalization that became known as twelve-tone technique. The ultimate systematic shape of that technique was achieved at the cost of the flexibility of the compositional elements to which it owed its existence; the unbroken coherence of twelve-tone composition was accompanied by the shadow of a reification that had not threatened its predecessors in the same way. A presentiment of this seems not to have escaped Schoenberg himself. On the occasion of his quarrel—later resolved—with Thomas Mann, he reproached Mann for having chosen an adviser other than himself to help him with the depiction of Leverkühn's works. He is said to have pointed out that if Mann had turned to him, he would have been able to think up countless other principles of construction for Adrian Leverkühn besides twelve-tone technique. It is easy to believe him once one has seen the examples in the early works of some of the many possibilities of constructivism in composition. Nevertheless, it was not a complete mistake for Mann to have based his description in that novel on the actual technique developed by Schoenberg, rather than on mere abstract possibilities: it put Schoenberg in the right against his own objections. The technique that has become a historical reality always has a certain superiority over alternative systems that remained mere possibilities. On the side of what actually happened were historical forces that wanted this particular development rather than others. Nevertheless, possible alternatives always include the forgotten, the oppressed, and the vanquished, and with them the potential for something better. An essential obligation of a potent historical consciousness, including a consciousness of artistic forms, is to preserve what has been forgotten. Such a contradiction is central not just in twelve-tone technique, but probably in all composition today. May these reflections on the prehistory of integral composition help to resolve it.

§ Alban Berg

At Christmas 1955, on 24 December, Berg had been dead for twenty years. The period since 1935 was not one of continuity and steady growth in experience; it was disrupted by catastrophes. People forced to emigrate cannot escape the feeling that long years have been torn out of their lives, and it is easy for them to succumb to the delusion that their present existence is just a continuation of what was destroyed then. That is why it is so difficult to convince oneself that Berg has been gone for so long and that we have to make an effort to remember a man whose absence we have never quite been able to admit to ourselves. A feeling of guilt must come over anyone who, in evoking the memory of Berg, sets a seal on the fact of his death. In addition to its subjective justification, this feeling may also be connected with the life that Berg has been granted since his death, in the afterlife of his works. For ten years, until the end of the war, his memory was expunged from public consciousness in Germany, and likewise in Austria. Following the premiere of the *Lulu* Symphony, which Kleiber dared to put on during the Hitler Reich, he was outlawed as a cultural Bolshevik, and from then on there were probably no further performances of his works. Although there was not anything that the fanatics of racism could have found to object to in him, he scorned to make any concessions to the healthy convictions of the people and to barbarism. After 1945 his music was frequently performed again, but in a very different context. During his lifetime he was a leading member of the avant-garde and would never have felt himself to be anything else. He now finds himself lumped together with others under the label of "modern classics," a label from which he would have recoiled. The kind of reception that would really have enabled him to represent new music in the way that was claimed for him was denied him.

His fate differed from that of the other representatives of musical modernity, however. Today it seems as if the public has made its decision in favor of Berg and against the experts, much as Wagner advocated in *Die Meistersinger*. But this is not entirely accurate either. Even during his lifetime Berg's music was appreciated for its expressive qualities, its human tone, and no doubt also its rich sensuousness, and he was compared favorably with Schoenberg in this respect. Berg always objected to such praise, not simply from loyalty to his older friend, but because he felt it to be based on the misapprehension that he was a conformist. He felt slighted in his claims to radicality. After the Berlin premiere of *Wozzeck* in December 1925 we walked around the town until late into the night, and I had to console him over his success, the greatest of his life. If the audience liked that, he said, there was something wrong. And in fact, the quality that brought him success then is the same one that makes it hard for musicians to accept him today. Although those who denounced him thirty years ago have now fallen silent, he is dismissed today as someone who already belongs to the past. The deepest reason for this rejection is probably that the standards he set for composition are felt to be extremely irksome. People would now like to escape from their constraints and from his insistence on the spontaneity of the imagination, an escape they would justify by appealing to the spirit of the age. At the same time, it was he who was responsible for one of the innovations about which so much fuss is made today, namely the inclusion of the element of rhythm as a constructive feature. Of all the composers of the Schoenberg school, it was he who was the most willing to involve himself in quasi-geometric formal experiments. It is perhaps not superfluous to remark that as early as *Wozzeck* he constructed an entire scene as a set of variations on a rhythm, and in the twelve-tone *Lulu* this procedure was expanded to a large form with [rhythmic] retrograde elements that he called "Monoritmica." In his later works he generally strives for elaborate symmetries that go from the measure-count proportions of entire movements down to the smallest units of phrase construction. This is particularly true of the Chamber Concerto and the Violin Concerto.—There is a particular hostility toward Berg in Germany from those who belong to the so-called *Sing- und Spielbewegung* and those who advocate both a collectivist attitude on the part of the musician and the contemporary relevance of the seventeenth century. They need only hear a few bars of Berg to start talking automatically of *Tristan*-like late Romanticism, as if chromaticism and the leading note were the most important aspects of Berg's mature music, and as if determining what his searching, infinitely subtle sensibility succeeded in making of such elements were irrelevant.

In the light of all this, our task must be to try and correct some of the current misconceptions about him, to compensate for some of the damage that he has suffered at the hands of public opinion, and to eliminate some of the phrases and clichés that have made the living experience of his work so fraught with problems nowadays. I am under no illusions about the difficulty of this task and the small prospects of success. I won't be surprised if tomorrow I read and hear once again that Berg is a neurasthenic late Romantic decadent whose overrefined subjectivity no longer speaks to the younger generation. And I shall be overjoyed if people who hear Berg's music and then read sentences of this kind cease to accept them at their face value, and if those who are still unable to change their views were to stop and think for a single second whether Berg's alleged weakness is not worth more than the security of the present day, in which none of those who talk about it so loudly have any real faith. But nothing would be more misguided than to achieve such modest success by denying those elements of Berg's music that every jackass can hear, to use Brahms's words, and that provide both a cheap and inexhaustible source of pleasure to those who wish to criticize him. What is more important is to be aware of the significance of these elements within the force field of Berg's music, to discover what he has made of them.

The fact is, of course, that Berg's origins do lie in *Jugendstil* and the fin de siècle. His affinity with neo-Romanticism and aestheticism was powerful enough to have left its mark even on his fragile physical existence. To convince oneself of that it is only necessary to glance at the 1908 photograph of Berg as a young man in Willi Reich's biography. Even the older Berg still retains a resemblance to Oscar Wilde. He was on friendly terms with Peter Altenberg. He would use a word like "secession" as if it were still current, and there are even links with Schreker, for whose *Der ferne Klang* he had made a piano reduction in his youth. We cannot imagine Berg's music without the element of opulence, of extravagance, especially in his orchestral sound. It has sublimated itself into that synthesis with structure, that seductive and refulgent sensuousness, that gives the instrumentation of the late Berg, above all in *Lulu*, its incomparable aura.

The fury that this quality, along with his passionate expressionism, unleashes today obeys a mechanism of repression, to use the language of psychology, which is all too appropriate here. This is because each of the expansive gestures in Berg's music reaches out in search of an unself-conscious happiness that refuses to conform to reality. Such happiness appears unattainable in the regimented condition that grants man happiness only on condition that he conforms. It is altogether appropriate if such happiness is made to look either childishly old-fashioned or else, in the contemporary climate of restoration, unworthy of authentic existence. Whoever wishes to hear Berg aright should not begin by asking after every beat whether this is not altogether too personal or whether it also speaks to other people, but rather should follow the logic of the music. He will then find in it more human qualities than in reflecting upon the effects that it may or may not have on others.

This human quality, however, its expressive substance, is diametrically opposed to the Wagnerian, with which insensitive ears confuse it. The degenerate, addicted aspect of Berg's music is not a feature of his own ego. It does not aim at narcissistic self-glorification. Rather, it is an erotic enslavement, the object of which is nothing other than beauty and which calls to mind a nature that has been oppressed and degraded by the taboos of culture. The two great operas, *Wozzeck* and *Lulu*, contain nothing heroic, and in them spirit puts on no airs. Instead their enslaved and lethal love attaches itself to the lower depths, to lost souls, to the half-demented and at the same time helplessly self-sacrificing soldier, to his beloved whose instincts rebel against him and whom he destroys together with himself. Later, that love attaches itself to Lulu, an image from the age of courtesans dressed up in the costume of 1890. She is a woman to whom dominant men succumb and whom they destroy in the course of brutally asserting their dominance. The choice of these texts and the standpoint from which he set them to music, the standpoint of universal sympathy with the oppressed, determines the pattern of his work down to the purest piece of instrumental music. His tone can be described as greathearted. "Compassionate" would be a poor, patronizing word for it. This music gives not alms, but total identification; without reservation it throws itself away for the sake of others, something we hear too in the greatest moments of Berg's kindred spirit, Robert Schumann. We become conscious of this Bergian tone as early as the beginning of the development section of the Piano Sonata, op. 1, and then again in the wistful tenderness of the second movement of the *Lyric Suite*, or in the nostalgic quotation, as if gazing backward in recollection, of the Carinthian folk song shortly before the end of the Violin Concerto. Such anachronistic yearning far transcends the unreserved willingness to join in and get on with the job that is acclaimed in so much other contemporary music under the misnomer of vitality. Even the inner structure of the Wagnerian yearning for death has undergone a decisive change in Berg. In Wagner the end of the world was the triumphant consummation of the destructive impulse, transposed into the supreme, unconstrained fantasy of power. In Berg this is translated into a kind of abdication, as if the living subject felt something of the injustice that arises simply because his life depends on stealing a place from someone else, and who would rather give up his life than continue to benefit from the theft. One of Berg's favorite words was "warmhearted" [*jovial*], and what he meant by this was not small-minded good nature and complacency, but precisely that gesture of selflessness and fellowship. What ultimately divides the tone of his music from Wagner and the rest of the new Germans is an element of acquiescence, a legacy perhaps of the south German or Austrian tradition. It has a strong admixture of nostalgic skepticism and irony and is full of the profound knowledge that there is no hope other than that contained in the gesture of bidding farewell to the world and its goods. If we are to talk about expression, and make judgments about it, we also have to take a view of what is expressed, and in Berg's case this is the reverse of private, subjective self-limitation. It is solidarity with mankind, made concrete as the irresistible approval of what mankind excludes from itself and what therefore stands in unconsciously for the image of a possible humanity. In his case, addiction includes the potential for freedom.

In this spirit, and in opposition to widespread and growing tendencies toward regression, he kept a firm hold on a crucial aspect of operatic form. But his artistic instincts also led him far beyond the empathetic techniques of the musical drama, the illustration of feelings and events by sound. His choice of remote subjects—one from the period before the 1848 Revolution, the other from the 1890s—as well as the fact that he salvaged them as ideas belonging to the past rather than simply attaching his music to them, is significant, for it adds a distancing element to works that he himself called operas. This is matched by the principle of construction that is employed consistently in both works and that confers a certain autonomy to the music, even as it follows the events. This is a principle that can scarcely be claimed for Stravinsky's works for theater, for all their use of miming techniques. In Berg the principle of musical drama, as the translation of music into a wealth of infinitely complex tensions, effectively became one of comprehensive development. In contrast to Wagner, he was the first to introduce into opera the truly dramatic feature of Viennese classicism, its variegated dialectic [*durchbrochene Arbeit*]. In his works, and perhaps in them alone, we can see the outlines of a kind of autonomous operatic music emerging from beneath the cloak of the musical drama. It is music that follows its own impulses right through to the end instead of exhausting itself in an ascetic rejection of empathy, and it derives its autonomy from its own internal relationship to the drama that it absorbs. Opera of this type fulfills itself musically, satisfying the logic of its own musical laws, for it does not just run alongside the drama, but follows the contours of all its impulses, developments, contrasts, and tensions. The music is absorbed into the drama more than ever before, and as a direct result it is articulated down to the last note and achieves the autonomy denied it in the old-style, tone-painting musical drama.

That is what distinguishes Berg's relationship to Wagner and to the musical heritage in general from that of the other masters of new music. Just as his compositions seek infinite internal correspondences and are hostile to contrast, so too on the historical plane Berg did not bluntly reject the world of his parents, the late nineteenth century. Loyalty stood at the apex of his moral heaven. Alberich's "Be true" in *Götterdämmerung* [act 2, scene 1] was something he would quote with emphatic approval, perhaps with a presentiment of the mythical, prehistorical origins of loyalty and also with a sense that loyalty is the quality best suited to twilights of gods. Just as he kept faith with the people and the cause to which he had committed himself freely, rather than under some instinctive compulsion, he also kept faith with the world from which he came. Little characterizes him better than the fact that, at the height of his maturity as a composer, he orchestrated and published the Seven Early Songs, which lie completely outside the confines of everything that had come to be associated so specifically with the Bergian style. He did not shy away from providing insensitive ears with the ammunition to denounce what he wrote subsequently. Berg's development did not consist in his repudiation of his musical heritage. Instead he consumed that heritage, much as in the nineteenth century people of private means lived off their capital. But this also implies that he did not cling to that heritage as if it were his private property. By so consuming it, he ended up destroying it. It is the dual character of this process that defines his uniqueness. The lineaments of his music will be most easily read by those searching to discover what has become of that heritage as a result of this process of dissolving and reconstituting it in the course of composition. Only today, when his constructivism, stripped of his recalcitrant musical language, threatens to relapse into decorative commercialism or to regress to an emphasis on content alien to art, does the truth element in Berg's shy smile and his measured treatment of the past emerge fully. The aspects of his music that do not appear to fit completely with the criteria of stylistic purity and logical consistency are the vestiges of a blindly accepted tradition that he has failed to illuminate. But this musical procedure is legitimated by the way it permeates the world of substance and expression that it confronts. An inexhaustible qualitative wealth characterizes Berg's whole method of composition and flows into it from a past that he does not reject as unmodern. He was undoubtedly very well aware of this tension. With his indescribably proud modesty he once responded to a compliment by saying that his achievement was to have preserved his own personal tone within the twelve-tone technique and its tendency to level out all distinctions. In the same way, when confronted with the critical question of why he almost always allowed elements of tonality to survive in his works, he answered that that was the way he did things and that he was disinclined to change them. We should add that his habit of harking back to the past did not show any signs of diminishing with time; indeed, it is particularly marked in the Alwa sections of *Lulu* and throughout the Violin Concerto. But nothing traditional emerges from his music unaltered. His energy as a composer tests itself on such material indefatigably, and regenerates itself in the process. Despite the junglelike density of its texture, and complementary to it, Berg's music is articulated down to the last note. No other contemporary music, not even that of Schoenberg, who followed his impulses more spontaneously, is so planned and masterfully worked out as Berg's, no doubt because of his spatial, architectonic gift in which his sense of articulated order outweighed the flow of feeling. That means that there is not a single movement, no section, no theme, no period, no motive, nor even a single note that fails to fulfill its wholly unambiguous and unmistakable formal meaning even in the most complex of contexts. In this respect he was not so very different from Webern, although the latter's reductive method relieved him of many of the burdens of creating large-scale structures. The more musical production today denies that dimension of composition, that is, the quasi-linguistic, the more Berg's works assume exemplary status for them, first and foremost the *Lyric Suite* for string quartet. However, his gift for the meaningful elaboration of the language of music, for authentic composition— something that has not received proper recognition even today—is nothing other than his highly wrought subjective sensibility and his refined sense of subtle nuance. Berg was able to translate those subjective reactions into the criteria of composition itself, thus displaying a highly civilized, we might even call it French, mastery; his much-criticized subjectivism gave the work its objective validity, the sublime solidity of form, with the consequence that, like Mörike's lamp, it seems "blessed in itself." From the outset, Berg's sensibility was determined by his relationship to objects. The loving and considerate way he treated them arose from a desire to look after created things. It was as if he wished to make good some of the damage done to them by people who altered them for their own purposes. As a forty-year-old he still used his first shaving set and was proud of having looked after it so well that it still looked new. The composer's hand worked with the same care. In his works, the world of prehistoric dreams, the monstrous, and what Goethe termed the dull [*das Dumpfe*] encounter what is brightest and full of sensitive artifice, the beauty of the wealth of forms. This is the riddle of Berg's music. We could scarcely describe it more simply or accurately than by saying that it resembled him.

If we compare Berg with those who were closest to him, with Schoenberg and Webern, and with the development of the radically new music of the last twenty years, it is easy to comprehend his achievement as having formed a link with the past, as securing the connection between the innovations of the moderns with tradition. And in fact the continuity lies closer to the surface in his case than in that of his friends, even though Schoenberg in particular punctiliously fulfilled the obligations that he had inherited from Bach and Viennese classicism down to Brahms and Wagner. Compared with such rigor we may say that Berg retained a certain urbanity, even in his inclusion of heterogeneous stylistic features, and the internal breadth of his composition gained from this. If in general the influence of Mahler on his school was much greater than appeared on the surface, in Berg's case we can see how often he openly echoes Mahler's intonation, particularly in sections of *Wozzeck* and the Violin Concerto. His ambivalent relationship to the folk song, in which his identification with the victims assumes musical shape, would be unthinkable without the Mahler whose marches resonate with sorrow for the deserter. And Berg's peculiar insatiability ensures that he himself finds it hard to endure the constructive constraints he imposes on himself: hence his constant efforts to extend the limits of sound with doublings, clusters, and parallel progressions, which create an affinity with Debussy that climaxes, above all in *Lulu*, in a veritable impressionist phantasmagoria. His ideal orchestra would have glowed and flashed iridescently, and that was not possible until impressionism had become a historical reality; then the idea of impressionism could be conjured up and made completely available, as if in a memory. We may recollect how the writings of Marcel Proust took possession of the entire technical repertoire of French painting at the moment when these techniques were recalled to mind like something long forgotten. But Berg's oeuvre always has something extraordinary about it, and we would subtly miss the essential point about it if, because of such links to the past, we were to listen to him as if he were the rearguard of modernism. That would be to measure him against a concept of progress that has since become far more dubious than the usual idea that plays the old truths, the eternal values, off against progress. Berg made no such pact with the old values, nor did he stock up on such eternally lasting goods in advance. His music is too strongly dedicated to death for that. However, at every one of its stages music suffers a loss at the hands of progress: the increasing control of its material, the expression of the increasing manipulation of nature, always entails a certain violence. Berg shrank from this, yet simultaneously entrusted himself to progress without reservation. This paradox is promoted by a feature of his musical makeup that prevents him from allowing anything to slip from his grasp and by his determination to retain a grip on anything that might advance his work. It is perhaps an anxiety, related to his affinity with death. But this desire to keep a hold on things is not unlike the attempt to square the circle; it is a piece of quixotry. It means that every one of his works is really an impossibility, attainable only through trickery, a tour de force. He who desires to salvage in progress the very thing that progress destroys must pay an exorbitant price. Berg heroically paid this price. False friends, who knew him well but understood him little, soon realized that an effect of the Schoenberg school had been to add an alien, heterogeneous ingredient to Berg's musical reactions, which were strongly defined early on, and that the fault lines of his work provided ample evidence of this. But these fault lines are the signature of his truth. He risked these fractures—stylistic breaks on which, in pieces like the concert aria "Der Wein" or the Violin Concerto, the clumsiest fingers could be placed—as an act of opposition to a consistency that threatened to devour itself and to a trust in what once had been. In a sense he returned to the past as a sacrifice to the future. Nowadays no artistic totality can be created from itself, and Berg knew that the aesthetic individual is no longer capable of a harmonious act of objectification merely through reliance on his own resources, while every external objectivity stands opposed to him and lacks any authentic power over him. But knowing this, he simply absorbed that antagonistic state of affairs into his work. Indeed, it became its supreme formal principle, as if Berg's boundless need for security preferred to accept the dissolution of his own work, to include the work's internal contradictions in his composition, rather than to throw himself on the mercy of history, which would confront the deluded claims of the work with its internal ruptures. Berg achieved an extreme consistency in composition but sacrificed consistency of style in the process, trusting the monadological eloquence of the work, which absorbs the irreconcilable into itself and forces it to express itself, more than the purity of an idiom in which ineradicable contradictions lie merely concealed. In consequence, alien, external material, even sometimes the traces of the conventional features of commodity music, have been built into this refined and noble music as a permanent source of irritation, even though its finely veined texture permeates them wholly. Not until the last act of *Lulu*, in the procurer scene and the street ballad that can be heard in the attic, did this aspect reveal its true character, that of surrealism. That sounds like dream—not like romantic dreams, but like those dreamed nowadays that depict the return of recent events in a darkened interior while high above a golden ribbon floats past. Such a tone was always part of Berg's spiritualized music. Stylistic purists imagine themselves superior to such things and talk about kitsch when it shocks them. They hope to protect themselves against the shock of the parental world and against a seductiveness that they feel as strongly as Berg, but they lack the strength to expose themselves to it while retaining their self-control. Thanks to this strength, Berg has something of what Wedekind, the author of *Lulu*, also possessed. Karl Kraus praised his *Pandora's Box* by saying that in it trashy poetry became the poetry of trash, which could be condemned only by certified idiocy. The greatest works of art do not exclude the lower depths, but kindle the flame of utopia on the smoking ruins of the past.

§ The Orchestration of Berg's Early Songs

Since the initial performances the songs have been generally criticized for still being Romantic. It has been claimed that there was no need for the composer of *Wozzeck* to disinter a work he had composed twenty years previously, to orchestrate it ambitiously and present it to the public. The work belongs properly at the end of the nineteenth century, so the criticisms went, and the critics are rather more eager to proceed with the liquidation of that age than might have seemed necessary if indeed it has been left behind. Some even think it possible to argue that *Wozzeck*, too, belongs to the impressionist or expressionist era, since it contained no authenticated New Objectivity and since even the fugues do not sound like the eighteenth century gone out of tune. In saying this, the distinction between expressionism and impressionism was apparently far less important than the intention of consigning to the glorious, obsolete past a work whose challenge had not yet been met. Yet in fact, Berg's intention in orchestrating these songs was not to disguise their unmodern exterior. The orchestration does not have the effect of bringing music composed in 1907 up to the orchestral standards of 1928. Instead it uncovers musical substance that, implicit from the start, points forward to beyond the period in which the songs were composed, thus forming the basis for a critique of post-Wagnerian orchestration. The distinguishing feature of the latter is its metaphorical, ornamental character: it is all dolled up. The Romantic orchestra, even the virtuoso orchestra of Strauss and Schreker, was never developed from the musical material. Rather, it is placed around the musical events, like a cloak; it adorns them, in the desire to extract from them the effect of plenitude and vigor that no longer resides within. At best, in the instances of advanced impressionism, the configuration of sonorities presents itself as musical structure.

However, the orchestra of the Early Songs has but one intention—and in this respect, the only comparable orchestra of its time was that of Mahler—and that is to convey the substance of the songs in a clear and intelligible manner. Clarity and intelligibility do not mean the neutral "registering" of the musical events; they mean that whatever is made real in the songs should be reflected in the orchestration. The aim should be harmony of sound and composition in interaction with each other, not simply harmony of sound in and of itself. The sound resembles the music it expresses; it is as differentiated and complexly arpeggiated. Yet it merely resembles it; it does not assert itself, pushing the music to one side, but always emerges visibly from the character of the musical material. In this respect it is also modern, not the sign of something other than itself, but simply the concrete precipitate of the musical events. They are made concrete by being communicated directly; for nothing strikes a harder blow at Romanticism than the unmediated givenness of music.

The first criticism of this approach to orchestration centers on the tutti sound. Romantic orchestration always involved trying to unify the multiplicity of harmonic and melodic arpeggiations into a coherent totality of sound. The music possessed too little structure to be able to dispense with the support of a homogeneous orchestral tone distinct from itself. In the Romantic orchestra the all-encompassing string tutti strives to smooth out every detail by incorporating it into a fictional infinity. Such a fiction is destroyed in the sonorities of Berg's songs; the musical structure allows it. The individual events possess their individual sound without regard to a preconceived totality; if a totality of sound is the end result, it is thanks to the musical construction.

This means first of all the thoroughgoing desubstantialization of the sound. The necessity of a piano setting is turned into the virtue of a disembodied orchestral style, without plushy excess or heaviness. It never outgrows the music or tries to be more meaningful than it. The all-encompassing string tutti is, if not totally eliminated, at least subject to constant and imaginative disruptions: muted with dampers, stifled in pizzicato, distributed over a number of solo instruments. On the other hand, it is not replaced by anything like a static wind sound, or even

baldly contrasted with it. A blended color predominates, blended between strings and winds, just as the music is composed of the blending
of the minutest units without the overall tonal pattern ever laying claim
to an archaic coherence that would be in conflict with the subjective dynamics of the songs.

Such blending is the principle governing not only simultaneous
sounds but successive ones as well. The songs are dissolved not just at
each moment in which they ring out, but in the sequence of sounds. The
chief means of orchestration is instrumental change: the constant change
of colors, which dissolve successively into the smallest possible units
without ever permitting the compact post-Wagnerian color pattern to
make its appearance. By stringing together the atoms of a sound that
might be highly Romantic in detail, the sound takes on a different character overall. The orchestration of the songs does for an earlier historical
stage what the style of *Erwartung* accomplished definitively for a later
one. Today, now that the barriers of tonality have fallen, a composer
standing in the free space that has opened out beyond it is better able to
make use of tonal methods than one remaining within the realm of
tonality. The situation was similar in 1928, for only after Schoenberg had
developed the *Klangfarbenmelodie* did it became possible to orchestrate
music composed before *Erwartung* "correctly" relative to what was possible in 1907.

The orchestration of the Early Songs is also correct in a strict sense. We
know from Berg's early works, particularly the Piano Sonata and the First
Quartet, but also *Wozzeck* and the *Lyric Suite*, that its form was dictated
by a principle of differentiation: by the imperceptible transformation of
one motivic unit into another. The functionalism of early Berg meant
that no musical event was conceived as standing alone, each one was determined by its place in the process, so that being was replaced by relationships. Harmonically, this functionalism was formed under the aegis
of chromatic procedures involving leading-tone and dominant-type relationships. It now discovered a viable structuring principle in an imperceptible transformation of motives that frequently reduced the motive to
a single note, in order then to make that remnant, that note, into the nu-
cleus of the new motive. This structuring principle now becomes the
principle of orchestration. It replaces the sequence of abruptly contrasting and heterogeneous sounds with a succession of blending sounds. In
his treatment of the principle of orchestral fluctuation [*Umschlag*] in the

songs,[1] Berg constantly changes the sonorities by preserving "remnants" of the preceding sonorities in the succeeding ones, thereby developing the new "fluctuating" sonority in an imperceptible transition from the previous one. This functional method of orchestration keeps the movement of sound in a constant flow; it loosens it up, but also continually binds it together, without ever using traditional sonorities—of the kind that even Strauss still tolerated—to restrain the dissolution of the sound pattern. Before the Early Songs Berg probably never implemented this style with such consistency. He fills a gap Schoenberg had left in his development from the post-Wagnerian tutti orchestra to the "nonfunctional" sound of *Erwartung*. In Berg the step from the traditional to the liberated sound is so marked because it is accomplished in an essentially harmonic setting that naturally favors the transformation of sounds into each other more than the separateness of contrapuntal, autonomous voices. The orchestration of the Early Songs looks back to the history of Berg's own harmonic style and retrospectively discovers the cogent orchestral formula for that style. Admittedly, this could be accomplished only following a

---

1. The idea of an imperceptible transition seems incompatible with a—necessarily sudden—change, fluctuation [*Umschlag*]. Psychology, however, posits the concept of a "threshold" that corresponds to a qualitative leap in the midst of a continuity. In the same way, Berg's music literally combines the ideas of transition and sudden change. That is nowhere clearer than in a passage in the Chamber Concerto that exaggerates Berg's method almost to the point of self-mockery. The beginning of the stormy cadenza after the gentle dying-away of the Adagio is the only sharp contrast in the entire work. But the infinite pains Berg takes to introduce mediations make him shy away even from this one. It, too, is to be incorporated into the Wagnerian "art of transition." The task he faced was both to confront an extreme pianissimo with an extreme fortissimo, but also to lead one gradually into the other. Berg ingeniously succeeded in achieving the impossible. While at the end of the Adagio the wind ensemble and the violin imperceptibly fade away, even before they stop the piano enters even more imperceptibly and rises to a mezzoforte, such that the great outburst of the piano remains as a continuation of that intensification. But it all happens as if behind the scenes: the piano, which is not used as a solo instrument in the second movement, scarcely makes an appearance, and even where it gains in strength in noiselike notes on the lowest register, it is the melodies, the voices of the piccolo and the violin, that remain the principal events in the forefront of our attention. In this way Berg actually does create both a complete fading-away and an abrupt, contrasting fortissimo, just as, conversely, the latter paves the way for an unconscious apperception. Nothing could demonstrate more incisively the unity of compositional stimulus and the art of orchestration in Berg.

radical breach, not in the course of a banal continuity. Only from the opposite shore does it become possible for the meaning of his harmonic evolution to be ratified by his orchestral method.

All of this calls for greater concreteness. We may think, for example,
how the beginning of the first song ["Nacht"] with the whole-tone effect
would have sounded in Reger's *Romantic Suite*, or even in Debussy: its
foundation would have been full, deep strings and horns. By contrast, in
Berg there is a very muffled woodwind sound—bassoons and clarinet in
the lowest register, doubled by pizzicati on the strings that break through
the dense wind sound without amplifying it; accompanying isolated
chordal attacks on muted horns, quite dematerialized, though not floating atmospherically, but rather remaining faithful to the musical events.
This is then followed at once by the characteristic technique of orchestral
fluctuation. Instead of developing the sound in broad expanses, it is at-
omized: it changes constantly. These sudden fluctuations are not made
with impressionist intentions. He does not just add flecks of color; instead, the orchestral changes serve to elaborate the changes in the musical figures. In Beethoven's day and during the Romantic period this constant change of color was not generally necessary, although the way was
prepared for it in Wagner through the principle of melodic segmentation.
The formal structure is created essentially by the harmonized and modulatory scheme. In tonal music the process of construction is largely comprehensible; today, however, with the extinction of tonality, it is color together with thematic characterization that constitutes form. Hence, wherever new thematic material makes its appearance, the color must be new
too; wherever identity prevails, the color must preserve that identity, however veiled. Consider, for example, m. 5 of the first song: we hear the entry, as a very inconspicuous accompanying voice, of a new thematic complex, the sixteenth-note figure of the first violins; this is then imitated by
the woodwinds and finally leads to the actual beginning of activity, the
main section in A major. This new thematic complex changes the entire
complexion of the orchestration. The whole-tone chords in eighths,
which up to then had belonged to the woodwinds, are transferred to the
warmer tone of the horns—with an almost imperceptible intensification
of motivic activity that brings about a thaw in the dark rigidity of the
opening. At the same time, the horns hold fast to the legato of the clarinets, while gradually modifying the sound in a series of tiny steps. The
string pizzicati are retained as a "remnant" of the varied basic sound. This

"differentiated" orchestral treatment is typical of the orchestration of the songs in general.—Furthermore, the specifically Romantic passage around m. 9 is likewise "dematerialized," thus avoiding the compact sonority that might have been expected. There are indeed harp arpeggios and a radiant entry of the first violins above them, but the chordal accompaniment has been relaxed and distributed among the strings and the horns, so that three eighths fall to the horns, while the violins produce one eighth, and even double the next one, thus binding the overall sonority together functionally while fragmenting the individual sounds. Then, in m. 11, there is a further transformation; the Romantic "blossoming" has reduced itself to the memory of the moment, remains economically confined to uniqueness, and is then absorbed into the immaterial, dreamy taciturnity of the dominant tone. The sound is neutralized by the woodwinds, the strings fade out entirely; flutter-tongue flutes and muted horns carry the sound. It is so arranged that mm. 11 and 12 are played by the deep strings alone, mm. 13 and 14 by the higher ones—in this way the saturated string chorus is expropriated, but at the same time, in the spirit of the functional sound that pervades the songs, he avoids an austerely contrasting wind sonority that would not be appropriate to the fluctuating, flowing style. Only with m. 15 does a kind of tutti reappear, but now minus the rounding-off of the horns; with the entry of the horns the first violins again disappear at once, having been allowed just to play themselves out in a higher register; at m. 19 the sound is neutralized once more, superposed only by the first violins playing piano. The resolution is driven further to combinations of solo instruments: at m. 21 a solo horn enters over the strings that here, exceptionally, act as "background," but as such appear muted right from the start, i.e., arpeggiated. Very ingenious, the orchestration at m. 24: flutter-tongue effect on the flutes, which descend chromatically to their deepest register; in addition, muted solo trumpet, harp arpeggios, combined with muted violas, a chordal horn pedal, with, by contrast, the string sound wholly opened out; the violins leading the melody in a higher register, the deep strings as continuo, the violas with those light arpeggios—hence without chordal heaviness. The result is an essentially soloistic, very delicate timbral combination. Even the harp, which appears here as a Romantic remnant, has a place in the structure. As a characteristic arpeggio instrument, it appears only in the middle section of the piece, which it grounds, though here too in an economical and light, airy way, binding it together as a unified sound without obtruding as a value in its own right. In the exposition and the close, where a dull, indistinct, natural sound is aimed at, its arpeggios cease entirely. The close clearly recalls the orchestration of the beginning, while varying it in accordance with subsequent events. The strings cannot remain as completely latent as they were at the beginning, but are released in line with the spirit of the middle section. Thus, while the combination of deep woodwind and pizzicato sound recurs like a recapitulation, the violins over them are given free rein to express themselves, and the eloquent string tone is preserved; likewise at the end, where the music disappears entirely into that of the opening section. The orchestration provides closure by reinstating the basic sound, but is able to inflect it to fit with the opening of the middle section. Whereas the piano version simply finished with a reprise, the orchestration has tracked down the inner form, made real the compulsive force of the musical events, and hence rethought and given backbone to the impressionistic design of the original song.

The principle of orchestral fluctuation [*Umschlag*] does not just predominate in each of the songs individually, but it also determines the relations between the songs: the large units are shaped according to the paradigm provided by the small ones. Each song has a completely different basic sound from the others, and these basic sounds stack up into a sort of architectural structure for the whole cycle: the full orchestra is used only in the first and last songs; in the second the strings play as solo instruments, while in the sixth there are neither flutes nor oboes; the third is just for string orchestra, the fifth just for wind instruments and harp; the fourth is without clarinets and trumpets. This specification is not imposed on the songs from outside, but grows out of their musical atmosphere. The second song ["Schilflied"] begins with a combination of soloistic timbres: a static horn, highlighted in unison by a harp to avoid the ominous "pounding" horn tone of the New Germans; in addition, a descending bass line on the solo cello, quite ethereal, a second stationary voice on the deep flute, whose muffled sound is very important throughout the songs, and finally, a light counterpoint on the oboe. Only at the word "Abendschein" do the five solo strings play tutti. The radically soloistic sound is not just contrasted with the somewhat more expansive tutti sound of the first song, but it is through this technique that the brooding, troubled character of the song is brought out—similarly, perhaps, to the instrumental idea in the scene in front of Marie's door, the adagio in *Wozzeck*. Technically, this procedure is justified by the way in which the entire soloistic, loose treatment of the wind section is disavowed by that string tutti. In the process we find the subtlest of combinations: at the start of the figured middle section the sound, including the soloistic string sound, fluctuates once more. In contrast to the first song, the strings here are mainly combined, so there are no long passages with only violin or cello; as a consequence, new methods of differentiation have to be found, whereas tying together the retained sound of the five solo strings suffices to unify the orchestral structure. This is why in the middle section this sound is moved close to the bridge and dematerialized, and at the same time, the arpeggiated sixteenth notes of the clarinets and bassoons are tied together by the pizzicati on the deep strings; then, after a sul tasto episode brought close to the wind tone, the "normal" sound of the string ensemble is very gradually retrieved. At m. 19 everything is differentiated once again: a soloistic section is formed that refers back to the opening but gives it a different timbre, as with the reprise of the first song; that is to say, it orchestrates it more richly, just as the composition itself is enriched and divided into smaller values with the continued aftereffect of the sixteenth notes of the middle section. This becomes more concentrated into an echo of the opening section with the concertante wind section and the sul tasto strings: horn and harp, together with the pure quintet sound, are all that remain.

The third song ["Die Nachtigall"] strengthens the contrast by eliminating the wind instruments used constantly hitherto and confining itself to the strings. They are not treated in the homophonic manner typical of all adagiettos since Bizet, however; indeed, the sound is as differentiated and incorporeal as before, it is simply modeled in a different material. This is achieved with persuasive simplicity. All the strings are subdivided, half of them muted, the other half not; the way it works is that the voices with movement, the harmonic counterpoint à la Schumann or Brahms (to whom this song comes nearest—it recalls "Wie Melodien") are entrusted to the unmuted strings, while the stationary voices, in other words the piano pedals, are given to the muted ones. As a result, the "background" of the songs is rendered completely transparent, while the more dynamic parts are split up, preventing the emergence of concentrated homogeneous sonorities. The middle section, one of the most inspired passages in the songs, is given over entirely to the muted strings; the unmuted ones occur only soloistically, producing brief imitations of the vocal part. In this way, despite the utter economy of the forces employed, the sound is completely transformed, though still tied to the original sonority. The reprise resembles the beginning, instrumentally as well; only at the end are muted and unmuted strings deployed in the same spirit, whereupon they melt into each other completely.

In "Traumgekrönt" [no. 4], probably the most mature and accomplished of the songs formally, a sort of tutti sound is permitted once again, admittedly on a greatly reduced scale; clarinets and trumpets are absent. The constructive themes—very much along the lines of Schoenberg's Chamber Symphony—that enclose the song with rich imitations and diminuted motifs, have been distributed through the orchestra with the greatest subtlety; through consistent assignment to a fresh timbral family, the imitative entrances stand out vividly. The two closely related principal themes, variants of each other and both diminuted, are initially presented by the vocal part, strings, and harp; after this the flutes imitate the close of the principal vocal theme, and the characteristic secondary motive appears on the oboe, to be taken up in the orchestral postlude on the first verse couplet by imitations of the muted trombone and the muted horn. The rest of the main theme is intoned by the woodwinds, though the sound has already been transformed: the tutti sound of the strings at the start is now extinguished. It returns only in the second half of the stanza, no longer quite so homogeneous, but disrupted by the diminuting of the principal supporting motive; only the muted first violins have the principal melody, the vocal theme of the first stanza, while the vocal part and the horn articulate a supple melodic counterpoint; in the consequent, the main theme appears on trombones and harps, and in conclusion the diminuted motive on the woodwinds. The second stanza is a variation of the first, its structure left intact but artfully varied at the level of detail; the secondary motive of the beginning is now moved into the vocal part, which repeats it and develops it into a new theme; the principal theme on the flutes, over the very transparent string sound, is answered by a beautiful imitation on the horns; from m. 19 on the reprise remains faithful, except the oboe imitation from m. 5 is now given to the solo cello; lastly, in the brief coda the inversion of the diminuted principal vocal theme enters on the horn. Appropriately, given the musical structure, the orchestration is consistently concerned more with clear, linear construction than with sonorities as such. However, the very nature of the clarity aspired to never degenerates into rigid registration; rather, changing and fluctuating, in obedience to the most sensitive impulses of the composition, of the line itself, that clarity displays the very greatest artistry: it too avoids homogeneous sound, only it does so by orchestrating out the individual voices and creating new color combinations from the linear construction.

The following, very brief song, "Im Zimmer" [no. 5], again displays extreme contrasts. Here the strings are missing completely; the orchestra limits itself, with the greatest subtlety, to the wind section, which is not self-contained, like the organ, but loosened up in the most delicate combinations, such as is normally possible only with the strings. Activity comes at first in the clarinets—which were absent in the previous song—with stationary notes on the flutes; and then in the oboe supported by the English horn, entirely without brass. In the more active part, the staccato harp joins the oboe and English horn, lightening the sound at the same time with a roll on the hanging suspended cymbal; at the climax, a kind of string effect is directly sought, and this is attempted via brief harp arpeggios and flutter-tongue flutes, whereupon the brass enters for the first time: horns, solo trumpet, and solo trombone, in the same relations to each other as the clarinets and flutes had at the start. The woodwinds come in gradually, and at the same time the bass clarinet in combination with the harp overcomes the stasis of the wind tone. The high-pitched clarinet sound over celesta staccato and soft clashes on the cymbals achieve total transparency; muted brass bring closure. The song produces a wealth of instrumental nuances in the briefest space and with the simplest harmonies.

In the sixth song, the "Liebesode," flutes, oboes, and the English horn are absent. After the introductory bars the sound is to a certain extent unarpeggiated, as was to be expected; string values predominate. Although on one occasion the constantly repeated string entries are replaced by clarinets, the string writing is so ingeniously maintained at different levels of density that it is concentrated only at decisive points, while at other times the phrases of the first violins rise above a basic sound that is constantly being modified in both register and fullness. The constantly repeated arpeggio figure is left to the harp as a basic sonic image, while the actual variation of sound is reserved for the woodwinds, which alternate between tremolo, light clarinet passages, flutter-tongue effects, and thematic and melodic voices. Horn chords "realize" the "figured bass"; the solo trumpet is assigned to the vocal part, rises out of the tutti sound, and forms the final cadence.

Only the last song ["Sommertage"], like the first, calls for the full orchestra. Moreover, in line with its constructivist, thematic plan, the orchestration is not unlike that of "Traumgekrönt," but with more emphasis on timbral variety because of its larger scale. The technique of clear "orchestrating-out" is combined with that of continual fluctuation. The strings often seem to be concentrated in chords so they can be relieved at any moment by a different sonority. At the beginning, for instance, their run-up is caught by the woodwinds, with the flow carried on by the flutes and clarinets; the sound of the strings, meanwhile, does not disappear, but is reduced to a solo effect. With the first entrance of the brass, the strings join in with pizzicati and are then broken up into arpeggiating figures carrying a woodwind theme; not until m. 13 is there another fully thematic entrance of the first violins. The entire song is orchestrated in this spirit. Even the tutti sound of the close is broken off immediately, after only two bars. The orchestration of the song points clearly to a linear style completely emancipated from traditional harmony, and after the essentially vertical treatment of the "Liebesode," its emphasis on the horizontal dimension is all the more striking.

The unity of composition and orchestration in the songs should not be understood crudely: the distinction between their compositional and orchestral style cannot be denied; they no more conceal it than does part 3 of the *Gurrelieder*, as Schoenberg points out. But only in his mature phase was it possible for Berg to do justice to the true compositional events inherent in the songs. Had they been orchestrated twenty years previously, it would have been done in a decorative manner. Paradoxically, they could be truly portrayed instrumentally only on a different formal plane from that of the songs themselves; on their original plane the orchestration would have become a mere as-if. This is what justifies the belated orchestration. Ultimately, the sound gives the music a name that, Rumpelstiltskin-like, it previously desired to conceal. For in the songs the pure structure lies in wait for the sound, which salvages it by appropriating it. It has added nothing, merely revealed something that was there. It has not refurbished the songs, merely confirmed them. Their authentic nature is proved by the rightness of the deferred orchestration.

§ Anton von Webern

While Anton von Webern was alive, and before the Fascist terror drove his music into obscurity, into which admittedly it had seemed to want to retreat of its own accord, he existed in the public consciousness either as a bogeyman or as something of a special case. A bogeyman because the shocking brevity of the majority of his compositions dismissed the listener into a silence before he had properly started to listen, and also because of their aphoristic nature. They denied him any guidance in the shape of visible, spun-out developments of the sort that Berg and even most of Schoenberg grant us. A special case, because his oeuvre is dominated by a single, isolated aspect of the music of his teacher, Schoenberg, namely that of radical concentration, an aspect taken to an absolute extreme with a pertinacity one would like to ascribe to the teacher-pupil relationship. Then, after a stray bullet brutally destroyed the pianissimo life of the composer in 1945, his esoteric fame became exoteric, and its function changed fundamentally. Whereas once he had been dismissed as the limited and overradical pupil of his master, he suddenly became the son who rules in the place of his father: Boulez's dictum *Schoenberg est mort* [Schoenberg is dead] cannot be separated from the elevation of his most faithful disciple to the vacant throne. Already for years there had been a tendency in the West to play Webern off against Schoenberg, both because the sound textures of his music did not reach so far back into the nineteenth century as that of the older composer and because his taste for *refus* [rejection of compromise] appealed to the French. Stravinsky is said to have esteemed his work even before he started to experiment with serial composition—which he evidently did because he was so impressed by

Webern. But Webern's posthumous reputation was really technical and stylistic and, above all, strategic, rather than dependent on his nature as a composer specifically. It focused more especially on his last phase, which had set in unmistakably with his Symphony, op. 21. In this Webern, who had up to then demonstrated his mastery of and individual approach to twelve-tone technique, now developed it to such a degree that it gave se- rial music a sort of seal of approval. From then on the row was no longer treated as something malleable. No longer did the arrangement of the in- tervals between the twelve notes merely provide the material on which the composer's intentions went to work; instead, it was made to supply all the structural elements and determining factors that would result in the creation of the work. The integration of the musical events, the unity of each and every work, surpasses everything achieved by Schoenberg's twelve-tone technique, and even the earlier works of Webern himself. Webern further intensified possibilities that had been opened up by Schoenberg, going well beyond his teacher in the process. Of course, in contrast to the serial composers who chose him as their patron, he never completely renounced the musical methods he had inherited from Schoenberg, which incorporated traditional elements in sublimated form. With all the talk about Webern's technical innovations and their applica- tion, however, the composer's central idea was neglected. Few composers of the present have had to endure seeing the interest in their works dis- placed to such a degree by curiosity about the trend they embody, even though the trend can be said to have substance only in the works. The image of Webern today is presented in the verdict contained in lines from *Der siebente Ring* by Stefan George, some of whose poems Webern him- self incomparably set to music. In this poem, "Schwelle" [Threshold], George writes: "Kaum legtet ihr aus eurer hand die kelle / Und saht zufrieden hin nach eurem baun: / War alles werk euch nur zum andren schwelle / Wofür noch nicht ein stein behaun" (You'd scarcely put the trowel aside / and gazed with pleasure at your work: / But a threshold only was all your toil / To a task for which no stone was cut). Even though it is not really possible to separate the composition from its tech- nical discoveries, the latter do point to the works from which they arose: to their idea. After all, what survives is the music itself, rather than its methods, however admirable.

The idea informing Webern's music is his absolute lyricism: the at- tempt to resolve all musical materiality, all the objective elements of musical form, into the pure sonority of the subject, without an alien remainder that refuses to be assimilated. As a composer, Webern never departed from this idea, whether consciously or not. To understand it requires that we reflect on the role of expressionism in the arts. Lyrical poetry was the first to produce expressionist works, but it soon ran up against its limit: that of the objective *concept* that, though tied to language, can never be fully translated into pure expression. As soon as poetry eliminates the concept so as to become sound and image, it transforms itself into a more impoverished, gray, two-dimensional music. But music stands under the spell of its architectonic nature, the idea of form it has inherited. It would be unwilling to renounce its task of articulating time; nor would it venture to foreshorten it come what may or to sacrifice expansiveness for the sake of greater intensity. This is why music never realized the ideal of pure lyricism without reservation, even though lyricism is inescapably present within it. Webern—and one is tempted to say, Webern alone—succeeded in doing this.

The precondition for this achievement lay as much in the state of composition that confronted him and that impressed him to the very core of his being, as in his own individual nature. Schoenberg's free atonality had expanded the expressive powers of music to an unprecedented degree. Statements of Webern's from the period around 1910 leave us in no doubt that this expressivity, the ability of music to express impulses reaching beyond the threshold accessed by other arts, was the central message he received from his teacher. Such an expansion of expressivity by no means confined itself to extremes of experience, to violent outbursts or barely perceptible tremors, but focused also on a mysterious dimension of an endlessly questioning contemplativeness, a terrain that Webern's music then made its home. The models here were some of Schoenberg's middle-period works, such as the conclusion of the first and second of the Piano Pieces op. 11, and also the second of the five Orchestral Pieces, op. 16. This new type of expressivity became possible because of the elimination of the linking categories that had hitherto existed between expression and the musical surface. Casting all its pre-existing forms to one side, music became direct expression. With the disappearance of tonality and its chordal, modulatory, metrical, and formal symmetries, together with the ban on repetition that composers felt was necessary, they could not but make their compositions shorter. Intensified expression coincided with a taboo on extension in time. The need to conquer time was inseparable from the fear that extension and development through time would jeopardize the purity of the expressive moment. This experience acquired a power over Webern, and in his music its destructive effects went hand in hand with the ferment of creativity. Throughout his life his sensibility resisted extension in time, against his will, even in the constructivist works of his late phase. Alban Berg, who in this respect was his exact opposite, remarked as early as 1925 that when Webern wrote his first twelve-tone pieces, his method of composition deprived him of the most palpable benefit that Schoenberg had derived from the new technique: namely, the benefit of writing extended pieces that could organize time without making use of tonality. In Hegel's *Phenomenology* we encounter at one point the disconcerting phrase "fury of disappearance." Webern's work converted this into his angel. The formal law presiding over his composing, in all its stages, is that of shrinkage: his pieces appear from their very first day to have the same sort of substance that one usually finds at the end of a historical process. Webern shares with Walter Benjamin a penchant for the micrological and the confidence that the concrete concentration of a fulfilled moment is worth more than any amount of development that is merely ordained abstractly from outside. The signatures of the two men, the philosopher and the musician who was fanatically tied to his material, two men who did not know each other or even very much about each other, were nevertheless very similar. Both were like letters received from a kingdom of dwarfs, in miniature format, which always looked as if they had been reduced from something of vast dimensions.

It is important in this context to discuss the formal laws governing Webern's work. His music tends to recede, but its center of gravity is located in the fact that it does not pursue its idea of pure expression in isolation. Instead it follows it into the heart of the musical shape, elaborating and articulating it to the point where it is capable of becoming pure expression. The whole of Webern's work revolves around the paradox of total construction as a means of achieving immediate utterance. Close on forty years ago, when Five Movements for String Quartet, op. 5, appeared, the work differed from Schoenberg's Little Pieces for Piano, op. 19, in a highly significant way, for all their similarities. The latter contained only a few motivic-thematic passages. In general the work belonged to the type of athematic pieces that consist instead of a series of associations linked together additively, much like the procedure that became known among the surrealists as automatic writing. The most comprehensive such attempt in music is the monodrama *Erwartung*, but the chamber song "Herzgewächse" is of the same type. In contrast, Webern's first expressionist miniatures, those same movements for quartet, are motivic-thematic in nature; the first is a rather comprehensive, even complete, sonata movement, though somehow reduced to its basic strata; the others, spun out of brief, extremely succinct motifs, make extensive use of imitations and inversions in which the rhythmic values and accented notes have been so displaced that the listener does not properly become aware of their motivic identity. Everything seems just to waft past, and yet a certain necessity is evident, thanks to this secret organization. This, then, becomes the trigger of everything one might call Webern's development, even though that concept is as inappropriate to his oeuvre as a whole as it is to his individual compositions. How to make the sound authoritative by perfect construction; and how, conversely, to reconcile the constructed work, through thoroughgoing animation, with the human subject—these, the innermost problems of new music, were the questions Webern grappled with ceaselessly in his late phase, with full theoretical consciousness. His insistence on this task is what gives his music its stature, that of the incorruptible who refuses to be deflected from his true path.

Without development, Webern begins with the Passacaglia, op. 1, a masterpiece of utter authenticity; this is in stark contrast to his friend Berg, who found composing much harder than the brooding ascetic, and who had to solve all sorts of problems before he could put himself and his powers of composition to work. Despite the formal rigors of the passacaglia form, to which Webern strictly adheres, the piece is infinitely expressive, and both colorful and yet serious in tone. The New German school, to which it is linked by virtue of its opulent harmony and color and its passionately wide-ranging melodic line, can claim nothing like it that is at the same time so bare of ornament and effects, even though at one point—the only one in Webern's life—there is a lush orchestral passage. As is only to be expected, the Passacaglia distantly evokes the finale of Brahms's Fourth Symphony, particularly the beginning. But it is much less taut, loosened up in a more Straussian manner. The material comes from the tonality used by Schoenberg in the period of the Second Quartet, but greatly extended and advancing harmoniously through an independent linear chromaticism. The first movement of Schoenberg's Chamber Symphony no. 2 is the closest to Webern's first work.

The double canon *Entflieht auf leichten Kähnen* [Take flight in light-
bodied barks], op. 2, set to a poem by Stefan George, uses similar material, but leans more toward lyrical condensation thanks to its artful use of
counterpoint. It is followed by two song cycles, both to poems by George.
They are among the most perfect of all the achievements of new music.
The songs of opus 3 comprise five of the most famous poems from *Der
siebente Ring*, and they are treated atonally, like Schoenberg's George settings. Webern's, however, differ in their slender lines, their youthful high
spirits, and a Latinate élan that would have delighted the poet and that is
seldom found elsewhere in German or Austrian music. Such youthful
lyricism had hitherto worked only in poetry. The second song especially,
"Im windesweben war meine frage nur träumerei" [In the weaving of the
wind my question was only a dream], is a particularly enchanting instance. No less captivating is the conclusion of the last song, with the
sweet light [of spring] illuminating crevasses [in the ice]. The second cycle [op. 4] is more static, less flowing, more somber overall, burying itself
in individual chords. It marks the entry into Webern's interior—which he
will never again leave. The transition is carried out with almost palpable
symbolism by the first, introductory song. Its frissons have outlived *Jugendstil*. The opening idea is unforgettable.

With the Five Movements for String Quartet, op. 5, we see the beginning of what we may call Webern's second period: that of the most extreme reduction to short forms. These movements have nothing of the
genre piece about them, nor have they been written down with the ominous silver stylus; the shock they triggered removes them from the sphere
of unobtrusive refinement. They disavow the nineteenth-century term
"miniature," with its overtones of cultural piety; but there is no better
term, for they fit into no established category. Their intensity of concentration is what makes them a totality: a sigh, as Schoenberg noted with
admiration, was worth an entire novel, a tense gesture of three notes on
the violin was literally the equal of a symphony. And the resistance Webern
encountered, until, like every other advanced artist, he was banished to a
pedestal and neutralized, is aroused by the scarcely endurable tension between the tender, fading surface of the music, which almost wishes it had
left the world behind, and the pathos of the work as a whole that inspires
this wish, a utopia of absolute desires that moderates them only because
all external show, all immodesty, seems too modest in its eyes. All of this
becomes almost palpable thanks to the prickliness, the unapproachabil-

ity, of Webern's music, a sensuous aspect of his uncompromising integrity. Only someone who has been involved in performances of Webern's music can properly appreciate that fact. If one approaches his music straightforwardly, like any other, to rehearse it or perform it, it recoils:
it shies away from a direct approach but must instead be played surrounded by that aura of stillness of which Schoenberg said, "May this
stillness ring in their ears." If it does not, it punishes the presumptuous
performer with a wounding absurdity or it simply takes flight. The exceptional difficulty of playing Webern, wholly disproportional to the simplicity of many of his pieces, to his sparing use of notes, stems from the
task of translating the distance between the performer and the work,
which belongs to the work itself, into precise demands on the performer.
In an age of what purports to be literal-minded, positivist fidelity to the
written score, the ability to respond to such imponderables, an ability that
matured with the great works of Romanticism, is dying out: Webern's
works reinstate them simply by existing. The extraordinary liberties he
took when performing his own works, and which furnish even the most
pared-down and economical score with an unexpected plausibility, doubtless arose out of deference to his profound aversion to musical literal-
mindedness. Only a two-dimensional musicality will reject as arbitrary
the way in which Webern performed his own music. His prickliness is the
expression of his refusal to bow to demands for communication, or any
demands of the here and now; it represents the claim of each of his works
to absolute uniqueness. As such, it ought to prevent the performance of a
number of his works in succession, something that would be possible
with almost all other composers. Each piece desires, as an intensive totality, to be alone in the world, incompatible with the mere existence of the
next one. A full Webern program would be like a congress of anchorites.
The totality of the particular distinguishes the specialist Webern from
mere speciality, from mannerism.

   With the quartet movements Webern enters visibly into his own do-
main: already the fourth is completely a miniature. Even so, there are
overarching melodic lines that take your breath away, especially in the last
and the second movements. The melodies have not yet been boiled down
to brief phrases or individual notes. Webern declared that the Movements
for Quartet, op. 5, and presumably also the Bagatelles, op. 9, were chosen from a large number of such pieces. In view of his importance for present-day music, it would be an urgent task to unearth all such unreleased

material and publish it. The Six Pieces for Large Orchestra, op. 6, are, if anything, simpler than the Movements for Quartet: the motivic-thematic work recedes, and they are relatively homophonic. At the end of the first piece the harp even plays a good old whole-tone glissando: almost a mistake in this environment. But it contains a truly extraordinary, in its way unique, and again rather more detailed, piece, a rudimentary funeral march, a distant echo of certain elements in Mahler, of whose music Webern was probably the most authentic interpreter. What he shares with Mahler is the tone of remoteness from the world, the gesture of fighting a losing battle, despite the contrast between Mahler's vast canvases and his own minimal ones, between the threefold fortissimo and the threefold pianissimo. This pianissimo should not be taken as it sounds, in other words, as the reflex of the most delicate stirrings of the soul, even though it is that as well. Frequently, and especially in the Orchestral Pieces, but also in some passages of the succeeding Pieces for Violin and Piano, op. 7, and the Pieces for Cello and Piano, op. 11, this threefold pianissimo, this almost inaudible sound, is nothing but the threatening shadow of an infinitely remote and infinitely powerful din. This was the sound of the rumble of artillery from Verdun in 1916 that carried as far as a forest avenue near Frankfurt. Here Webern comes close to Georg Heym and Georg Trakl, the prophets of the war of 1914: the falling leaf becomes the harbinger of catastrophes to come. The treatment of the percussion in the two cycles of orchestral pieces is the most tangible evidence of this. The second, op. 10, is for chamber orchestra with solo strings, and so has contracted even further compared to the first; for the most part, the individual pieces amount to only a few bars. The power of their delicacy could be experienced by anyone who heard them in Kranichstein in 1957 alongside members of the younger generation who revered them. Their effect surpassed everything else: they revealed for the first time before a large audience that music that had been abused for its subjectivity and its remoteness in fact possessed universality.

During this phase the possibility of musical objectivity became narrowed down to the logical consistency of the subject, which, by virtue of total consistency, is reversed, even in music, into its opposite. The pure sound to which the subject is drawn as its vehicle of expression is freed from the violence that the shaping subject otherwise inflicts on the material. By resounding, without any mediation on the part of the language of music, the music resounds as nature, and ceases to be subjective. This, no doubt, is how we should understand the natural sounds that found their way into his works at around that time, above all the Mahlerian cowbells in one of the Pieces for Orchestra, op. 10 [no. 3]. The Bagatelles for String Quartet, op. 9, perhaps the most slimmed-down pieces in this phase, represent the consummation of that which can be uttered only in music, absolute expression, of which Schoenberg spoke in his Preface. Subsequently, they became the model of what was sometimes called pointillist. But they never separate the notes out mechanically. No doubt they, too, are sparsely dabbed on in contrasting shades, and sometimes that intensified monody emerges from the polyphony which dominated in the later Webern and the early years of the Darmstadt school, after 1945. But here too there is no tone, no pizzicato, no noise close to the bridge, no pause, that did not have a specific function in the *moments musicaux* of the bagatelles as precise and unambiguous to the active listener as forms or phrases in a movement by Beethoven or Brahms: three notes can represent an elaboration, a simple tone can be a coda, without the ear doubting its formal significance. The process of paring down becomes even more radical, if that is possible, in the Cello Pieces of 1914; and yet the few measures they each contain are articulated with a conciseness that elevates them to great architecture. Such conciseness is the fruit of a reduction of what is heard that makes use of silence to create space for subtle differentiation.

With the Four Songs, op. 12, there begins an almost imperceptible change. Webern's music secretly expands; in his own way he registers what Schoenberg first noted in *Pierrot lunaire* and the Songs, op. 22: that you cannot stand fast on a single spot, lest the spiritual reduction of music turn into a physical withering away. The new expansiveness is merely hinted at; the first and last songs are still aphoristic through and through, though they do have a little freedom of movement, and the two middle songs, one from *The Chinese Flute*, the other from Strindberg's *Ghost Sonata*, to which Webern felt particularly close, have more developed vocal lines, admittedly of a subtlety in which the process of dissolution is contained from the outset. All this is openly intensified in the hitherto rarely performed Four Songs, op. 13. Webern's six Trakl songs, op. 14, likewise with a chamber ensemble, are probably the most important of this period, Webern's third, together with the two choral songs to poems from Goethe's *Chinesisch-Deutsche Jahres- und Tageszeiten*, op. 19. The condensation of expression and compositional method coincide with an expan-

sionary expressive impulse that feeds on the congenial poems: it is a matter of return without retreat. With the climax at the end of the last song,
the internal musical substance collapses. The Trakl songs, with their completely plowed-under construction, sound like twelve-tone music, freed
from every trace of the traditional language of music, every predominance
of one tone or another, and yet able to fill the time. Webern proved on
that occasion that the distance from here to twelve-tone music was minimal, that it was no alien principle. His first twelve-tone pieces, likewise
chamber songs, and the last freely atonal ones merge into one another
without a break. The numerous vocal compositions of this time were often canonic and mostly called for small chamber ensembles, in which
preference was given to the clarinet with its mobility, its potential for creating contrasts and sudden leaps. They now often sound particularly brit-
tle because of the frequent piling on of large intervals in the vocal lines.
Not only is it very difficult for the ear to synthesize the disparate notes
into a melody, but the priority given to achieving the right note constantly threatens to make the result sound shrill and compulsively over-
anxious. This disrupts our consciousness of character and meaning. The
true revelation of these pieces is a function of the way they are performed;
only when they are performed without anxiety and bravura will their substance be properly revealed.

   The String Trio, op. 20 [1927], one of the twelve-tone works of those
years, is Webern's first instrumental composition since the Cello Pieces,
and probably the pinnacle of his achievement. It completely realizes his
ideal. The entire flexibility, the entire wealth of musical shapes, the entire
expressive plenitude of the earlier works are here for the first time transformed into extended time in two brief movements, including one in
strict sonata form. The trio is constructed down to its very last note, but
has nothing constructed about it: the power of the shaping spirit and the
nonviolence of an ear that simply listens passively to its own composition
while composing come together in a single identity. An irrepressible mis-
trust toward the active intervention of the subject in his material, as a
shaping presence, might well serve to define Webern's stance, one in
which he was closer to reconciliation than was Schoenberg. It is the stance
implied in his motivic micro-work in the first miniatures: its aim was the
defense against the arbitrary, against caprice. The need for security, a kind
of wariness, is something he shared with his friend Berg. Possibly a response to the pressure exerted by Schoenberg's authority, it brought both

of them into opposition to the dominating, patriarchal manner of his music. The caution with which the early Webern made use of the new sonorities, as if he hesitated to let go of any of them and allow it to be absorbed into the self-evident routine of the "material," is probably a related phenomenon. The authenticity of the impact he has made derives from such a lack of violence, from the absence of the composer as sovereign subject. For the more compellingly the composer dominates, the more he assumes the quality of the blind ruler issuing decrees, with the emerging realization that everything could just as well have been different. Webern's music, however, wanted to appear from the outset as if it were absolute, to be accepted as an existing thing and nothing more.

This appearance, however, is accompanied by the temptation to be taken literally. This is why the ideal of nonviolent composition—and this is the last of Webern's paradoxes—inaugurates that late phase that fortified his successors in their efforts to achieve total domination of the musical material. Complete nonviolence turns into complete violence. This process is inaugurated with a much more clear-cut caesura than the one between the last atonal and the first twelve-tone compositions—with the Symphony, op. 21. From now on—so that the music should unreservedly place itself in the hands of the musical material, without intervention—he ceases to compose with the twelve-tone rows on the Schoenbergian model. Instead the rows are supposed virtually to do the work themselves. Logically, it was possible to determine the entire composition in advance once the serial program had been selected, with its basic material and the initial guiding formal principle. Webern now arranged the rows so that they broke down into subsets that established relationships among themselves—retrogrades, inversions, and retrograde inversions that hitherto had to be derived from the row as a whole. This gives rise to a rich interplay never before encountered in twelve-tone technique. The most complex canonic formations emerge from the use of the row in different, related, and sometimes overlapping subsets: Webern's lifelong predilection for canon is twinned here with his love of microforms. It cannot be denied that he wrote very important works in this phase too, especially when he remained true to the lyrical ideal and followed the texts expressively. This was the case with the Three Songs, op. 23, to texts from *Viae inviae* by Hildegard Jone. The poems of this writer are at the heart of all the vocal works of his later years. He regarded her as the continuation of Goethe in his old age, though he undoubtedly overestimated her vastly. Similarly, much is authentic in the instrumental works of this phase—such as the sonata model of the first movement of the Concerto for Nine Instruments, op. 24, or the sublimated *Ländler* from the Saxophone Quartet, op. 22. But after works like the Trakl songs or the String Trio, the sense that his powers are on the wane won't really go away. The wealth of relationships pushed back into the material and that now lie naked on the surface, more or less unprocessed, like a piece of second nature, seems to have been achieved at the expense of music that has been really composed. Harmonic and polyphonic sonorities become increasingly impoverished, and the rhythmic patterns, too, are increasingly austere, inflexible, and monotonous, with almost rigid durations as building blocks. Anyone who was unaware of the processes and modifications at work in these pieces would suspect that Webern was composing mechanically—as, for example, in a variation in the symphony, where despite the mass of serial relationships he just ends up recycling the same group. In the same way, he seems to be running in place in the strangely repetitive beginning of the String Quartet, op. 28. In the first movement of the Variations for Piano, op. 27, a foursquare three-part song form, the serial fireworks peter out in a pale imitation of a Brahmsian intermezzo. The fear that the act of composition might damage the notes leads to a sclerosis that no longer has anything in common with the earlier pieces: hardly anything happens anymore; the composer's intentions scarcely make any impression, and instead he sits in front of his notes and their basic relationships with his hands folded as if in prayer. Thanks to his total surrender to the objective compositional process, his music is threatened with the loss of the element in which it lived.

Nevertheless, the String Quartet, op. 28, was a piece that Webern held in particularly high esteem. He expected nothing less of it than that it would bridge the gulf in the history of Western music between objectivity and the subject, a gulf that seemed to him to be embodied in the historical forms of the fugue and the sonata. Webern's music requires patience. It would be rash to make confident judgments about the quartet and the closely related Variations for Piano. Nothing is harder in music than such simplicity: namely, the judgment of whether it represents the latest achievement or the fatal recurrence of something preartistic. Webern may have been in the right after all; our understanding may just have failed to catch up with his. But it would be unworthy of him, and it would be to ignore his claims to our attention, were we to conceal the fact that his last works, when compared to the freedom of necessity in his earlier ones, arouse the suspicion of an alienation, a fetishism of the material, comparable only with the late works of Kandinsky and also Klee. What someone once called the charged atmosphere [*Knistern*] of Klee's paintings, something that might be attributed with equal justice to Webern's works up to opus 20, has been barely perceptible, up to now at any rate, in his later works. It is conceivable that in their literalness and their subservience to the notes—which formed such a powerful contrast to the earlier shorthand—something of the naive peasant in Webern broke through to the surface, something of the pigheadedness of the believer in natural medicine. We may perhaps surmise that he was not quite up to the boundless sublimation that his oeuvre demanded and that, like a man about to break down, he regressed to a stage on this side of the sublimation process. His tendency to specialize, arising from both the inhibitions of the unreflective craftsman and the excessive demands imposed on him by his own single-mindedness, fits in with the idea that as a whole person he was unable to keep pace with himself as a particular being. A regression to the primitive would be the revenge of an intellectual rejuvenating himself to the point of total differentiation, and who had fended off too much, left too much on the outside, to be able truly to assert himself against the outside world pressing in. Exhaustion may have been the price he had to pay for the timeless perfection of his early works. A factor here may also have been the personal isolation he must have experienced after Berg's death and, later, with Hitler's occupation of Austria. That he had no one to provide productive opposition undoubtedly strengthened the lure of the mathematical speculations that dangled the mirage of cosmic being before the eyes of the lonely composer. At the very last, in the Variations for Orchestra, op. 30, and in the Second Cantata [op. 31], he obviously felt the need to expand once again. In their organization the variations are indeed barely richer than the pieces written following opus 21, but the timbres coruscate more. The cantata, however, is noticeably more complex in every respect, not shrinking from high-chord diversities and displaying a melodic freedom that soars beyond all rhythmic schemata, in a way not seen in Webern before. This was probably the direct model for Boulez's handling of melody. What is striking is the varied succession of settings, from homophonically accompanied songs right through to radical examples of canon. Not since the symphony had Webern permitted himself such a plenitude of either simultaneous or contrasting events. The breakthrough of the Second Cantata contains a productive critique of the works that preceded it.

~

It is not for nothing that Webern puts us in mind of Paul Klee. It helps us to specify more exactly the idea of absolute lyricism that guided him. His affinity with the painter extends more deeply than the mere analogy between approaches that led both in their middle years to abandon all impasto and everything voluminous and to confine themselves to line. In their use of line, too, they are related, both displaying an eccentric graphic style, a calligraphy both definite and enigmatic. Its name is scribbling; it is how, with a beggar's pride, Kafka chose to describe his prose. Furthermore, both Klee and Webern explore an imaginary twilight world somewhere between line and color. The works of both are tinted, not colored. Never does color become autonomous, never does it even assert its role explicitly as a definite compositional stratum, nor is it a sound pattern. But it captures the spirit of scribbling, just as children's drawings feed on the delight that springs from the paper they have colored. The oeuvres of the two men in their respective media migrate from the established genres into this twilight world. They project a fragile, transcendental ideal type that cannot be assigned to any recognizable location; of Schoenberg's works, *Pierrot* had come closest to this no-man's-land of art. As early as the Six Pieces for Orchestra, op. 6, the relations of the instrumental values to each other had formed part of the construction: for all its precise sensuous vision, this also creates something suprasensuous, something not just disembodied but almost devoid of physical sonority. But at the same time, Webern also resembles Klee in his rejection of abstraction. His expressivity does not correspond to what is meant by abstract painting, or to what is commonly condemned as abstract in music: he realizes the idea of desensualization in a sensuous way. Webern's musical minimalism is founded on the expressive requirement that excludes any independent phenomenon that is not at the same time expressive. This economy comes to influence expression itself—to the point of silence. It is for this that he finally shows understanding. The absolute voice of the soul, which enables it to become conscious of itself as mere nature, is a simile in his music for the moment of death. His music presents this moment in accordance with the tradition in which the soul, fleeting and ephemeral, flutters out of the body like a butterfly. It is a tombstone inscription. Webern's expressivity is his obsession with the imitation of the sound made by something disembodied. The absolutely transitory, the toneless beating of wings, as it were, becomes in his music the faintest, but most persistent, seal of hope. Disappearance, an ephemerality that fixes on nothing that exists anymore, or even that objectifies itself, becomes the refuge of a defenseless eternity. Webern set many religious texts, and his oeuvre can be said to be religious like that of scarcely any other composer since Bach; but it also bespeaks the incorruptible abandonment of all established religious commitment, of every positive religiosity that objectively destroys what it says by saying it, destroying at the same time the only thing that matters to him. His mind felt its way toward that goal in lines like the one from the Song to the Virgin from opus 12, "Gib auch den Verstorbenen die ewige Ruh" [Grant also to the dead an eternal peace], Trakl's "Strahlender Arme Erbarmen umfängt ein brechendes Herz" [The pity of radiant arms embraces a breaking heart], and the indescribably composed last words of the songs in opus 23, "Und, ewig Schlafende, auch euch erwartet Tag" [And, eternal sleepers, you too the day awaits]. But even more precisely than it could ever be said even in the texts of the composer, who could say it only in music, it was said by Kafka in the story about Odradek, that creature who might have figured in a picture of Klee's: "Of course, you don't ask him any difficult questions, but treat him—as his diminutive stature encourages you to do—like a child. 'What's your name?' you ask him. 'Odradek,' he says. 'And where do you live?' 'No fixed address,' he says and laughs; but it is a kind of laughter that you can produce only without lungs. It sounds rather like the rustling of fallen leaves. And that is generally the end of the conversation."

§ Classicism, Romanticism, New Music

There is a widespread view that places new music in straightforward opposition to Romanticism, in line with a change in attitude of the kind parodied by Schoenberg in the *Satires*: "No longer shall I write Romantic music; I hate the Romantic." Romanticism is understood here as an exaggerated, ecstatic cult of the ego: composers are said to be fed up with its adventitious, arbitrary nature. Instead they are said to be taking a new interest in the objectivity and binding nature of musical forms that had been so neglected in the nineteenth and early twentieth centuries. This *fable convenu*, tailored to Stravinsky and Hindemith in the first instance, and extended subsequently to twelve-tone and serial technique, continues to inform critical attitudes toward new music. Every ostensible reminder of Romanticism is said to be old-fashioned, passé, Makart. It is evidently no longer to be endured, however modern a piece it may be in other respects. Conversely, even crude attempts to appropriate long-past historical fashions find it easy to masquerade as new music, as long as they are presented as stylistic innovations. For such mentalities everything from Schubert to Mahler and Richard Strauss is called Romantic, with at best a further classification as early Romanticism, high Romanticism, late Romanticism, and impressionism. In this process the concept of Romanticism is taken over, more or less uncritically, from literature and also painting. There is a tacit endorsement of the aesthetic formulated first, in all likelihood, by Schumann and later on reiterated by philosophers such as Croce, based on the principle that the aesthetics of one art is the aesthetics of all the others and the aesthetic categories of one can be readily imported into the rest.

This belief is both right and wrong. It follows an idea of the artistic as embracing the poetic, as found in the term *Tondichter*, tone poet, which Beethoven claimed for himself. The suspicion that this name is itself Romantic cannot be denied. Its justification is that the arts are in fact being brought closer together by their increasing subjectivization, a process that penetrates material of the most varied kinds and is complemented by the intensified rationalization of that material. The plural form "the arts" already sounds archaic. The more the historically maturing subject appropriates art as its own medium, the more each individual art becomes the language, the bearer of expression, of that same subject. This leads to an intensification of what the philosophers call aesthetic illusion [*Schein*]: art fakes a reality, it stands in as a sign for the subject governing it. The concept of a *musica ficta* provides the earliest evidence of such a tendency. On the objective side, that of control of the material, there is also a progressive disqualification, an emancipation from the supposedly arbitrary nature of aesthetic subject matter. As everywhere in society, artistic rationalization, the planned control of means, implies their increasing unification, their growing resemblance within each sphere of art, as well as of the different arts to one another. In modern times especially, it is illuminating to see how the techniques involved in the different arts begin to enter into mutual relations: musical Classicism at the turn of the eighteenth and nineteenth centuries, for example Cherubini and Beethoven, in their relation to contemporary painting and architecture; the emancipation of color in Berlioz paralleling that of Delacroix; the impressionist approach to painting as compared with the musical impressionism of Debussy; Strauss in relation to the German *Jugendstil* variant of impressionism; finally, Webern in comparison with Klee and, in a different way, with Mondrian. There is an element of truth in all these elective affinities, but none is free from the shadow of mere analogy; they are never to be taken entirely literally. And later on especially, music, a young art, and one that is known to lag behind the others, often borrowed aspects of technique from painting, rather than developing them independently. To a certain extent this is true of Debussy, but it quite definitely applies to Stravinsky's Neoclassicism, which doggedly clung to a passing phase of Picasso's for over thirty-five years. How far Schoenberg's free atonality was inspired by Kandinsky around 1910 still awaits investigation. It could be shown that both have transformed the *Jugendstil* ornament into a principle of construction. For all the complications, however, there can be no doubt that over the centuries the different arts have proved increasingly capable of expressing and objectifying the sustaining, common experiences of the social subject in related ways.

At the same time, however, this talk of the unity of the aesthetics of the arts is equally false. It reflects the neutralizing tendency that became the destiny of all intellectual endeavors under the general rubric of culture as a consequence of the irrevocable separation of intellectual production from its immediate function in the real world. Just as the term "culture" reduced to a single formula very different and even incompatible phenomena such as religion, philosophy, science, art, law, and God knows what else—in short, the totality of activities that do not serve the immediate reproduction of life—the same development can be observed in the subordination of the arts to the concept of art. While this subordination reflects the real tendency toward the integration of the activities of the mind, it remains restricted to the human subject that motivates and affirms it. In the process it is forgotten that art always implies a dialectical relationship between the subject and its opposite number, its material. Its objectivity is what arises from this complex of mediations. The artistic materials present the subject that exerts control over them with demands that spring from their historical origins, while the subject has its own requirements of them. If art has its roots in mimetic, prerational behavior, if it represents the memory of that behavior in the midst of the process of rationalization, this element of the qualitative, of difference, of whatever is not entirely subsumed into the rational, never relinquishes its claims. Whenever in the name of spirit it becomes completely spiritualized, it violates its own spirit, that is, the memory of what cannot be entirely reduced to rationality and to what has been subjugated by it. The unity of art is always also inimical to art. The most extreme caricature of this negativity is the cultural mishmash that ends up absorbing every artistic utterance within a comprehensive timetable of all the seasonal festivals a tourist can visit without one clashing with the others. Whatever subjective profundity and objective authority the arts may acquire through their subordination to the integral idea of art, they risk losing in terms of specific authority.

With a certain monomaniacal zeal Rudolf Borchardt has recognized this in literature, but it is no less true of music. In the first place, music is not "aesthetic illusion"; it is no image of an other, but a spiritual entity in its own right that does not point a priori to something else. If in the course of history it has come to resemble the other arts in many respects, this process—which is a process of being permeated with language [*Versprachlichung*]—has left it scarred. The unconscious suffering resulting from those scars is not the least of the reasons for the rebellion against this linguistic affinity that has been detectable ever since the emergence of new music. This can be seen at its most drastic in the inappropriateness of the stylistic concepts that have migrated into music from the other arts, concepts such as the Baroque. It has been shown in a far too little known study by G. F. Hartlaub, *Fragen an die Kunst* [Questions for art], that the talk about Baroque music is invalid. It is primarily a method employed by music historians to confer on some of the less fascinating products of the seventeenth and eighteenth centuries something of the authority of contemporary painting. But the largely undeveloped, primitive, rudimentary, and undifferentiated music of the thorough-bass period really has nothing in common with the highly subjective, in Hartlaub's term, "late" painting style of Mannerism, nor with the opulent wealth of forms of the architecture of the period—apart from the fact that they all existed at the same time—unless you include quite modest analogies, such as elements of stately pomp in Purcell or Handel. If one wishes to discover the Baroque in music, it would be better to look for it 150 years later in Bruckner, who did not choose to be buried in St. Florian for nothing. In his case many Baroque features belong genuinely to his mode of composition and are not simply an attempt to ingratiate themselves with a different artistic medium. Scarcely less problematic in music, however, are stylist categories like Romantic and Classical, which have an even longer history. It would probably be foolish to try and dismiss these as merely transitional. Concepts are only constituted at their margins, and not at the point where they are contiguous. The fact that Mozart's six quartets dedicated to Haydn have something of a classical quality about them— albeit one in need of further development—is no more to be denied than the specific affinity of great works by Schumann—the Fantasia in C, the *Kreisleriana*, the song cycle based on poems by Eichendorff—with the immediately preceding phase of literary Romanticism. The concept of the classical could in fact be applied more readily to Mozart than to literary figures such as Goethe or Alfieri because he is free from the programmatic links with antiquity that have been taken from the cultural tradition and that dominate literary Classicism. Mozart's Classicism can be accepted precisely because it makes no conscious claims to it. Nevertheless, "Classicism" and "Romanticism" are dubious stylistic categories in music. An essential and by no means accidental feature of the Classical is that impulses of its type should not be poured into fixed, ready-made, so-called objective forms, but that its forms should be partly constituted in the course of a conflict with an untrammeled subjectivity. They become authoritative only where inherited formal conventions, alienated from consciousness, become impregnated with critical subjectivity, with the very substance that the stylistic cliché ascribes to Romanticism. The Romantic dimension is, strictly speaking, an a priori of Classicism. Just as the alienation of Wilhelm Meister would have no force in the absence of Mignon as a counterweight; and just as Hegel's *Phenomenology* both bears the Romantic consciousness within itself and criticizes it in Schelling— the same phenomenon is to be found in great music, especially Beethoven's. The most palpable, if not the most important, example is the first movement of the C# Minor Sonata, made famous as the *Moonlight* Sonata. It defines the character of the late Chopin nocturnes once and for all. In a more subtle and more sublimated form, however, this element survives as a component of Beethoven's oeuvre as a whole. It even survives in the unapproachable and unconciliatory late works. Wagnerian Beethoven biographers such as Ludwig Nohl have not failed to criticize short forms like the cavatina from the great B-flat Major Quartet [op. 130] for coming too close to Romantic genre conventions like *Songs without Words*. That was doubtless the misunderstanding of an overzealous partisan. But the most characteristic passage of the Andante con moto quasi allegretto of the C Major Quartet, op. 59, no. 3, does indeed have a thematic figure that sounds like a Schubertian idea. And in general the intimate middle movements of the quartets—including the Adagio of opus 74—are particularly rich in such inflections. A further instance of Romanticism would be the lyricism in the piano works, such as the first movement of the A Major Sonata, op. 101, and even the Rondo of the little E Minor Sonata, op. 90, if it had remained self-contained, instead of being subsumed into the subjectively created objectivity of the form as a whole. The cycle *An die ferne Geliebte* follows the entire trajectory from the Romantic lied through to the postlude, which is on a symphonic scale.

All this has a crucial relevance for the interpretation of new music as a reaction to Romanticism. That interpretation keeps adjusting the concept of Classicism, robbing it of a decisive element in order to harness it to the needs of the polemic. This probably explains why musical Neoclassicism in the broadest sense attached itself to that of preclassicism—the term is itself crudely makeshift—instead of Viennese Classicism. From the outset Neoclassicism had something anachronistic about it that could pass muster as long as it was used polemically and with self-irony. But it became intolerable the moment a serious attempt was made to infer from it an objectivity that rode roughshod over the indispensable, historically emancipated subject with a cheerfully perfunctory gesture. The pathetically harmless concept of the neo-Baroque ought to suffice to place all this in a clear light; the traces of Wilhelminian neo-Gothic are frightening.

Conversely, however, even the concept of musical Romanticism falters when confronted by its meaning. Some of the great orchestral movements of the mature Schubert—the Andante of the C Major Symphony springs immediately to mind—could just as well be called classical. Again, this points not to the occasional coincidence of fundamentally different conceptions of music, but to the extent to which they are mutually intertwined. After Schumann, musical Romanticism became what the New German school attacked as mere academicism, and specifically in its Schumannian variant. This was no simple onslaught from outside, nor did it mean simply that Romanticism had become sclerotic. It is a moot point today whether Brahms's works—like those of Ingres, perhaps—should be dismissed as academic, or whether their constructive, objective features enable them to point beyond Romanticism, as might be supposed from the central role played by Brahms in Schoenberg's inner formation as a composer, as Schoenberg himself stated. In Brahms, the effort to objectivize music through its structure, its formal density, and not through the transplantation of categories external to it, was at its most advanced. The modernity of what the official progressives dismissed as reactionary exposes the failings of the musical concept of style. Music that is Romantic thanks to its subjective and expressive impulses gains its authority, and provides itself with backbone, by means of a musical Classicism to which Schumann's *Davidsbündler* were already committed when, owing to a misunderstanding, they called themselves followers of Beethoven. This same Classicism then led to the resumption and intensification of Beethoven's principle of analytical, motivic, and thematic work in Brahms. The music of high Romanticism necessarily possesses a Classical dimension. But in that case new music, with its objective principles of construction, can hardly be said to have come out of the blue; it is not merely an arbitrary riposte to a Romanticism to which in fact it is indebted for so many of its own informal principles, not excluding that of the tone row.

Furthermore, the concept of Romanticism that became established in music was far too broad and unspecific. The incorporeity of music, which actually rules out the crude alternative of Romanticism or realism from the outset, has facilitated this vagueness. Music appears to be a pure realm of the soul, free of the world of things, and as soon as it can be more or less made to fit this pattern it is routinely called Romantic. However, much of what goes under the name of Romantic is really, when looked at more closely, part of the current of anti-Romanticism, or even realism, in a Romantic disguise. Berlioz was a Byronist in his attitudes, and projected himself as a Romantic dreamer: he was also Romantic in his use of a certain irrationalist musical *Gestus*. Yet the emancipation of the orchestra that he promoted, the incipient trend toward technification, was anti-Romantic. On the New German wing of so-called Romantic music this aspect has continued to gain in influence. The Wagnerian *Gesamtkunstwerk*, as a phantasmagoria of Romanticism, is technological and even positivistic at the same time. "Many of Wagner's culture-loving and civilization-hating opponents . . . criticize him for having adopted without reservation the technical achievements of the nineteenth century, despite his alleged 'struggle' against them. They enumerate the sins of the Bayreuth 'stage mechanic,' and would undoubtedly come to even more disconcerting conclusions if they could read a score. Wagner's intention of integrating the individual arts into the *Gesamtkunstwerk* ends up by achieving a division of labor unprecedented in the history of music. 'The wound is healed only by the spear that caused it' [*Parsifal*, act 3]—this might be the motto for Wagner's mode of composition. And it is precisely the religious *Parsifal*, which makes use of the filmlike technique of scene transformation, that marks the climax of this dialectic: the magic work of art dreams its antithesis, the mechanical work of art."[1] In Strauss especially, in whom the work of art is rationally organized as a totality of precisely planned and calculated effects, the Romantic and expressive ele-

---

1. Theodor W. Adorno, *Versuch über Wagner* (Frankfurt am Main, 1952), 138ff. [also in *Gesammelte Schriften*, vol. 13: *Die musikalischen Monographien*, 2d ed. (Frankfurt am Main: Suhrkamp, 1977), 104; translation from Adorno, *In Search of Wagner*, trans. Rodney Livingstone (London: NLB, 1981), 109—Trans.].

ments—although they are admittedly neo-Romantic *Jugendstil*, the romanticism of Romanticism, and internally inconsistent—are juxtaposed to completely anti-Romantic motifs. This rupture, one inherent in the New German school from the outset, is what makes the Straussian oeuvre so shocking, though it is also the source of its dignity. Even the expressive element, something that schematic thinkers today simply lump together with the Romantic, has undergone an internal development that places it in opposition to the older Romantic expressive ideal. Schumannesque exuberance, which regards itself as an infinitely sovereign, outflowing subject, becomes reified into the psychological person whose individual impulses—*Elektra* is exemplary in this respect—are registered and reflected by the music. This element of the expressive protocol that then provided the decisive turn in new music was already part of Strauss's palette. In terms of both stylistic category and tonal material, *Elektra* and Schoenberg's roughly contemporary *Erwartung* are not too far apart from each other. But a history of music that draws the triumphant conclusion that *Erwartung* is not really so new after all, and that the restrained products of Neoclassicism constitute the true line of progress, would soon have to eat its words. It would have to do violence to progressive music by dating its material development back to the Romantic period, while attempting through sophistry to smuggle into modernity what is no more than a regression to the music of the previous generation but one. Developments in composing in the last decade, which settled accounts with an attitude-based Neoclassicism and concentrated instead on the constructive treatment of material, passed a death sentence on such ideological ventures.

That so-called Romantic music can be subsumed only inadequately under the category of Romanticism is the revenge for the fact that all Romantic aesthetics crucially uses music as its model. To make a plausible case for carving a Romantic sector out of music is difficult specifically because Romanticism used music as its paradigm. By that yardstick, all music has Romantic features; by the light of Romantic poetics, then, Bach is as much a Romantic as Beethoven, for otherwise Schumann's productive love for Bach would be incomprehensible. It is not without reason that, in book 3 of *Die Welt als Wille und Vorstellung* [The world as will and idea], Schopenhauer paid homage to music as the queen of the arts; it is not without reason that, from Tieck on—and he was indebted in his turn to Wackenroder—the program of early Romanticism was musical, and that Jean Paul cannot be imagined without music as an ideal. The Romantic conception of the immediate expression of subjectivity, unhampered by thinglike objectivities, was a product of the musical experience of the generation around 1800. Twinned with this are the experience of transcendence, of floating, of sound not rigidly fixed to any individual support, and, ultimately, the irrationalist ideal itself, which the Romantic movement set up in opposition to the rationalism of eighteenth-century enlightenment. Romanticism, of course, cannot be automatically summed up in such formulas, just as in general, like all phenomena of the mind, it cannot be reduced to simple definitions. It can only be grasped as the determinate configuration of a multiplicity of elements. Much in it—historicism is a case in point—was primarily antimusical and could only enter music via the intellectual mediation of the Romantic movement as a whole. But when in the true late Romantic phase Verlaine, in his *Art poétique*, called for "de la musique avant toute chose" ["music above all else"], he retrospectively hit upon something that is not absent from any Romantic work of art. But if the musicalization of all art is a core element of the Romantic idea of style, then the idea of Romantic music as a style contrasted with other music is scarcely sustainable. Romantic music—though affected by the Romantic movement as a whole—and Romanticism as a specific idea are distinct, in the sense that the former possesses characteristics in which the musical material harmonizes with Romanticism from the outset. Hence the sonorities that cannot be localized specifically, that one cannot put one's finger on, the lack of concreteness; and at the deepest level, the fact that in developed music no event is purely itself, but receives its meaning from what is absent—from the past and the future—which it then influences in its turn. Prior to all specification of style there is something in music that Romanticism then claimed as its own, without its having had anything to do with the process of selection that every concept of style requires. And this a priori Romantic feature of music cannot be eliminated by any stylistic trend, however fanatical. The dubious aspect of the fashion for objectivizing Bach—which admittedly is already on the wane—can be understood in this context: under the pretext of de-Romanticizing Bach, scholars are demusicalizing him, that is to say, depriving him of those features without which no meaningful musical whole can be created. He is being subjected to norms of counting and measuring that are made irrelevant by the literally ephemeral aspect of music, the aspect that is consti-

tuted only in its own demise. Otherwise, it would have been impossible
to conceive of the happiness that medieval monks must have experienced
when for the first time they played a note together with its fifth. Pure
sonority itself—and it is a great achievement on the part of the serial
composers to have emphasized this—has a temporal, dynamic element,
something of the nonidentity of identity, as the philosophers would say,
and whoever imagines that he can ignore this in the name of transsub-
jective being and effect the absolute spatialization of music will become
the victim of sterile misconceptions.

All of this leads us to the conclusion that the categories of style that
have been imported more or less unthinkingly from the history of literature or art are not only a poor fit with music, but in fact are completely
incompatible with it. The concrete meaning of the assertion that the arts
taken together do not add up to art as such is that the stylistic categories
of one art are quite inappropriate to others. This is why important contemporary musicians, such as Schoenberg, have rebelled so vehemently
against the notion of style, opposing to it the "idea" of the objectively
binding truth of each individual work. It is possible to call a truce on the
at present rather overextended concept of musical style without necessarily closing one's eyes to the stylistic unity of certain epochs. This concept
of musical style thrives on a false, wrongly contemplative distance, on an
overview that lives at the expense of a relationship to the object. For the
most part, the concept of style today serves to eliminate things that don't
fit into neat categories. The critic makes use of cultural and historical ra-
tionalizations that confuse the wish to make authoritative judgments with
the authority that derives from specific successful works. This enables him
to gaze down on them from above with the arrogance of the mediocre. In
recent times the music that came closest, even in its own consciousness,
to a style of its own, the music of the mature Wagner, owes its achievement to the polemical impulse underpinning it, namely the critique of
historical syncretism that Wagner and Nietzsche together aimed at the
nineteenth century. Wagner's style, like that of *Jugendstil* with which it
has so much in common, was in fact the function of a lack of style of
which the renegade Nietzsche subsequently accused him: the will to style,
then and now, is the absolute antithesis of style. Conversely, wherever
music surrenders unreservedly to the demands of its historical material,
without any stylistic ambitions, without, as it were, peering hopefully beyond the horizon of its own intrinsic problems, it is there that it seems

most likely to discover something like a style, and to achieve something authentic while rising above the quarrels about style that still rage today. Schoenberg, Berg, and Webern, three composers very different from one another in both tone and character, really do have something of the sort in common, even though they all despised the idea.

Now, all this goes to the very heart of new music. It can no longer be described as a classical wave, however interpreted, following upon a Romanticism that is far too dialectical to be able to supply the thesis for such an antithesis. Moreover, the most cursory glance at the contemporary Classicism of the visual arts—a Classicism that has no authority whatsoever—reveals its irrelevance to the established musical scheme. The critique of a new classicism in music coincides with the social insight that the underlying preconditions for everything that might rationally be called classical are as absent now as they were in the nineteenth century. A "classical" style, however defined, would be no more than the product of cultural philosophy. There exists no meaningful order of human affairs that the aesthetic subject might be able to experience so much as his very own, so much so that it might confirm what he could see with his own eyes even prior to any effort on his part. Nor has a state of consciousness been achieved that is higher than the subjective one from which so-called Romantic music arose: at best there has been a regression to an even earlier, lower stage. The new art does not discover its utopia in the desire to repress such subjectivity; on the contrary, the wish to extinguish the subject only redounds to the benefit of that regression. In a would-be classical style today, the subject would not be preserved as positive and reconciled, but would be suppressed in favor of blind, alien, collective forces. A new classicism would not conceive the subject within itself and represent its cause, but would confine itself to abstract negation, to a mere polemic against the element of illusion in the subject, which, it must be admitted, has become ever more apparent since the nineteenth century. Perhaps Stravinsky's preeminence when compared to other musical Neoclassicists is that he emphasized the abstract and polemical nature of his own stylistic ideal as a ferment of effects, instead of implying that an authoritative style had now arrived and was available in concrete form. If anything in music may be called Romantic, it is the yearning for such an authoritative style. Anyone who entertains notions of *ordo* and the guild system today is in thrall to that same Novalis who glorified the Middle Ages in his treatise on Christendom or Europe; he is at the mercy of the very ideas the Neoclassicists most abhor. Only they of course deprive Novalis of his truth, the dream of a nonpresent and nonreconstructible society, which they drag down to their administered world and allow to freeze in a merely given reality.

Nor does new music simply form a contrast with the nineteenth century. The summary eagerness to see just that occur is itself suspect. When past phenomena are said, without relevant explanation, to be obsolete and passé, as if the mere passage of time could be made responsible for cultural developments, the presence of unfinished business, often of a traumatic nature, is almost invariably revealed. Efforts to forget the nineteenth century aim to make us forget that the promise to emancipate mankind was never redeemed. This promise had once been announced in a subjectivism that reached deep into such frail movements as women's emancipation, but its reputation was blackened more recently by the emergence of a prefascist tendency. Today one would like to overcome that ceaselessly denounced spirit of individualism, to use that embarrassing expression, if only because its real precondition, the conflict of interests between individuals who are both alienated from and chained to one another, still endures; meanwhile, however, they are prevented from achieving individuality by the prevailing pressures and would be only too happy to present their weakness as a strength. High-sounding proclamations of order and social bonds, said to be long overdue in the realm of culture, only conceal the attempt to justify a desperate weakness. People force themselves to rationalize an act of repression. The changes that have taken place since the nineteenth century, however, cannot be interpreted as an altered style of thought or feeling that now calls for a different spiritual expression. Instead such changes can be legitimated only through criticism of the age, of the ideology of the past, though hardly by intellectuals who are assiduously concerned to make their obeisance to the so-called spirit of the age. A start should be made not with the excessive complexity and frayed quality of so-called late Romantic music, which sounds Romantic only to unsophisticated ears. What really call for correction are the kind of failings seen in Brahms, for example, where the principle of construction actually leaves the material of the music untouched, such that there is a gaping void between the two. Or again, in many instances the material has been revolutionized but the compositional methods fail to take this properly into account and remain backward in the face of the highly differentiated material, much as Wagner's sequencing technique does in contrast to his discoveries in harmony and orchestration. In other words, if new music arose out of technical problems of the later nineteenth century, it did so as a response to questions that failed to find answers then. No doubt, all of this also has a substantive meaning that goes beyond questions of technique. The subjectivist position of so-called Romantic music was revealed as mere delusion when it became apparent that, behind the loneliness that, in *Palestrina*, the ideologically Romantic Pfitzner called the innermost center of the world, the rule of objectivity held sway: the principle of individuation is itself social. But movement beyond this delusion is not achieved by a change of ideology or an artistic gesture. An artistic solution is needed to settle those issues that were not settled in the nineteenth and early twentieth centuries because of the weight of tradition. The unfinished business related to appearances, the decorative element, the surplus of sensuous effects over their constructive justification; it was what none other than Wagner found the fitting formulation for in the middle of the nineteenth century when he talked about effects without causes. In contrast to that, all qualitatively new music undoubtedly brings an iconoclastic, anti-Romantic element to the surface. Reduction to structural essentials, elimination of inflated extras, and even an element of polemical primitiveness cannot be removed from it. But new music could no more make its home in this cult of the primitive, or nurture it, than could fauvism in painting. It was forced to define the supposedly elemental features as something mediated, as the bearer of expression, and as the precondition of the new structuring principle that it required as well. Its own logic has driven it to transcend the flirtation with the primitive which the cliché of its opposition to the nineteenth century would have wished to preserve. The distinction between polemically reduced music, such as Schoenberg's first atonal Piano Pieces, op. 11, and the complacent simplification of Neoclassic structures in Stravinsky's *Apollo Musagetes* or his Piano Serenade, goes to the very heart of the matter, for it forces us to inquire whether the reductive process manages to preserve the differentiation it has temporarily abolished, or whether it proclaims that positively impoverished, vacuous, preindividualistic styles, of which the human spirit had rightly been ashamed, are in fact innovative simply because they flout that sense of shame. It is no accident that the emancipation of new music coincides in time with psychoanalysis, a theory in which the painful conflict with parents and the process of breaking away from them found their way into consciousness. Both artistically and psychologically, however, this process of breaking away is not achieved by repressing the memory of one's parents and seeking refuge with one's kind grandparents, like a child. That would scarcely be less infantile in music than it would in reality. After all, new music, as a reaction against late Romantic music, inherited the task that crystallized in the latter: a state of consciousness that can no longer rely on any objectively valid canon of forms and must therefore objectivize itself from its own resources, from its own force of gravity, from the laws governing its own subjectivity. Every other—and that means every other stylistic attempt at musical objectification—would be nugatory, the victim of the very arbitrariness of which the preceding epoch stands accused and which new music imagined it had left behind.

The relationship of new music to inherited stylistic concepts like Classicism and Romanticism changes in line with the revision that those concepts themselves stand in need of. New music shares in both these concepts because they preceded it, but not because it looks up to them or imitates them, or because it would be good to be able to shelter within an established style, but only because in its reflection upon itself and the preconditions specific to itself it releases the latent energy that those styles have stored up. In any case, they never achieved the reconciliation of the artistic elements that has secretly been intended by the ideal of integral composition since the onset of the modern era. The element worth salvaging from what passes for musical Classicism is not the preclassical manner, with its semblance of architectonic symmetry and embellishment. Just as such an order lacked a community, it also lacked the musical material and the canon of forms that could sustain it. And since it was alien, external, and repressive toward the human subject, what was wanted was not an order of that kind, but rather its opposite. Nevertheless, the postulate still survives of an objectivity that passes through the subject, is mediated by it, and receives it unto itself once more, an objectivity that Viennese Classicism aspired to make real. What the great composers of the Viennese school wanted, from Haydn to Schubert, was music that was perfectly structured, absolutely right, absolutely authoritative, and yet at every moment still subjective—liberated humanity. But music like this has never yet found its voice. It remains as a challenge, as the anticipation of an image of society in which the interest of the community as a whole would be identical with that of each individual, and in which coercion and oppression would be things of the past.

On the other hand, because an actual reconciliation proves to be constantly receding into the distance, thus assuming an increasing air of utopianism, the idea of new music enters into a decisive opposition to everything affirmative or positively transfiguring, everything that implies a spiritual order already exists. It is furrowed with pain and with the negativity that the cliché attributes to Romanticism. New music keeps reopening the wound, instead of affirming the world as it exists, and this attracts the entrenched hatred of those who appeal to the pseudoargument that it must be obsolete and old-fashioned because it clings to sounds that are dissonant both literally and metaphorically, that are strikingly "modern" to the ear. This criticism is itself overlaid by a powerful trend of reality, that of the coercive integration that constantly cuts off the voice and the right to live of anyone who fails to conform. To that extent the Romantic element, long since declared dead by the theoreticians of style, is still alive as an unwavering impulse in new music. It must measure itself against that perennial situation instead of decreeing it out of existence. The historical material it must come to terms with, the twelve successive semitones of equal value, available in every combination, was the result of the process of differentiation that took place in the so-called Romantic era in the shape of chromaticism. This achievement cannot be reversed; no new tonality, mixed with church modes, for example, would be possible now. Every prescribed musical language would have something unreal about it; music is left with nothing other than the bare twelve tones. And even these have not transcended the process that brought about their emancipation; it has left its mark on them, and keeps on going. Whatever is done with the twelve tones still contains something of the tensions that once characterized Romantic chromaticism. Whether advanced music is more than mere bricolage is determined by the extent to which it shapes these tensions in a more radical manner than did the nineteenth century. At the same time, however, the historical process generated a specific sensitivity to what the chromaticism of the time left unarticulated, the sheer monotony of the smallest steps. The wealth of intervals of highly usable twelve-tone rows—in contrast to the chromatic scale that functions as the "row" in *Tristan*—is perhaps the most important feature differentiating new music from the Romantic material out of which it has grown. It was only with the progressive refinement of the intervallic consciousness that it became possible to go beyond Romantic chromaticism: not toward a restoration of the diatonic, but toward the further articulation and independence of the twelve tones through exploitation of the wealth of possible intervallic relationships between them. As in this basic stratum of composition, musical Romanticism in general has produced a sensibility, a dynamism and complexity, a freedom and lack of inhibition in listening that ever since has contained the promise of happiness of all musical composition and that must remain unconfined if the objectifying impulse of emancipated music is not to repeat itself endlessly or end up in obscurantism. It will be meaningful, and non-superfluous, to objectivize music only when the following conditions are satisfied, conditions that the superficial gaze would ascribe to Romanticism: all divergent individual elements must simultaneously resist the principle of form that their own nature conjures up; the complex must stand in genuine need of constructive articulation in order to be represented in all its purity; and finally, the dynamic force must be so powerful that, to remain dynamic at all, something fixed must be opposed to it, even if that fixed thing is the dynamic force itself.

Romanticism must not simply be rejected by new music: that is how it might have appeared at the moment of transition, but not today, when the old has long since become visible again in the new, where it had lain dormant. If new music is antithetical to Romanticism, this is only so as to make the Romantic fully conscious of itself. Above all, then, the goal of new music must be the complete liberation of the human subject. For thanks to the bourgeois controls on Romantic composition, right down to and including Strauss, this liberation had been hampered in the expression of suffering by expressive conventions whose musical language was permeated until recently with a variety of residues. The truth contained in the matter-of-factness of new music, its resistance to mere illusion, is also a resistance to such conventions. If anything, such resistance lends support to the subject instead of expelling it, as would suit so many people. Because music calls the emancipated aesthetic subject by its true name—in other words, expresses it directly—that subject is able to achieve its own objectivity, out of its own inner being, by saying what it in truth is. This calls for no dilution of Romanticism by any sort of complicity, but for the intensification of those impulses that have been placed under a taboo by bourgeois mediocrity.

It is hard, after all that, to dismiss the concept of a synthesis, badly compromised though it is. The time may well be ripe for regarding new music as such a synthesis, in contrast to the legacies of both the Roman-

tic and Classical. But if we are to accept that glib, soothing word and simply deny what actually inspired new music, we should do so only in the
dialectical sense that connects Romanticism to Classicism, not externally,
but in terms of its own potential, its integral character. Nothing is to be
expected from forcing different styles together, as versatile composers, including some famous ones, have attempted. Classicism and Romanticism
can only be reconciled, if at all, through their extremes. But even then the
idea of a synthesis has its repugnant side, namely the hope that unity and
peace can be achieved in art, even though they missed their moment in
reality. Music that aims at reconciliation is at its most sensitive when confronted by the illusion of reconciliation: this can be seen from the anxiety performers display in the presence of kitsch. What is wanted is not a
peacefulness above all conflicts, but the pure, uncompromising representation of absolute conflict.

§ The Function of Counterpoint in New Music

For Rudolf Kolisch, in true friendship

Just as the speculative eye sees things together, so the speculative ear hears things together.
—Søren Kierkegaard, *Either/Or*

The choice of a technical subject, or one with elements of craftsmanship, instead of a philosophical and aesthetic one is itself the expression of a philosophical intention. In his *Theory of Harmony*, Arnold Schoenberg, whose work in the arena of the "functional counterpoint" still awaits interpretation, went out of his way to define the theory of harmony as a craft theory, as opposed to an aesthetics. That was possible because his book provided a new and productive account of traditional tonal harmony. He assumed such knowledge as a precondition of composition, just as the painter presupposes an ability to draw nudes. But it could not claim to supply the norms for current composition, any more than a faithful reproduction of human anatomy can set the standard for contemporary painting. His textbook differed from an aesthetic tract because of its retrospective nature. It had every interest in underlining this fact. For the development of composition and its historical material at that time—the period of cubism—had superseded not just the traditional tonal harmony, but also an aesthetic that had elevated historically conditioned tonal procedures into more or less eternal laws. Fifty years on, the situation in composition can no longer accept the separation between handicraft and aesthetics that Schoenberg had called for in response to a spontaneous artistic need. On the one hand, the committed and progressive younger composers of today are inclined to give their technical problems, particularly questions of musical language and its organization, a normative status, to regard them as artistic, and to make no bones about substituting technical criteria for aesthetic ones. On the other hand, philosophical aesthetics nowadays lags even further behind artistic practice than it did in the days of Debussy, whose works could not really be imagined without the theories of symbolism and impressionism. This is why there is a need to rethink the relationship between the aesthetics and the craft of music. It would not be legitimate to devise an aesthetics from above with quasi-ontological status, one that was unconcerned with the laws governing musical language and the concrete musical structures in which alone those laws are crystallized. Nor would it be sufficient to give a positivist description of the technical facts and then to tack on to it retrospectively a theory that would lose all sense of its own meaning once it had ceased to grasp its truth or falsity. Only the philistine keeps questions of musical technique and aesthetic meaning in separate compartments; only the unrepentant technofreak or resolute idealist confuses the two. But neither will the solution be found in a middle course between speculative thought remote from musical practice and a diligent craftsmanship. It is not for nothing that artists reserve a particular detestation for the sensitive listener who approaches music from outside, but with taste, and who, while always refusing to submit to its discipline, immerses himself in it without feeling the resistance that derives from knowledge. Such people belong to a bygone age, lost beyond recall—their prototypes were collectors and amateurs—and what is true socially, holds good musically as well. The work of art is not best served by a compromise between the extremes of the internal and external, of spirit and technicality. True mediation can result only from preserving the extremes as such. The theoretical idea has to penetrate into the blindest center of the monads, which is what works of art are, into those of their aspects that are the opposite of spiritual and yet remain in control of them as spirit. The site of the philosophy of art is its technological force fields: the tensions that every work of art objectively contains within itself are also the medium of its truth and hence of philosophical interpretation.

A valid musical aesthetics would have to show how the spiritual substance of a work of art—what traditional philosophy called the artistic idea—is constituted in the life of its components, in the way in which they continually modify each other, forming ever new constellations. It may seem astonishing to offer up counterpoint as a paradigm for this, with its simultaneous spinning out and fitting together of relatively autonomous voices. For ever since Schoenberg, new music has been moving objectively in the direction of total organization, integral unity. This is why it no longer allows the individual dimensions of music—harmony, counterpoint, form, tone color—the autonomy they enjoyed as subjects in the traditional academic syllabuses. Instead it strives to unify all these elements, above all the horizontal and vertical dimensions, and where possible to derive them from an identical core. This trend is by no means confined to the Schoenbergian twelve-tone technique and the subsequent shift toward a serial structure that even incorporates time in the total organization. At the very best, the awareness of the inadequacy of the old, strictly segregated categories has today become more or less universal. Even Hindemith, who is on the extreme conservative wing of new music, has avoided the old divisions in his *Unterweisung im Tonsatz* [Instruction in composition] and operates instead with overarching concepts like "scale degrees" and "gradients." But genuine though the desire may be to create a theory of music that does justice to the structure as a totality and does not simply add together such elements as melody, harmony, counterpoint, rhythm, instrumentation, and form, an unarticulated synthesis is only purchased at the cost of a bad simplification. The task of raising the latent play of opposing forces to the plane of consciousness is a matter of the way these different aspects relate to one another. Synthesis is no mere matter of the lowest common denominator; to degrade these aspects to that is one of the disasters of contemporary practice. Instead its substantial reality is in its ability to work out the conflicts and contradictions between the different strata or domains. And in general the concept of musical material in *The Philosophy of Modern Music* should not be used to refer to any naturally given material, to physical and technological possibilities that can be deployed absolutely and at any point in time. Instead the thinking there was mediated through and through: every musical language contains the entire history of music and ultimately the whole of society. The simplest reflection teaches us that, historically, horizontals and verticals pointed in different directions, that successive and simultaneous sounds are not identical, and that they were not organized according to the same rules, however closely connected they may have been in the major works. The distinction between harmony and counterpoint was an appropriate reflection of this fact. To imagine that it was enough to fold melodies into harmonies, or unfold harmonies back into melodies, would be mechanistic and would reduce the twelve-tone method to an abstract preartistic procedure. To recognize counterpoint as the stratum of composition in which verticals and horizontals are interwoven may help us to counter the superficiality of such ideas and of compositions based on such assumptions. In this context we should perhaps also follow a suggestion of Heinrich Jalowetz that a distinction be drawn between counterpoint and polyphony, although it is not entirely compelling. Polyphony is to be the name for the relationship between several more or less independent parts that are all of more or less equal importance in terms of their relative weight and melodic definition. Counterpoint is the procedure that adds to one or more principal voices one or more independent voices that are secondary in comparison, and on a graduated scale. The second type, like the first, is of medieval origin, but it is more important for contemporary practice because it preserves monody as it has dominated music ever since the beginning of the age of harmony, that is, for the last four centuries. It preserves, in other words, the principle of an accompanied main melody, instead of sacrificing it to an older practice. To put it crudely, we might say that counterpoint holds fast to the idea of the songlike melody in the midst of genuinely worked-through polyphony, and thereby to the idea of the sovereign subject, rather than suppressing it in the spirit of a prebourgeois collectivity.

It is beyond dispute that alongside, and as a corollary to, the emancipation of harmony, the use of counterpoint is what distinguishes new music from that which went before, much as modern painting dates from the priority given to the constructivist principle. This holds good for all responsible representatives of the new music movement, with the possible exception of Stravinsky. In the latter's early works there is no real use of polyphony; subsequently, it appears only intermittently. His official separation from new music, one that was maintained until recently, springs ultimately from the absence of the contrapuntal spirit: in this respect, he is essentially rooted in the nineteenth century—the very last thing he wanted. But earlier explanations of the new trend toward counterpoint are quite inadequate. Better ones are urgently needed, all the more so as the old premises of counterpoint—a relatively homogeneous, static, and closed society that can be represented and disciplined in polyphonic song—are no more valid at the end of the bourgeois epoch than they were at its beginning. The human subject that took up arms openly and on his own against the idea of a self-contained plurality is still the reference point of all creative productivity: no contrapuntal cosmos today could be the echo of a social one, and no sooner do so-called revivals of polyphony aim at creating one than they turn out to be doomed. Simultaneously violent and impotent, the contemporary evolution of the contrapuntal spirit offers us the paradox of a multivoiced music without a community.

Instead of facing up to this paradox, people, if they did not simply insist, with a modest sense of pride, that a revival of the polyphonic spirit was taking place, were content to note the fact and to explain it historically, even though this merely deferred a confrontation with the problem. Among the historical explanations, the best known, and probably the most important, is the one tracing it back to motivic-thematic work. In the development sections of the essentially homophonic works of Viennese Classicism—there, where thematic material is "elaborated," where something actually happens in the music, and where further sections are not just added but are dialectically created—composers often had recourse to the polyphonic treatment of so-called thematic paradigms, of the kind that had come, after a long prehistory, to dominate the mature fugal form. This is the only point at which Viennese Classicism was able to benefit from the quickly buried legacy of Bach. In Brahms, for example, whose compositional method became increasingly differentiated, we see how the art of thematic work begins to spread out from the development section to permeate the movement as a whole. And at the same time, we find the spirit of counterpoint also beginning to stir. More or less outside his own compositions, Brahms occupied himself with exercises in counterpoint. An additional factor was a trend toward something completely opposed to polyphonic texture [*durchbrochene Arbeit*]: the emergence of harmony, which from the seventeenth century on had increasingly supplanted counterpoint. The more harmony freed itself from the triad, or more generally from the scheme of superimposed thirds; the more chords were created by simultaneously sounded notes; and above all, the more each note in the chord was able to maintain its separate identity, instead of melting into the homogeneous sonorities that operate with the simplest harmonic combinations—the more the chords became polyphonic in themselves. With the increasingly dissonant character of harmony, the tension in individual sonorities also increased. No sonority was self-contained, like the old consonance, the "resolution" [*Auflösung*]. Every sonority seemed to be laden with energy, to point beyond itself, and every one of the distinct individual notes contained within it required an independent "melodic" continuation of its own, instead of there being a succession of one synthesized overall sonority after another. This emancipation of individual notes from their chord was probably what Schoenberg had in mind when he spoke of the instinctual life of sonorities.

Moreover, it is not necessary to focus on the late phase of this tendency of harmony to emancipate itself to become aware of the countervailing forces emerging in thorough-bass thinking. Particularly on the conservative wing in the later nineteenth century, in other words, in Brahms, the more harmonic progression relinquished ordinary smooth dominant and leading-tone relationships in favor of progress by energetically differentiated and balanced steps, the more did the fundamental voices—the bass, in other words—gain a certain autonomy, definite contours, and an element of "melody." So-called spectacle basses [*Brillenbässe*] and the like become taboo. This trend is already very far advanced in an early work of Schoenberg's, his First Quartet, where the bass accompaniment, which was supposed to strengthen the chief subject harmonically, is itself so sharply defined that it involuntarily condenses into counterpoint and then continues to play a major role in the rest of the work as an independent countersubject. Such sharp definition of what had previously been a matter of indifference or had passed more or less unnoticed requires in its turn a sharper profile for everything else that takes place at the same time, lest any disproportion arise in the relative significance of simultaneously appearing voices. In general, when any element of the music is intensified or becomes more independent, it affects everything else, so that between the elements the equilibrium is established, which the mature Schoenberg once defined as the desirable goal to be striven for anew in every composition. Hence, if the complex, internally articulated single sonorities with many notes release articulated parts, then conversely the chords need consistent part-writing so that they may be heard as their logical consequence. In what unimaginative traditionalists think of as a youthful Wagnerian work of Schoenberg's, the *Gurrelieder*, the dissonances in the Spirit Chorus in the third part are so drawn into the tonal flow that the individual voices merge involuntarily in those sonorities. Since the early phase of new music, harmony and polyphony have been in a state of constant friction, with each element intensified by the demands of the other.

This definition of the new counterpoint as one required by the interaction of the different elements of composition proves valid right down to the practical rules of thumb. Thus Richard Strauss, in his revised version of Berlioz's *Traité de l'instrumentation*, added the comment that his own primary interest, the emancipation of orchestral color, was possible only in the presence of meaningful polyphony of the kind he found—with some justification, when compared to Viennese Classicism—in Richard Wagner. Every instrument, every group of instruments, must have something musically vibrant of its own, a genuine "voice," and not, apart from the melody, be just a matter of basso continuo or fill-in parts to round out the work as a whole. Even the most recent achievement of traditional music, the emancipation of timbre, can only be realized where simultaneous voices are able to unfold freely in tonal space. But this needs counterpoint, even though the fact that counterpoint is tied to a tonal, harmonic system may give it an ornamental appearance. A related feature is encountered in Schoenberg. The more complex the sources of the composition in its own impulses, from within, the more urgently compositional clarity is required as a corrective. Throughout Western aesthetic experience, an essential characteristic of a work of art is that what takes place at its core should appear on the surface. Schoenberg always insisted emphatically on the need for clarity both in composition and in performance. It was one of his most cherished criteria, and incidentally, one his school shared with Mahler, a claim that always comes as a surprise to the neophyte who attaches such importance to the surface impact of the music. Schoenberg's aim as a composer, unlike that of so many of his younger contemporaries, was never simply to produce an obvious unity at the expense of the differentiation that prevailed in the late nineteenth and early twentieth centuries. From the outset he was guided by the unconscious realization that in works of art above all, unity can be made substantial only as the result of a struggle; and only if it does not dourly assert itself, and run on automatically, without any countervailing resistance, as in music that is mechanically propelled. The indescribable tension of the musical forces in Schoenberg's oeuvre and his immediate school springs from the fact that their works possess not only a total constructed unity, but also all the nuances and contrasts of the soul divided against itself, as it is against the world; and that this legacy of a subjectivism, which is all too cheaply derided today, is not abstractly negated, but is preserved and raised to a higher level, as the double meaning of the Hegelian *Aufhebung* would have it. While all the elements interpenetrate, they also remain distinct, and the unity comes into being only through the function each of them has and by virtue of which it influences the others. It is not an immediate unity, but a unity of opposites. It is this, however, that arouses the constant anxieties about clarity. Only when every form fragment, every phrase and half-phrase, every note unambiguously proclaims what its function is in the whole will the totally organized work be protected against lapsing into its opposite, chaos. It is for this reason that nothing may remain unarticulated in the relations of the parts to each other; they must be contrasted clearly and distinctly, and achieve full plasticity. Similarly, an alert polyphonic thinking is required at every moment, as is also that capacity for transparency, for classifying the individual parts into main event, secondary event, and mere background, that shows Schoenberg the contrapuntalist to have been a polyphonic composer in the narrower sense. All counterpoint also has an analytical function, the dissection of the complex into distinct parts, the articulation of simultaneous events in accordance with the relative weight of its components and according to similarity and contrast. Its external sign is the marking, introduced by Schoenberg, of principal part [*Hauptstimme*], secondary part [*Nebenstimme*], and background parts. In his music a pause becomes an artistic device to let in air so that the voices do not stifle each other; the technique of thematic separation [*durchbrochene Arbeit*], modeled on the string quartet, aims to clarify as much as to condense. It had always been the case that continuous counterpoint, like all too-luxuriant counterpoint, appearing obtrusively in the wrong place, was as bad as the wishy-washy variety; with Schoenberg, this becomes a regulative principle. Counterpoint is a necessary principle not merely for the consistent structuring of new music, but also, if we may put it so, for its representation. This need arises as much in the centers of the music as in the commandment to place these centers at the periphery, in other words, to make them manifest. To that extent, polyphony today is the exact opposite of the "paper music" it is claimed to be in the abusive phrase of musical reactionaries. All this points to the irresistible conclusion that counterpoint arose from the needs of so-called late Romanticism, in contrast to the childish cliché with its rigid and facile distinction between Romanticism and Neoclassicism, between subjective and objective. The resurrection of counterpoint is not the product of historicism; it is no mere excavation of prebourgeois and early bourgeois music. Similarly, the notion of a generation shift is far too simplistic. This would do absolutely nothing to explain why a series of composers with a special talent for counterpoint should have suddenly descended from heaven. Talented people are created in line with the objective state of the forces of production. Counterpoint is the product of the immanent laws of composition, of the very music to which the new contrapuntal music then emerged as an antidote. The transition is not a matter of talent, or conviction, or even of what is known as style, which is no more a given in music today than it is in the plastic arts. Instead, it is a matter of the logic of music, the inexorable advance in the organization of the work of art. Historically, the relationship of new music to that of the preceding epoch is neither one of unmediated reaction on the part of those who are fed up with the existing situation, nor one of a steady, but dialectical, transition. An older procedure provokes its antithesis thanks to its own nature.

This makes the genealogy of the new counterpoint a question of function: the problems created by history become embedded in those of aesthetic validity, of true and false, in the logic of composition. The difficulties of new music are unquestionably caused largely by counterpoint, because it taxes the ear to have to separate out several independent voices simultaneously while also listening for their interrelationship. But whoever wishes to throw light on them cannot rest content with showing how this counterpoint came into being. In art, just as in reality, the logic of history may sometimes lead to absurdity. However much this modern counterpoint is historically determined, it has to make sense in its own right, in terms of its own needs. This means taking a closer look at the concept of thematic work, whose subcutaneous dissemination and expansion took place in Brahms. Strange though it may seem in a composer labeled academic, Brahms's role in the origins of new music is roughly comparable to that of Cézanne in modern painting. The complete thematization of his compositions was not the result of any backward-looking learnedness. Faithful to Beethoven, it was designed to bridge the stylistic gulf between, on the one hand, the exposition and recapitulation that were more or less loosely strung together and, on the other, a dynamic, condensed, and yet in many ways rudimentary middle section in which the most important events were concentrated. As early as Brahms, in whose most responsible works there is scarcely a note that is not thematic, not related to thematic material underpinning the whole, the older Classicism's idea of development becomes all-embracing, even though he respected the traditional distinction between exposition, development, and recapitulation, as, for that matter, did Schoenberg in the majority of his works, well into his old age.

But even in Brahms, the thematic work is seldom radically contrapuntal. It is distinguished crucially from the modern version by its relation to musical space. This is, to expand the linguistic usage of musicians, who like to speak of sonic space [*Klangraum*], the unity-creating reference system of all simultaneous events, in which two different things may no more occupy the same space than they would do in the realm of the external senses; and, in addition, it provides the functional framework for the unfolding of simultaneous sonorities, the "perspective." This space was already firmly established and unproblematic in Brahms. The individual sonorities were vocabulary items, identically repeatable playing chips—even in the majority of the works of Richard Strauss, whose harmonic discoveries barely modified the harmonic reference system, in which they appeared as no more than deviations, clusters that were awaiting the triumph of the system. The absence of coherence, which lies on the surface in Strauss but dates back for centuries, is, however, merely a symptom of something deeper, of a lack of congruity in the different dimensions of the language of music. The realm of freedom, of subjectivity, of a specific artistic shaping without convention, was that of the horizontal dimension, which is reflected in harmonic arpeggiation and differentiation but in principle does not include harmony itself. This remains the residue of a quasi–a priori universality. In earlier periods, at least from Bach down to Viennese Classicism, it had a decisive function, and perhaps made possible the most important solutions. But when confronted by the enhanced freedom the horizontal dimension has since acquired, it has ossified and failed to adjust to the inner nature of the main events. The horizontal and vertical dimensions in music were never truly homogeneous; in the end they parted company altogether. A gulf opened up between conventional pattern and subjective shaping. Correcting this gap is the function of counterpoint. In tonal music that is not yet emancipated harmonically, thematic work, the process of becoming that is the very life of music, takes place in a guaranteed space. Articulated by its relationships, such work is mainly content to give shape to sounds in succession. Individual paradigms are established and then spun out in sequences, abbreviated, expanded, intensified, and resolved. New music has to create its own space from within itself. It is no longer a reference system for thematic work, but its product. That propels it in the direction of simultaneity, of polyphony. There was a time when even thematically highly organized music succeeded in becoming essentially homophonic; throughout Viennese Classicism, including late Beethoven despite all assertions to the contrary, polyphonic passages are the exception, and even where they do occur, they are rarely genuinely complex. Frequently, the main motive leaps from one instrument to the other in fragmented orchestration [*durchbrochene Arbeit*], achieving a kind of pseudopolyphony that does not aspire to a serious articulation of the individual parts. There is an analogy here with the tendency of Baroque architecture to use decorative features to create the appearance of structural solutions. Such a pretense, however, is paid for with the integrity of the work: not just with impurities in setting, which are not absent even from Beethoven, but with the consequence from the outset that the obligation entered into by every use of counterpoint is not fulfilled, and that what ought to be followed through to its logical conclusion remains a mere transitory episode. New music is truly objective in refusing to tolerate this any longer. The moment when it can no longer swim with the harmonic current, and can no longer even travel along firm harmonic tracks, it must acknowledge the compulsion to total construction that ultimately leads to reciprocal relationships between the different voices and thereby to the radical dominance of counterpoint.

In this the shape of the themes themselves, the melodic detail, is involved. In Viennese Classicism, as is well known, the themes consisted to a great extent partly of triads, partly of seconds that provided a cantabile filling for the gaps in the triad intervals. These relatively simple paradigms could easily be fitted into the harmonic pattern, even simultaneously, as in the occasional stretto passages. They were in themselves so closely based on harmonic formulas that they scarcely offered resistance. Melodies of this kind hardly ever laid claim to full plasticity and autonomy. Such restraint, the renunciation of the unconditioned subjective definition of the basic figures subjectively chosen for each work, is what gave the Viennese school around 1800 its rounded perfection, saturated in resignation and the glory of seamless mastery that is conveyed by the concept of Classicism. The Romantic triumph of subjectivity cast off that restraint. After the lied of Schubert and Schumann, above all, instrumental themes too became genuine melodies. And that remained the case with Schoenberg, in all the phases of his work. The combination of well-defined linearities is far more difficult and also conspicuous than the manipulation of unraveled triads and interpolated seconds. Only now is thematic work transformed from a game into contrapuntal seriousness. The more strongly characterized the principal voices are, the more independent the secondary voices become, if they are not to fall away and if disparities are not to arise between the degrees of intensity of the different strands of the composition. Thus the primacy of counterpoint ought not to achieve less than was achieved by the individual composition purely from its own resources, its own specific progress. This is thanks to the authority, coherence, and objectivity that in former times came from outside and had been promised by the tried and the tested language of music. In the new music that counts, it is as untrue that the subject has merely emancipated itself as it is that music has simply invoked objectivity. Its ideal is autonomy. It adheres to nothing that is alien to its own impulse, its own coherence, and that has been merely imposed upon it. It desires to become objective out of its own subjectivity, through the unreserved immersion in its unique self, without external supports and borrowings.

Eduard Steuermann has handed down a statement of Schoenberg's to the effect that with good counterpoint, you actually forget the harmony. Undoubtedly, Schoenberg was thinking as much of Bach as of his own compositions. It might be objected that in the case of Bach, the archexponent of tonality, even in the most highly condensed and terse contrapuntal pieces, such as the D major stretto fugue from book 2 of *The Well-Tempered Clavier*, the harmonic degrees and chord relations are so unmistakable that one could forget the harmony only because it was so self-evident. But this objection does not so much disentangle the obvious relationship between harmony and counterpoint in Bach as describe it. A further aid is to think of the relatively casual harmony in everyday singing of canons. The force with which one voice impinges on another, the way it contrasts with one in the present and reflects one that has past, cancels out that other force which melts the parts down into an undifferentiated, simultaneous sonority. The more densely the network of distinct strands becomes intertwined, the more superfluous does it become to emphasize the abstract harmonic unity of simultaneous sounds and of progressive chord sequences. This corresponds in the listener to the necessary concentration of attention on the direction of the parts and their relationship to one another, something that banishes a merely harmonic consciousness to the background. This shift, however, is not just "psychological." Because the only thing that can be said to be artistically shaped is what has found its way into the experienced musical phenomenon, the primacy of counterpoint is the place where objective construction encounters human perception. Nothing else is meant by Schoenberg's statement that a discussion of harmony is not on the agenda at present. It is no longer constitutive, it no longer steers composition, but presides only as a negative factor. Of course, anything that makes harmonic nonsense must not be allowed to stand; the harmonic flow must not come to a halt or cease to glide forward automatically, it must not make unmotivated leaps, and nothing must sound "wrong" in a sense immediately familiar to the composer's ear. But harmony no longer determines the general direction of the work as it did in the thorough-bass system, or as does what Schoenberg terms the "chorale." Undoubtedly, we may compare the contrapuntal arts that have flourished in new music, to an extent that has baffled many people, with artistic tricks, just as modern composers have cited such artistic gymnastics as the medieval retrograde and mirror canons: new music shares with the acrobat's tricks the fact that gravity is abolished and the burden of the harmonic system, the fluctuations of mere chordal connections, is eliminated. Kurth's phrase about linear counterpoint hints at some of this, except that the composers who naively embraced it tended to neglect harmony as a negative criterion and simply stuck voices together without concerning themselves with the logic of the resultant harmonic flow. Such voices are always bad counterpoint. Successful, though by no means foregrounded harmonic coherence remains the test of counterpoint itself.

At issue here is the overcoming of harmonic gravity, the suspension of harmonic space. This was shown by the older contrapuntal practice in its use of double and multiple counterpoint, on which the fugue form as such is based. In the higher contrapuntal techniques the voices proceeding according to the thorough-bass system can change register: what was at the top can be put on the bottom line, in the middle, or vice versa. Even though Bach built this principle into the thorough-bass notation, it nevertheless is in profound contradiction to it; a figured bass with a succession of chords as a basis is irreconcilable with a procedure in which the concept of the chord basis itself is devalued, along with the complementary concept of the top voice carrying the melody because one element can turn into another. It is well known that in contrast to all of the music that he wrote based on dance types, Bach's fugal elaborations are seldom symmetrical and can be made to fit Riemann's eight-measure scheme only with great difficulty. Likewise, the school rule warns against using a regular phrase with a half cadence in the middle. Such irregularity is in

Bach's case no mere archaism, but highly meaningful: the primacy of figured-bass thinking, which uses rhythmic symmetry to underscore the harmonic articulation in terms of half and full closure, is prudently pushed back. He resists the idea of harmonic listening, the notion that the listener who has heard the question posed by the antecedent phrase should automatically anticipate the reply in the consequent. The impotence of later fugues, by Schumann and Mendelssohn, and occasionally even Mozart, is caused by the fact that with composers who approach music with homophonic hearing, what holds sway unchallenged in their minds is the harmonic space together with its rhythmic equivalents, the critique of which is an intrinsic aspect of the principle of counterpoint. In tendency, at least in multiple counterpoint, the vertical dimension is subjected to the primacy of the horizontal. Schoenberg's counterpoint always adhered to this and other equally stringent requirements, and by no means only with the advent of twelve-tone technique. Already in the relatively early First Chamber Symphony, op. 9, centered on E major, there begins at cue 27 a passage in triple counterpoint with a twice-inverted combination of a melodically defined, thematic principal part [*Hauptstimme*], an equally important figure in sixteenths, and an accompanying figure in eighths. Later on, around cue 68, in the middle of the great elaboration, there is a three-part canon with a fourth, independent and likewise thematic, part that is immediately repeated in quadruple counterpoint (cue 69). In twelve-tone technique every row is related both horizontally and vertically, and hence, like the technique of "developing variation," it is indebted to the principle of multiple counterpoint that envisages in principle that unification of the horizontal and vertical dimensions which then becomes the premise of all composition. "Developing variation" and counterpoint came very close together as early as the period of free atonality, following the emancipation of harmony, when Schoenberg first turned his mind again toward motivic economy. The middle section of the Second Orchestral Piece, op. 16, is based on a figure that is at once freely imitated and developed with a countersubject in the spirit of double counterpoint, but that undergoes countless variations in intervals, note values, and rhythm in the process. Even though it always remains recognizable, the theme never acquires definitive shape; instead it is kept ingeniously noncommittal, as if improvised. For this reason it can be taken over into the recapitulation of the homophonic exposition section without doing violence to it.

As contrapuntalist, Schoenberg consistently preferred the so-called higher forms of counterpoint.[1] His insubordinate imagination was set alight from the outset by the element of discipline, of rigor, and the formulation of twelve-tone technique might justifiably be regarded as the attempt to satisfy the requirements of strict multiple counterpoint within the framework of the twelve notes of equal value of the chromatic scale. In no sense is Schoenberg's revolution of the language of music a mere escape from school. It is rather the unceasing effort to take its claims seriously and to test them radically—right up to the breaking point, in fact. His treatment of tonality is comparable, and the paradoxical threat to the Schoenbergian oeuvre, the academic threat, doubtless springs from this fact. Counterpoint and thematic work are welded together without leaving any residue: a procedure that strives to imbue every event with thematic significance must also thematize the relations of the voices to one another, and will not put up with anything extraneous, anything not related to the identical thematic core. Aside from multiple counterpoint, a further means of achieving this is the combining of themes. In modern times, the first composer to do this was Wagner (the most famous, if not the most important instance comes toward the end of the overture to *Die Meistersinger*), but it was then ceaselessly belabored by the entire New German school, especially Strauss, with the use of program music to illustrate complexities, and by Reger, who used it as a sort of fugal bombshell. Early on, Schoenberg made thematic combination available to his constructivist method. It is very closely related to multiple counterpoint, in which a number of voices likewise assert equal, thematic claims. Thus, late in the long, single movement of the First Quartet, where the form calls for abbreviation and condensation, the main themes of the slow section and the rondo appear simultaneously. Similar things are to be found in the First Chamber Symphony in the repeat of the scherzo after the trio. In contrast to such thematically strict pieces of counterpoint, there is less

---

1. This is confirmed by a posthumous essay of Schoenberg's dated August 1931 and published by Josef Rufer in the December issue of *Melos*. He says that what he learned from Bach was "contrapuntal thought, i.e. the art of finding figures [*Tongestalten*] that can accompany themselves"—in other words, he did not learn to add to a given part an absolutely independent one. This implies that Schoenberg's contrapuntal thinking had always been concerned with the idea of integrated composition, or, in Schoenberg's own words from the same essay, with "the art of creating everything from itself."

emphasis in Schoenberg on the so-called free counterpoint that was so productive in Mahler, namely the invention of completely novel melodies to add to those already displayed. One of the rare exceptions is the start of the recapitulation in the first movement of the Fourth Quartet [m. 165]. It demonstrates the connection between counterpoint and formal shaping, for which Schoenberg was always careful to show his concern by translating the architectonic structures, from the shortest phrases right up to major sections, into precise serial events. The moment of that recapitulation involves a recognizable restatement, here, of the original rhythm of the theme. But such a restatement, like all faithful repetition, is illegitimate where it is not supported by harmonic symmetries. Schoenberg contrives to escape from the impasse by modifying the identical figure in line with the form by adding an entirely new element—the fresh counterpoint on the second violin—as if it were part of the dynamics of the development section. But it is no accident that such inventions are rare. If the counterpoint really wishes to create that authority out of itself, out of its thematic content, since it can have no other source, then the counterpoint must itself be authoritative: it must be wholly thematic. The category of authoritativeness [*Verbindlichkeit*] was, according to Kolisch, the contrapuntal category that Schoenberg valued the most highly, in his teaching as well. Schoenberg's rank above almost every other contemporary composer—including some of the most important—is established by this inability to accept anything but a pure relationship between the different voices. What is authentic about him is the authoritative counterpoint, ultimately in the supreme sense that the form results from the relations of the voices to one another, the behavior of the contrapuntal elements, the interaction of the voices. Form itself becomes a function of counterpoint, as it had not been since Bach, whose fugues once proclaimed the all-embracing nature of contrapuntal method.

The authoritativeness of Schoenberg's counterpoint can perhaps be best described by two antithetical demands that pervade his practice and converge in a synthesis. On the one side, counterpoint has always insisted on the mutual independence of voices that resound simultaneously. If one is the mere shadow of the other, or even just too similar, the counterpoint in which each voice claims to be independent becomes a fraud. It loses the oppositional power on which the integration of the contrapuntal structure depends. Incidentally, in accordance with the criterion of clarity, two voices that are not succinctly distinguished from each other cannot be regarded as contrapuntal at all. Conversely, however, the distinct voices must come together again in a unity; in other words, they must form a fit. By virtue of the consistent distinction between them, each must become visible when the other fades into the background. The external characteristic of this is in the complementary rhythms: the new counterpoint is precisely not a *punctum contra punctum*, but a *lucus a non lucendo*. The length of the note values in the different voices; the, for the most part, audible entry of the individual notes; and finally the accents—none of these should coincide. Quite early on, the Hungarian composer Alexander Jemnitz realized that rhythmic variety in counterpoint, providing every beat with an entry note, results in rhythmical monotony. Nevertheless, it is only this seamless fitting together that makes possible a synthesis of contrasts. The voices are joined together by a process of mutual exclusion, and as a result the contrapuntal principle finally feels its way toward welding the different voices together into a single melody. But through this, the principle in twelve-tone technique of seamless polyphonic interlocking, a total multiplicity, threatens to revert to simplicity. The whole dominates the individual parts of which it is composed and in which it has its being without a letup. Twelve-tone technique, which represents the consummation of the spirit of counterpoint, also contains the potential for its demise. The completely determined nature of the independently opposed and wholly complementary voices negates their very autonomy. The last frontier of contrapuntal thinking becomes visible on the horizon. Because the concept of counterpoint is now all-embracing, because everything that is not counterpoint vanishes from composition, something must change in the concept itself. The fact that it is eliminating its opposite also impugns its own validity. As a unity in diversity, the idea of counterpoint was essentially, in a true Hegelian sense, the identity of the nonidentical. With the arrival of total counterpoint, the nonidentical element begins to evaporate. It is true enough that even though the different voices are heard simultaneously, their tones and rhythms never coincide, and hence they are absolutely to be distinguished from one another. But this very absoluteness makes the differences between them problematic. Not only does everything go back to a unified, identical basic material, so that distinctions collapse into sameness; but also the all-inclusive nature of the distinguishing principle turns everything into one single thing. Differences are eroded into complementarities; the antithetical nature of counterpoint, the representative of freedom, is submerged in synthesis without retaining its identity. However, the achievement of counterpoint as an artistic economy, the very thing that made composers feel the labor was worthwhile, had been to bring free, autonomous shapes [*Gestalten*] together through the very power of artistic organization. If Schoenberg always despised "free counterpoint," so now the residue of contrapuntal freedom is being liquidated. It is as if all counterpoint had now found itself beneath a single roof, instead of spontaneously erecting the building. In aesthetic terms, no doubt, the totality retains the primacy over the individual components. Given this primacy, this unity, the independence of the voices was always illusory. But aesthetic semblance [*Schein*] and a technically illusory method of composition not carried out in full seriousness are not one and the same thing. The legitimacy of a work depends on whether the interaction of the parts and the whole within the aesthetic semblance, within the realm marked out by the composition, actually takes place or not. It is in the latter case that the aesthetic semblance is destroyed. From semblance it turns into illusion, as soon as it ceases to incorporate that dialectic. If the intrinsic logic of authoritative contrapuntal thinking terminates in total constructivity, the total constructivity ends up by liquidating the living substance of counterpoint. This inescapable contradiction is profoundly conditioned by the element of caprice, of self-assertion, of force, that is inherent in the logical consistency of serial composition. This is its negative side: that under the spell of unfreedom no art can find unscathed an authoritative mode of being that would be at one with freedom.

Imitation and canon, devices that twelve-tone counterpoint also uses extensively, are subject to comparable limitations. They, too, were chosen because they were felt to be authoritative and able to make visible the relations between the voices, not just latently, through the row, but also overtly, by means of thematic work in the most forceful and precise sense. Instances of twelve-tone counterpoint that simply follow from the row, mostly without imitating each other—one example is in the very difficult first movement of Schoenberg's Wind Quintet [op. 26]—obviously eluded, to his critical ear, the inescapable interrelationship that was supposed to substitute for the authoritativeness of traditional harmony. But because the universal relations of all the elements to the row are themselves latent thematic work, the additional audible imitations double the overt thematic work, that is, what the composition had already achieved: they prove something already proven. In the rondo of the Wind Quintet,

Schoenberg ingeniously resolved the contradiction between twelve-tone technique and imitation, or thematic work in general, by using it as the source of an artistic effect in its own right. "Theme" here is a merely rhythmical but almost too clearly defined shape. It fills up with various tones and intervals, in obedience to what the row and its transformations require at any given moment. The effect is parodic—as if an indefatigable imagination were always proclaiming the same message with different words—and parody of this sort is proclaimed by the tone of the entire movement. It becomes all the more striking, the more different melodic concretizations of the intentionally rigid thematic rhythm pile up; what happens then is that the regularity of the row ensures that the imitation, which makes the claim of absolute fidelity, turns out to be "free," as if the imitating voice could not quite recollect its model. The principle of developing variation in twelve-tone technique seems to imply a sort of free imitation; but here this imitation mocks that freedom by claiming rigor for itself: the authoritative ends up sounding unauthoritative.

Twelve-tone counterpoint has fallen between two stools. On the one hand, it is indeed prescribed by the row, but its regularity is not immediately graspable, and it seems to be "free," if not arbitrary, at the level of experience. On the other hand, it is strict, canonic, but no longer necessary in terms of its internal principle of construction. With rising confidence in his use of twelve-tone technique, Schoenberg met this difficulty by reserving manifest imitations (apart from exceptions such as the late Prelude for Orchestra, op. 44) for highly stylized dance types of the kind he cultivated from the scherzo of the Wind Quintet on, which appeared less authoritative from the outset. These imitations playfully create what had been guaranteed by rhythmic and harmonic symmetries in traditional dances.

Conflicts between an entirely "free" twelve-tone composition, purified of all external formal categories, and the conservation of traditional imitations are not explicable as the expression of the artist's uncontrollable constructivist ambitions—whether naive or Alexandrian. Nor are they symptomatic of deficiencies in a sense of style that might be corrected by artistic mastery. Rather, what is expected of counterpoint, the creation of a specific coherence as authentic as the old universal system of tonality, remains a precarious project. For all the rigor with which the twelve-tone organization prepares for the actual act of composition in the here and now, it does not suffice to put its stamp on the actual composition in

such a way as to render it necessarily transparent. Additional contrapuntal arts are called upon to eliminate the arbitrariness that lurks in emancipated music, however it predisposes its material in advance. However,
the plight of the particular in its relations with the general goes much
deeper than is indicated by this technical dilemma in new music. It can
be formulated fundamentally as a question: How can the particular become authoritative without proposing any general, objective purpose that
is itself subjectively reflected? In other words, how can subjectivity become objective without force or fraud? The antinomy that this question
points to is dictated by the relation of art, indeed of all forms of human
spirit, to society. A valid order of art does not appear possible in the absence of a constitutive social order that the artistic one would resemble.
Subject and object cannot be reconciled in art as long as they are not reconciled in the real world, and the present state of affairs is the straight opposite of that, increasingly antagonistic, despite the illusion of unity that
is created by the overwhelming power of objective relations over each and
every subject. Precisely because of the deception involved in such posi-
tivity, however, the idea of art today is to transcend the existing society
critically, and to uphold the concrete image of a nonconformist, meaningful possibility. The more reality hardens against possibility, the more
urgent and real the idea of art becomes. Art now finds itself, at the end
of the bourgeois era, forced into the role played by Don Quixote at its
beginning: a role that is at once impossible and necessary. This is registered by the composer's work without any need for him to be conscious
of it himself. New music has its insoluble aspect, but its open horizon also
contains its good fortune because it forces it ceaselessly to make decisions,
as if with eyes closed about the rightness or wrongness of every strategy,
of every note, without externally imposed standards. Any other procedure
today would be barbaric. With the migration of objectivity and its claims
into the very realm that was uncovered by the rebellion against the oth-
erness of the objective, the rigid antithesis of the productive and the critical, itself increasingly ideological in nature, has begun to break up. Good
composing has changed into the process of the permanent critique of
composition, and the ability to criticize has become part of productivity.
Every direct productive impulse, every "inspiration" [*Einfall*], must contain a critical dimension if it wishes to be productive and no mere unconscious copy of unconfirmed generalities, of stereotypes. Such productive critique—with the word taken more literally than in Lessing's us-

age—opens up the only route to transcending the limits of the arbitrary without deception. It is the aesthetic manifestation of what the great philosophers described as positive negation. New music has not been vouchsafed any "model" [*Leitbild*], and where it seeks one, it merely reveals its own weakness. A good man, in his dark bewildered stress, still knows the path from which he should not stray; but he no longer knows of any historical models or tried and tested recipes that he might follow. Searching for something to hold on to is itself a sign of weakness. What is evident, however, is the concrete consciousness of the false. In composition, the dark bewildered stress coincides with the unreserved acceptance of the nature of the problem that every composition affirms at every moment. Music in the medium of positive negation—that is precisely how we should think of counterpoint: simultaneously as the negation and affirmation of the voice to which it is added. Without making concessions to a bad utopia, it is not wholly illegitimate to imagine that music may hope through spontaneous receptivity, through immersion in the unique, to become more than a mere existent thing. What artists do involves more than the impotent desires springing from their own isolation. In a deeply concealed sense, all musical subjectivity, even the pure fact of the individual composition, is objectively mediated. The more the work tries to forget, to rid itself of preordained, and hence unauthoritative, formal categories, the more it will inevitably discover such authoritative categories within its own structure: it is here that talk of monads turns out to bear truth. The most hidden, most fleeting impulses of the human subject that a composition tries to capture contain general concepts of musical coherence, in sublimated form and transformed beyond all recognition. Only because of them do ephemeral subjective impulses acquire any meaning; only through them are such impulses able to participate in a comprehensive framework that they themselves help to create. Both the secret and the criterion of new music that counts is that the path of its specificity leads into a core of universality; that at the heart of its individuation, the interplay of universal and particular springs to life once more, after having been overthrown as a relationship to a purely external norm. This may well have been in the mind of Anton von Webern when he remarked of a piece that unfolded in an unprecedented manner: this is a waltz—as if it were the most plausible thing in the world. In analogy to philosophical usage, we may think of realism in music as a state of consciousness that conceives of a universal concept as an existent being; nominalism is one that thinks of it as no more than something affirmed by the human subject. If these definitions are acceptable, we must infer that in new music, as in modernity generally, nominalism is unavoidable. New music was the first to appropriate this nominalist position without mental reservation, and it is unable to escape it. What it regards as authoritative are not norms imposed from outside, but only those that arise from within itself, as if from beneath. That, however, takes it beyond the bounds of nominalism and so holds out the promise of reconciliation. For absolute individuality is a delusion, just as much as absolute universality: in contrast, reconciliation would be the truth. The utopia of such an aesthetic challenge is the primal image of a future real condition, and precisely because the real situation today refuses reconciliation, we must retain the idea of it in an image.

§ Criteria of New Music

For my dear friend
Eduard Steuermann,
in memory of July 1957

The question of criteria by which to judge new music calls for reflection not directly on the criteria themselves, but on the methods needed to discover them, if we are to avoid the standard strategies of resistance. But we can scarcely begin by talking of methods as a matter of principle. For the methods cannot be separated from the subject and treated as something ready-made and external, but must be produced in the course of a process of interaction with their subject. In the first instance this means the term "dialectics" as applied to music, to its intrinsic development and to the consciousness of it. The word has been taken up by critics so as to discredit what it means, as if dialectics were an intellectual game that philosophers play with art from their own so-called standpoint, without really getting to know what art is. In contrast to that, Hegel understood dialectics not as a particular philosophical standpoint, but as the sustained attempt to follow the movement of the object under discussion and to help it find expression. If, nevertheless, reflections on criteria cannot always be translated directly into quarter notes and sharps, this is because, wherever music is to be taken seriously, it has undermined any simple relationship to its basic material. Reflection has even become an integral feature of the practice of the composer. Whatever is right for the physicist, who reflects on energy, matter, and causality, must be perfectly proper for the musician, too. To complain about this and to bewail the loss of the old naïveté will not do. Instead of refusing to raise music to the level of consciousness, of intrinsic rationality, spontaneous subjects should rather intensify that process until it reaches the point where it underpins aesthetic quality. Anyone who has not yet lost his musical virgin-ity cannot be wished anything better than that he should lose it as quickly as possible.

At present, the question of criteria in music is caught up in a polarity that is as sterile as it is problematic. On the one side are those who appeal to firm, even rigid values postulated externally, a kind of hierarchy in the style of the middle Scheler, and who aspire to make musical decisions through confrontations with such values. Such a fixed theory is massively contradicted by the history of music, which constantly proves that what claims to be purely natural turns out to have been the product of creative transformation. For the past few decades, such static value systems have been pleased to call themselves an ontology. The more arbitrary they are, the less they are able to do justice to the living movement of their object; and the more they owe their existence to subjective desire or the will to power, the more violently they claim absolute validity and unchallengeable authority. These thinkers can be contrasted with vulgar relativists who hold that nothing authoritative can be said about the quality of works of art and that there is no arguing about matters of taste, though they neglect the evidence that people incessantly quarrel about such matters and that such a thing as art education does exist. If the relativists were right, then the girl gymnasts who refuse to learn the techniques of dancing lest they suppress their own personality would be proclaiming a profound truth. In reality, the relativists are not entirely in earnest. They pass judgments all the time, often insisting on them with no less obstinacy than the apologists of eternal values; they hope, however, to be able to evade responsibility for their views by proclaiming their skepticism about making value judgments. Now, the dialectical contemplation of music aims to transcend this alternative by dint of the labor and effort needed to investigate the challenges and tendencies inherent in music. It aims to confront them with the concepts of true and false in their objective, concrete workings, as these are present to the conscious ear of the composer in every measure and every musical solution. To confront music consciously is not to intellectualize it. Moreover, living art was hardly ever as free of intellectual elements as the philosophers maintained when their ignorance of art led them to reserve it for the sphere of pure contemplation. Where art went beyond mere enjoyment, it was never fully identifiable with its immediate sensuous appearance, and our treatment of it must reflect this. As soon as one starts to discuss music, one enters the realm of thought, and no power on earth has the right to silence this.

Moreover, even though theoretical reflection is not to be confused with the artistic process of production, the latter contains more reflection nowadays than operetta composers might imagine when they picture Mozart in their minds.

There is considerable force in the idea that the given language of music stands in need of reappraisal, that it has become problematic. It is not simply that traditional tonality has gone out of fashion and that anyone who considers himself up to date would be embarrassed to compose using such methods. The fact is, these methods have become objectively false. It is not possible to ignore the mental climate of the age. Even if a composer in the provinces has not learned of the fate of tonality, what he writes does not thereby retain its integrity; it is still flawed and incoherent from start to finish. This is the case with Sibelius's symphonies, perhaps the last ambitious products of tonality in Western art. But the implications of this situation extend well beyond a simple prohibition on tonal melodies and chords. As in a maelstrom, tonality drags to their doom categories that had once been thought independent of particular materials of composition, but which turn out in fact to be intimately intertwined with tonality. This refers above all to categories of musical language and syntax: the traditional methods of constructing forms. Their familiarity seduces us into thinking of them as part of the general logic of music as such, and not just tonality. Nevertheless, they cannot simply be transported unscathed from the world of tonality into something newer. A first, crude idea can be gleaned from reference to the most important traditional form, that of the sonata. Proportion among different parts in the sonata referred fundamentally to proportion among the keys, a matter of modulation and harmony. As soon as the sonata form loses its substance in terms of harmonic content, it is left more or less hanging in thin air. It becomes a construct in the questionable sense that it no longer follows inexorably from the internal musical events, it no longer coheres with them naturally, let alone harmonizes with them, but is imposed on the textures of sound from outside, organizing them as if from memory. And this cannot fail to have an impact on even the minutest formal cells of music, literally its linguistic structure, which is saturated with tonality, much as, for example, the relationship between antecedent and consequent parallels that of tonic and dominant. This is why it is scarcely an exaggeration to claim that all the categories capable of establishing musical meaning have lost their autonomy and need to be thought through and formulated anew. Whatever happens musically nowadays is problematic in the full sense of the word, that of a task that cries out for a solution, and one, moreover, in which the difficulty of finding a solution is inscribed in the problem. To treat music dialectically means to submit to this situation. To object to the proponent of such a view is to criticize the observer for something that is dictated to him by the facts of the case.

What is really at stake in the matter of criteria was anticipated by a difficult, and by no means wholly unambiguous, thesis of the *Critique of Judgment*, at a time when such developments were not yet visible in artistic practice. And in general, Kant's immersion in the medium of thought far surpassed the experience of art that was available to him at the time, and that he was striving to explain in philosophical terms. He teaches that judgments of taste possess the character of subjective universality, indeed a kind of "necessity" [*Nötigung*]. Aesthetic judgments appear as if in obedience to a rule, as if thought were governed by a law. But the law, the rule, contained in artistic judgment is, to paraphrase Kant's idea, not given, but unknown; judgments are passed as if in the dark, and yet with a reasoned consciousness of objectivity. Our search for musical criteria today should also proceed along much the same paradoxical lines; in other words, we should search for an experience of necessity that imposes itself step by step, but which can make no claim to any transparent universal law. Actually, we miss the point if, as is inevitable in language, we subsume the experience of necessity implicit in the concrete monads of the works under universal concepts, if, in other words, we posit something like rules where none can exist, but only an infinitely sensitive and fragile logic, one that points to tendencies rather than fixed norms governing what should be done or not done.

The semblance of aesthetic relativity is dissipated as soon as we enter the works themselves and their discipline, as if we were entering Goethe's chapel. But even when we are inside, if we adhere to that theorem of Kant's, we must abstain from thinking of the objectivity of aesthetic judgments as something fixed and thinglike. This abstinence is precisely the demand that the dialectical approach makes on normal ways of thinking. Aesthetic objectivity is itself a process, of which anyone who conceives of the work of art as a force field is aware. What is required for this is not a set of dogmatic points of orientation, but the introduction of subjective experience—the very thing the prevailing view wishes to eliminate in favor of universal norms. Nevertheless, the element of compulsion, the fact that something in a piece of music is as it is and cannot be any other way, is perfectly comprehensible, and is not a matter of an individual chance. It can be judged much as a composer makes precise judgments about what is right, insofar as he proceeds in a meaningful, rational manner. Of course, this idea allows for a certain latitude of rightness; there may be several solutions in any one instance. But in comparison with, say, Mozart, this latitude seems lately to have shrunk. At the same time, the artistic principle of individuation has been intensified to the point where it colonizes every aspect of a work, so that every work, and each of its aspects, must be unique and no longer permits the wealth of deviations that were tolerated, even required, by a universal musical language capable of establishing its objective validity. For new music that concept of rightness [*Richtigkeit*] will be crucial, as will the ability not to confuse it with any preartistic, preintellectual determinants of the material or abstract arrangements of the notes. In reality there is an overabundance of compositions that are "right" according to explicitly controllable arrangements, but wrong or senseless in artistic terms. Music has many layers of rightness. More recently, even in the tighter circle of the serial school, there is a growing tendency to insist on a more differentiated, intellectualized conception of rightness.

However, at least some of the habits of thought still widespread on the subject of musical criteria have disastrous consequences. Compelling though it is to require each work to legitimate itself in terms of its initial assumptions and its consistency, and even though serious composers have proved their willingness to submit to this requirement, it nevertheless remains quite alien to the prevailing climate of opinion. The "cultural lag" between production and reception has recently increased to the point where it has destroyed the consensus about what constitutes musical culture. And this lag has a bearing not just on our immediate musical experience but on our standards of judgment as well. There is a continuum of stale cultural responses, stretching from the consumer who insists that he cannot understand a new work because he does not know anything about harmony theory—whereas in reality a knowledge of abstract theoretical prescriptions would be of little assistance in confronting the particular work—and extending to those critics who even now cannot rid themselves of the habit of throwing their weight around with talk of superbly crafted fugues or enthusing about the glittering orchestration in which a composer has dressed up his piece of music—which for the most part then sounds as though that is exactly what has happened. Admittedly, the music profession today requires more than ever the traditional skills that the music academies used to transmit before they were laid waste by the ethos of community. But the knowledge thus acquired, together with additional qualities such as originality and inspiration, does not of itself produce important music, as the cultural philistines would wish, but has become irrelevant to it. The instant application of fugal technique, for example, something that, like the sonata, depended on the constructive function of tonal relationships, is no longer acceptable today. The same can be said of an "orchestration" that adds the tone color retrospectively, much as attractive packaging is added to a standard product—for it negates the principle of a through-constructed composition. The fugues from *Wozzeck*, which are of critical dramatic significance, are genuine exceptions that prove the rule, and the fugues to be found in Schoenberg are either a virtuoso parody, as in the choral satire *Der neue Klassizismus*, or, as in the Suite for String Orchestra, a didactic *jeu d'esprit*. There is scarcely a philistine still alive who would dare to praise a writer for his scintillating style; but in music the intellectual manners that resist such mental stereotypes have yet to be acquired by critics, who listen to music in a way that has not progressed even as far as Croce's aesthetic nominalism. Competence is no longer what it was once supposed to be, but in reality never was, namely a treasure trove of acquired methods that could be exploited by talent. Instead, every element of the structure, from the smallest up to the totality, has to spring from the sustaining intuition of the specific musical insight, without regard to traditional skills. And conversely, every musical intuition, every involuntary, subjective impulse, must be transmuted into the rule-bound procedure that retroactively takes over what had started out as an irrational origin. Only by means of such a process of particularization, as a force that draws itself together into particularity, can the universal still claim a place in the work of art; only through the discipline of the overarching totality, which it enters into by virtue of its own impulse, can the particular maintain itself. Criteria that fail to live up to this ideal are anachronistic and almost inevitably end up by representing laxity or pedantry as good.

This is above all the besetting sin of aesthetic pluralism, which is deluded into believing that every conceivable type of music can coincide with any other and with equal validity—Schoenberg and his successors, Stravinsky, ultimately even Britten. Such claims are supported by pointing to the sharply different characters of composers of earlier times. Anyone who is incapable of taking pleasure in such variety is dismissed as doctrinaire; he is said to lack any understanding of the overworked notion of the complexities of art. These, however, are in the first instance qualitative. "Complex," that is to say, lacking any straightforward "message," is a word that can be applied to any work of art worthy of the name, but hardly to art as a whole. Nor can it mean that high art and low art, truly shaped works alongside mere artistic burblings, rich works and threadbare ones, can all be allowed to vegetate harmoniously side by side, simply because human beings and consumers can be found to fit each of these categories. The plurality that is found so refreshing today is a parody of the plurality that once, in a highly developed musical language like that of Viennese classicism, sanctioned the distinctions between Haydn, Mozart, Beethoven, and Schubert, even though their works are mutually rather intolerant; even though Schubert, for example, leaves himself open to criticism when he attempts to live up to criteria appropriate to Beethoven. The present variety, however, is not one of comparable but diverse products on a single plane, but one of disparate objects. It owes its existence to inconsistency. Some composers simply press on from all sides with the innovations implicit in the state of the musical material, without leaving any preexisting "parameters" in place, while others merely tackle one particular sector, leaving the others untouched, as if nothing else had changed. Still others call upon old-fashioned practices in a more or less literary spirit, while simultaneously doing them violence. Such diversity is spurious, and consciousness should resist it rather than chase after it. It lies on the wrong side of the threshold to a discipline that really ought to provide a proving ground for authentic wealth, a wealth not to be limited to crude characteristics. The diversity in the Schoenberg school, extending from Schoenberg, Berg, and Webern through the second generation and down to the responsible serial composers of the present, appears more securely established than the chaotic variety of music festival composers, who simultaneously embody historically diverse positions and whose syncretism merely perpetuates the stylistic confusions of the nineteenth century, which these days are such an easy target for derision. Variety exists only in unity, not as an agglomeration of "styles"; what is true of each composition applies with equal force to the relationships between compositions. The expansive gesture that embraces everything and finds good everywhere belongs in the realm of assiduous information collecting, not that of critical consciousness. The fact that every possible variant of art can thrive simultaneously, and that they all somehow or other express the age—the ghastly expression reflects the ghastly reality— no more confers legitimacy on them than does the fact of mere existence legitimate anything. Were this not the case, then the Siegesallee [Victory Avenue in Berlin], though undoubtedly a highly representative creation of the Wilhelminian era, could be put on the same plane, aesthetically or philosophically, as the paintings of Monet, Pissarro, and Renoir. The two administratively sanctioned levels of music today—serious and light— are nothing more than the marks of an antagonistic society, and the observer's task is to explain how they came about, not to defend them as such. That variety which is the life of art is only authentic if it measures up to the logic of music, the necessary interrelationship of all its elements, the integral work. Individuality that evades this, that balks at the challenge, is impotent in its privacy, a mere relic. Hardly anywhere is the inadequacy of mere judgments of taste so complete as in this sphere. If an audience finds a contemporary piece pretty, and responds with a delicious tingling of the spine because it sounds pleasant or unfolds smoothly or captivates through similar qualities, all this is based largely on the compulsion to repeat, the pleasure of mere recognition: a regressive phenomenon, a piece of unresolved childhood, the very antithesis of the redemption of that childhood through art.

This unreflecting inclusiveness is complemented by hollow claims to competence. Nowadays many people, whose sole qualification is an education in music history, possess authority and are able to influence musical opinion. They often regard those unlike them as experimenters in need of lectures from their betters, who inform them that every revolution has to be followed by a reaction, that great catastrophes have now been mended, and that the appeal to tradition will be able to "heal" music once more, provided one has the requisite philological expertise. This attitude should be attacked, not defended. Whoever still places his trust in a discredited tradition and continues to muddle on in the style of the nineteenth century or simply copies the styles of long-defunct social conditions in a spirit of craftsmanship, while confusing the results with "classicism," is no more on safe ground than is the latest prepared piano. A self-advertising tradition merely jeopardizes itself; a new security merely mocks its own idea. Beyond that is only the belief that history will itself make the judgments and put things right; in years to come a fool with a diploma will understand more than a rational contemporary who keeps his ears open. This is blind faith, and it is given credence so that people who have no specific relationship to music, or who have failed to keep up with events, should still have enough status to lend weight to their opinions. In music, unlike the visual arts, compositions before a certain date are completely unavailable for direct inspection, but instead are cloaked in an aura of the archaic that creates misunderstandings as soon as the attempt is made to revive them, as the phrase goes, or to infer norms from them. Anyone who is aware of the element of internal historical compulsion in music will dismiss the illusion that an overview of historical developments has any direct connection with truth. Musical historicism, of course, is not much concerned with the truth. In Wilhelm Dilthey's late work on the structure of the historical world in the arts, a book that is prototypical for the historicist point of view, he declares at one point: "Historical consciousness of the finiteness of every historical phenomenon, of every human or social condition, of the relativity of belief of every kind, is the last step toward the liberation of mankind. With it mankind achieves the sovereign power to discover the meaning of every experience, to give himself up to it fully, without inhibition, as if there were no system of philosophy or belief that could obligate human beings. Life becomes free from conceptual knowledge. The mind remains sovereign in the face of all the spiderwebs of dogmatic thought. Every thing of beauty, every sacred object, every sacrifice, once experienced and interpreted, opens up perspectives that disclose a reality. And in like fashion we absorb the bad, the terrible, and the ugly within ourselves as things that occupy a place in the world, that constitute realities whose existence is necessarily justified in a universal context."

In the tirades of this most recent newcomer on the German philosophical scene we can see with unusual clarity what is at stake in the ideology of historicism, the residue of Hegel: it is the justification of the bad. They sell their soul to the past and capitulate before it; they sanction what has occurred, the power of facts. Aesthetic historicism is the scientific mask of relativism. It can plunder the junk room of the past at will for arguments with which to fend off the new—claiming, for example, that all of this has been done before, and that the Florentine *ars nova* was similarly unrestrained in its use of counterpoint—whereas the truth is that modern society is so radically different from the conditions to which music history devotes its energies that every analogy drawn from history can be no more than an impotent Romantic gesture. Others present the old—which in fact does not need to be very old at all—as a source of higher truth because of its sacred origins; or act as if they were experts on the vital energies of the nation; or, finally, exploit their overview of history to demonstrate that musical judgments have always been fallible. They then conclude that all judgments are invalid and worthless, in order to promote uncritical acceptance of the line of least resistance and of what lies immediately at hand, "free from conceptual knowledge." No doubt there is a need for knowledge of the historical force fields of music; but the arena of such knowledge is the works themselves, not the historical coordinates in which the works are inscribed, or even the succession of different styles. Without wishing to undervalue the achievements of musicology, it remains barely indisputable that up to now it has made little headway in grasping the crucial phenomenon, namely the structural understanding of the works themselves. Those of its exponents who did make the attempt, such as Heinrich Schenker and Ernst Kurth, were relegated to the status of outsiders. However that may be, it is still impossible to draw inferences from historical phenomena of whatever sort about what music ought to be in the present. What knowledge has to confront is the configuration that arises out of the past but has never yet existed; it cannot be concerned with the fatal recurrence of the same.

The rejection of surrogate criteria does not constitute an answer to the search for legitimate ones. It cannot simply be asserted that the new, or even the logically consistent, is better, and logical consistency can contain a dialectic—that which was discussed in *The Dialectics of Enlightenment*—that turns into regression. The search for inner coherence does not necessarily involve an identification with the abstract path of progress. No doubt all aesthetic questions, all the questions that decide whether music is a work of art, are technical questions, having to do with method. But they also coincide with supratechnical questions, spiritual ones. Nothing possesses aesthetic value unless, as Kolisch once stated, it has a precise technical correlative. At the same time, the concept of technical coherence [*Stimmen*],[1] which lays down the canon for the integral organization of the work of art, is no more than the vehicle of the artistic, not the artistic itself. The problem of criteria would have to be specified further, depending on how far technical yardsticks of overall coherence

---

1. Cf. "Music and Technique" [pp. 197–99 in this volume—Trans.].

[*Stimmigkeit*] and constructivity relate concretely to the work of art as a spiritual reality. Aesthetic objectivity is in the first instance a surface manifestation [*ein Scheinen*], not a literal factual reality. Constructivity in art has the primary meaning of creating the illusion [*Schein*] that the work is something essentially objective, universally valid, necessary, and authentic, something that cannot be anything other than it is. The work of art cannot crudely be equated to a thing that might subject the logic of its structure to any sort of proof, as for example one might ask whether an object which has a purpose fulfills that purpose. This apparent inconsistency in the concept of structure must first be understood. If you produce an artifact that functions precisely in strict conformity with scientific laws, this is still a long way from creating a work of art. To regard it as one is the regressive aspect of recent advances; it is the relapse from the realm of art into collecting objects, the opposite of the concept of "intellectualism" so favored by reactionaries. The development of new tonal materials and principles of construction should not be inhibited, but should be pushed beyond the preoccupation with technique for its own sake—in other words, beyond a particular type of infantilism that is especially seductive when it is fused with positivistic science or its terminology, something that resists from the outset the dimension of meaning in works of art, the dimension of objective spirit that they contain. Blindness toward meaning or renunciation of meaning of any kind, in contrast to sheer activity, has meanwhile become so widespread that simply to call for meaning exposes one to the suspicion of reactionary Romanticism, whereas in truth what is being offered is a reflection on the raison d'être of art. That regression, however, the act of forgetting that works of art are not just words but are the vehicles of the spiritual, is tempting precisely because it is combined with an inexorable determination to rationalize artistic procedures. Preartistic objects are able, thanks to the technological labor stored up in them, to create the impression of extreme sublimation. They are based on a primitive view of the relationship between art and science. Needless to say, art has always played a role in scientific progress. Foolish though it would be to equate the two, it would be equally misguided to fall into line with what in American parlance might be called the "escapist" belief that the more science and technology advance, the more art must retreat into a world of supposedly pure feeling and turn its back on the scientific spirit. Such a retreat of art into itself would only lead it back into its own past. But the legitimate and un-

avoidable acceptance of scientific methods and techniques will neither
guarantee the work of art nor eliminate what distinguishes it from the
empirical reality in which such methods are rooted. Thus French impressionist painters can be said to have worked with the psychological and
physiological analyses of the mechanisms of perception and linked them
up with the techniques of painting. But their task was not to organize
works of art like events in the retina, or to transform pictures into docu-
ments of sense perception. Instead painters used science to teach themselves to see things in a new way as painters, and after they had done so,
the world itself looked different. The energizing and functionalizing of
perception was spiritual, historical, and intimately bound up with the
process of subjectivization. It was this that attracted those perceptual discoveries like a magnet. The impressionist painters fragmented the objects
into dots because dots were needed to convey the new experience of a
bustling boulevard with its omnibuses and trees, and not in order to comply with the laws of optics that discovered analogous processes in the
retina. In short, the absorption of aspects of the new technology suited
the artists' intentions. They wanted to open up subliminal strata of experience and make them available to art, which would not have been possible without those techniques. Doubtless, this was not a conscious strategy on the part of the impressionist painters; many of them likely
adopted these techniques intuitively, much as many composers do today.
But the relationship between technological advance and those experiences
is visible as the objective content of their paintings. It cannot be claimed
that an analogous procedure is evident throughout recent musical production, particularly since at times composers have defended the view
that the work of art is entirely separate from the human subject, without
being able, however, to escape the question of whether music is "heard"
or whether it breaks free of the imagination and becomes fetishized. The
term "heard" here is no psychological category, but an objective one belonging to the thing itself, namely the relationship between music and its
manifestation as sound, as the experienced ear registers it at first, say, in
the orchestration, and then in the other layers of the composition. But it
is this very objectivity, the aspect that Cézanne called the *réalisé*, that always points back to subjective mediation—whether to the artist's happily
adequate idea or to a supervisory process in which he laboriously tests and
reexperiences his ideas.

Meanwhile, we cannot stop short at this contradiction in the idea of aesthetic objectivity—that is, as illusion or as a literally thinglike phenomenon. Anyone who opposes spirit and technology to each other in good bourgeois fashion is as far behind the times as the person who simply conflates the two, treating intellectual questions as wholly reducible to questions of manipulating material. Where a work of art fails to achieve an overall coherence in material terms, it will be affected aesthetically too. Our sharpened sensibilities today are upset by what Wagner had called effects without cause, far beyond the ambience of the effects themselves that Wagner had in mind with his dictum. The five-part triple fugue in C# minor from volume 1 of *The Well-Tempered Clavier* contains, toward the end, a so-called pseudo-ten-part stretto, in other words, a succession of ten imitative entries, even though the movement only has five parts. Bach—and in this respect he was baroque, to use the historical term wrongly applied in general to the music of the seventeenth and early eighteenth centuries—acted here somewhat like the mythical director who had only a few extras at his disposal and, needing an impressive army to march across the stage, made his soldiers run back behind the set and make a repeat appearance so as to create the illusion of large numbers. Of course, this passage in Bach is undoubtedly convincing thanks above all to its energetic rhythms. But at the same time, the alert listener will become aware of a certain feeling of illusion, of the kind very familiar from baroque architecture, with its use of ornament to convey the impression of structural features, but that is only just making its appearance in music with its use of all sorts of possible motives, particularly those of Viennese classicism. The present-day ideal of integral composition is probably also the attempt to do justice to this new sensibility and to produce music in which aesthetic and technological objectivity coincide. The contradiction here is no less significant than the fact that today, as always, art is a semblance and yet everything about it that seems to be mere illusion has become unbearable. All new music struggles to discover whether and how far it is able to overcome this contradiction. The presentiment of an antiartistic element in this dimension of illusion in art, a presentiment that once became manifest in Adolf Loos's criticism of the ornament, has now advanced to the idea that art is in principle a matter of ornamentation. The aesthetic sensibility ends up in conjuring the threat of antiart, a kind of vulgar materialism once removed which vainly boasts that art works all right when it works, whereas we only know that it doesn't work when it doesn't work.

~

In an all too clear-cut antithesis between now and then, it could be said that traditional music asked how meaning was to be objectified in the aesthetic phenomenon, whereas new music, at least in its most recent phase, asks how an objectively determined musical shape can acquire meaning. At the same time, the concept of musical meaning cannot be anticipated by any definition; it can, however, be made more specific. Superficially, at least, traditional music had no need to concern itself with how meaningful it was, as long as the existing idiom appeared to guarantee a meaning. The vocabulary, grammar, syntax, and logic of harmonic progression in particular were as familiar through long practice as those of spoken language; they made it possible to judge whether a performance spoke the language of the music or whether it sounded like someone reading something he does not understand. The popular distinction between musical and unmusical comes very close to this: it is supported in the first instance by such phenomena as phrasing and accenting, which also structure the compositions themselves. The concept of musical meaning derives from the experience of such matters, which must still be mastered by anyone who wishes to make the concept his own. Nowadays, however, when the musical context arises out of a specific structure and is no longer laid down by fixed universal rules, that initial idea of meaning no longer suffices, even in the case of music of the past. A piece that glides effortlessly along with the flow of the sound frequently arouses the suspicion that it is lacking in meaning. The idea of musical meaning ceases to appear self-evident—both in composition and as a criterion of reflection. What is certain, however, is that it cannot be split off from our sense of the inevitability of the musical flow, which is created by the way it is articulated. Music remains meaningful if it is organized in such a way that it must be as it is, that it cannot possibly be otherwise—only now this is achieved without the assistance of abstract norms. The difficulties, however, arise because the categories that have created meaning up to now, even when they go beyond the palpable stock of formulas in the traditional language of music, no longer guarantee what they once promised. The model here is the development section. The fact that in the middle of a piece the thematic material can become dialectical, can break up into its possibilities and antitheses, transcending itself and reinstating itself, appears scarcely capable of being separated from the idea of the elaboration of great music, as long as, in Schoenberg's words, that music embodies the "history of a theme," in other words, a self-contained historical process. But as early as Beethoven, and certainly no later than Brahms, the dialectical principle of development had begun to encroach on the sonata form as a whole, rather than simply confining itself to the development section. At the beginning of Brahms's Piano Quintet, for example, is the passage in sixteenths that after a few measures of the opening melody spurs the action on, a double diminution modifying the initial melody: "thematic work," then, the immediate development of what had happened previously. The fiber of the music in Brahms is already so differentiated that the need for integration is correspondingly intensified so as to compensate. It cannot wait for the development before condensing the relationships. But the effect of this is virtually to make the development itself superfluous: where everything is development, no special development is really needed. Berg, who in this respect was perhaps less of a traditionalist than Schoenberg, dispensed entirely with the development in his mature orchestral works. Just as the fugue died out, so too are we now witnessing the death of the sonata, the central musical form of the bourgeois era. A sonata without development is scarcely a sonata any longer. As it wanes, it drags to its doom its own material, namely the theme; indeed, to "state" a theme no longer makes sense, now that it is deprived of its development. With atonality the turn to athematic composition has become unstoppable; total thematization collapses into its opposite. In this way the structural elements on which meaning might be founded are being swept away, and their absence makes the task of creating a rigorous musical totality almost prohibitive. Nearly every one of the elements that generate meaning, even the most abstract results of a bare musical "logic," grow up in parallel with the traditional language of forms. Composers today take note of this, and do not wish to hang on to outdated tenets, but discover that the more radically their critical ear dismisses as inadequate the means that enable inscribed meaning to function, the more inexorably they are confronted by something alien to meaning. They are thus faced as individuals with the task of breathing meaning into their music, a task formerly carried out by the objective spirit. If, when confronted by a self-evidently senseless constructivist composition, one asks the composer to explain where the antecedent and where the consequent are in a particular phrase, or what the logical function of each note is, he will answer with talk about some parallel or other between pitch levels, volumes, lengths, timbres, and the like, all of which remain external to the flow of the music and are unable to create meaning as long as they fail to articulate the musical phenomenon itself. But to call composers to account in this way is unfair because musical meaning today can probably no longer be readily captured in concepts such as antecedent and consequent that arise indirectly from particular kinds of musical material. Furthermore, the more general such concepts become, and the more they distance themselves from the historically determined musical material, the more they lose their power to influence it. Principles such as similarity and contrast and their interrelation are too abstract to create meaning on their own; music can pay careful attention to such concepts while still losing sight of their inner significance. Nevertheless, the traditional formal categories of musical language and their abstract silhouettes should be retained rather than simply jettisoned. Webern's superiority stems from the fact that, however far removed from the traditional categories they may be, even his most fragmented pieces allow the listener to reconstruct the meaning of every note. To cut the connecting thread completely would signal the end of any meaning. So what is needed is the most extreme sublimation of those categories, the most absolute clarity about the changes they undergo in the course of the composition. They should no more be conserved than thrown overboard, but instead should be transformed to the point where they come into agreement with the new language of music in the force field of the works. This is possible because musical material itself is not natural material, nothing physical that remains constantly itself, but something historical. Meaning is history that has migrated into music, and this is why the material is not as alien to meaning as it may seem to the outsider who just seizes it blindly. This becomes most obvious in harmony. Nowadays a well-harmonized piece is not one that ignores the fact that tonality ever existed, but one that specifically negates it; and by avoiding sonorities or structures borrowed from tonality, such music preserves them within itself through the very process of exclusion. The same thing also applies to the more remote formal categories of musical meaning. The composer's vigilance must activate the power of the universal in the radicality of the particular. As long as no other concepts offer themselves—they may be generated by the logic of a piece composed in sections, in accordance with "characterizing formulas" [*Intonationen*]—we should still ask about antecedent and consequent, the statement [*Setzung*] and mediation of themes, principal and secondary ideas, melodic development and contrast, and the like. But we should also ask about the difference between all these and the present state of musical material, right down to the point of prohibition.

The element of universality, without which musical meaning would be almost inconceivable, stands opposed to the bad universality of musical types. This is the universality at the heart of individuation, not the all-inclusive universality of logic, and certainly not that of established genres. Ernst Bloch wrote somewhere that it is essential for a piece of music entitled Barcarole to be just that and nothing else: the universality of the category "barcarole" is a necessary part of its definition. The concept referred to here, however, is not an integral part of the thing itself, as it is for Hegel, but mainly something that is just stuck on from outside, for orientation. The drained Barcarole in Bartók's piano cycle *Out of Doors* has only a tenuous connection to its title, not to mention those influential works that have been divested of any link with such universals. The mere inclusion in a type is not enough for it to express the inner life of a composition: whether a piece is an authentic barcarole has to be expressed in its internal structure. Even in Chopin's Barcarole, which does its title credit, nothing of its specific quality—its meaning—can be heard if one expects to interpret it in the light of its title. But if the piece is properly listened to, one may even—if we can use the Romantic metaphor—secure a vision of the glowing evening Venetian sky, which is only alluded to in the title.

Musical meaning must also be distinguished from expression. Expression is not related to musical sound as language is to a referent, or a symbol to what is symbolized; rather, it is what arises out of configurations and developments. Meaningful music is not necessarily expressive. Expression, the mimetic element in music, the thing that, to use Eimert's term, the music "resembles," is only one element of its meaning, and is to be held in tension with a further aspect, that of construction and logic. No doubt these opposed elements are dialectically interrelated. The thrust of a piece, the power of its form, the compelling nature of a structure, tend to be translated into expression, no matter whether the individual parts or phrases are expressive or not. The expressive power of Beethoven's great recapitulations is brought about not only by the increased intensity with which the main theme is presented, but also by the fact that the theme recurs as a product, the culmination of the development—in other words, it is created by its formal organization. With its sense of a shattering inexorability, the form confirms in the work as a whole what was merely stated at the outset and was then subjected to a historical development. If all the formal elements of music are nothing but inscribed contents, then conversely all successful formal features contain expressiveness within themselves, even if it is rigorously excluded at the level of detail. In the heroic period of new music, and as early as Mahler, one could sometimes find the performance direction *non espressivo*, "without expression." But even this marking has an expressive character, whether it intends it or not, and it would be naive to think it could avoid it. In much music, especially loosely constructed music, the unity of meaning is directly precipitated by the expression, by the unambiguously articulated representation of a feeling. The last movement of Schumann's Fantasia owes its expansiveness to the expression of lack of restraint, of giving of itself, of pouring itself out; what takes place in it redounds to this feeling. But new music is familiar with radically different works, like the first movement of Schoenberg's Third Quartet. Its meaning stems from its iron control. For all its formal freedom, its denial of conventions, a radical control seems to have been ordained by sheer will, and this is where its eloquence lies: the image conjured up of an inexorable determinism, almost devoid of lyrical expression, veers around finally into expressivity. Only when it has been conceded that integral musical shape is the consequence of the rational ideal of music in the West, and not the ideal itself, and only when the potential for disintegration has again been acknowledged, will we be able to see greater opportunities for the assertion that expression can create meaning. Only then will it be possible for harmony to regain a significance that it lacks today but that was at times more potent in free atonality. Of course, such disintegration would occur within a context that creates meaning. Meaning does not always imply that everything coexists in concord; but it does adhere to the overall context, even where that context is itself incoherent.—Lastly, the concept of meaning does not resemble that of the poetic idea that dominated the New German school thanks to their misunderstanding of Beethoven. The idea of music, the spiritual content through which every sensuous phenomenon is transcended—these are not ideas that somehow run parallel to the flow of the music. If they intervene, as in Schoenberg's Piano Concerto, the composition casts them aside, like crutches, once it moves ahead freely of its own volition. Here, too, purism would be too restrictive; a work like the admittedly backward-looking Chamber Symphony no. 2 presents us with a strikingly vivid poetic idea, instead of surrendering to noncommittal imaginings. But that aside, meaning, the spiritual dimension in music, is the kind of transcendence in which its immanent structures gradually culminate: it is more than the sensuous. Indeed, it is created by the dynamism of the sensuous, while not asserting anything other than what it is, what it moves, and what it negates.

With all this the concept of musical meaning still remains too formal. As a criterion it is not sufficient to establish whether meaning enables the individual sensuous elements to transcend themselves; what is needed is a decision about the substantial content of this transcendence. In Beethoven, for example, this substantial content can be summed up under the concept of humanity, such that the whole takes precedence over the individual parts of which, by a sort of ruse of reason, it is itself composed. In the same way, humanity takes precedence over individuals existing merely for themselves, of whom it nevertheless consists. Such a definition of musical meaning includes a "higher criticism" (to adapt a term taken from the historical sciences), a criticism of the truth of this meaningful content. The priority of the whole, which is asserted in Beethoven's form and which implies the negation of all singularities, is testimony to the repressive aspect of an assertive bourgeois society, and the quality of Beethoven's music cannot simply be isolated from it: the drumbeats that are all that remain of some of his overtures when heard from outside reveal something of what is not heard. In the same way, the sensuous musical context of Wagner's works can be seen to be essentially identical with the blind, circular, and profoundly ahistorical poetic content of Schopenhauer's philosophy, in which blind will becomes individuated, but only to devour the individual once again.[2] The unity of Wagner's methods of composition and the philosophy thematized in it both gives it its power and marks the point where a critique can begin: the untruth of that philosophy is the untruth of his music and enables us to pinpoint its flaw, namely its purely illusory development. However, the unfolding of musical meaning to the point where critique becomes possible needs time. It would be mere poetic wish-fulfillment to think of providing a critique of contemporary music in the same way. Whether its meaning is an integral

---

2. Cf. Theodor W. Adorno, *Versuch über Wagner* (Frankfurt am Main, 1952), 158ff. [also in *Gesammelte Schriften*, vol. 13: *Die musikalischen Monographien*, 2d ed. (Frankfurt am Main: Suhrkamp, 1977), 118ff.; translation from Adorno, *In Search of Wagner*, trans. Rodney Livingstone (London: NLB, 1981), 123ff.—Trans.].

totality, whether the traces of its disintegration anticipate a situation that points beyond modern individualism, or whether they point to the regression to an earlier phase and hence represent the denunciation of the idea that the course of the world can be seen as an intelligible historical process—in all this the individual work may proffer crucial insights to the critical ear, but it allows of no conclusive judgment. Even traditional music is resistant to higher criticism. In Brahms, for example, it would have to ascertain whether his specific tone and the impressive energy with which his music is realized are justified in terms of meaningful content; whether, in short, his mood of resignation, his retreat into the private sphere, is a weakness that mocks the vigor of his creative power and ultimately infects the music itself. Nietzsche's critique of Wagner was higher criticism of this kind. But he failed to make it stick because even though the questions he asked went beyond mere sensuous experience to the deeper underlying truth, he failed to penetrate to the music's innermost workings. There is something unconvincing about the Nietzschean questions, for all their apparent mastery, and it fits in well with the reactionary quality inherent in the music: Nietzsche was superior to what happens in Wagner, but at the same time he was not quite up to it, in the same way that the dialectics of progress almost always thrust the avant-garde back behind the very stage of development that it advances beyond. All higher criticism threatens to degenerate into ideology, into cultural politics, or alternatively to become condensed into an immanent critique, a critique of musical coherence. Nevertheless, there are inevitably limits even to the highest criteria. In Nietzsche's invectives against Wagner's decadence and play-acting, for example, one cannot escape the nagging sense that they are not free of a latent philistinism, even though he had a sharp eye for the philistine aspects of Wagner's own nationalist worldview. For it is unclear whether artistic quality and the truth content of works of art coincide so perfectly. There is a great temptation to regard works of the highest rank as slightly less meritorious if they embody a "negative" consciousness of whatever kind, than those allegedly more positive. In that event, the work of art is sacrificed to a deluded preference for positive values to which it has already objected. The thesis that Beethoven's music is superior to Wagner's because it articulates the idea of freedom and humanity as a whole, while Wagner's music, regardless of its inner tendency, resonates with the loss of these categories, leads the critic into a disastrous flirtation with art philosophy in the style of the *Verlust der Mitte*. Music historians often deplore Mahler's discordant nature from similar motives. The truth of the work of art is rather that its meaning registers the ideological stage that has been reached, the contradictions of the situation right down to the depths of the technical contradictions that have to be mastered, and may even surpass them by articulating directly the truth of philosophical consciousness. Its truth can be encapsulated in the fidelity with which it holds fast to a negative state of affairs without polemics, as if with its eyes shut, and it achieves a positive transcendence only through such fidelity, in determinate negation. But even that is not absolutely conclusive. Even though it can be said that Webern's songs are far more differentiated, tender, and full of meaning than Schubert's, even so, and perhaps for that very reason, Schubert's contain a moment of authenticity, of objective necessity, that has not yet become visible in Webern's late songs even today. The objective authority of Schubert's musical language, which has now been legitimately criticized and which therefore cannot be restored by an act of will, nevertheless redounded to the benefit of the pieces themselves. This antinomy cannot be eliminated. In the most important questions about musical quality we truly find ourselves on the track of that relativity to which common sense wrongly subscribes when judging the value or nonvalue of a composition: the same relativity that follows from the ambiguity of art, and that art preserves in contrast to the unambiguousness of rational thought. This relativity is none other than that of aesthetic illusion itself.

The concept of meaning recently became the subject of controversy: the subject of the debate was the relation of artistic means to ends. According to Heinz-Klaus Metzger, "The fact that works of art once had a purpose, social or liturgical, is something that today, when listening with a musician's ear, we must force ourselves to call laboriously to mind, a memory that is historical only in a dubious sense. Ever since art broke free from the service of rulers, legitimate works have ceased to pursue any very obvious goal external to themselves, and this necessarily has repercussions in their internal technical composition: there is no longer any distinction between articulation and what is articulated, between representation and what is represented. It may well be that art no longer has a purpose, and even that its meaning is its purpose. In fact, no one can say any longer with any assurance what art really is about. All the more anachronistic is the question of the relation between ends and means in its inner technical makeup. But does not its freedom—*l'art pour l'art*—

point to its determinate antithesis to society?" In general Metzger finds the question of musical quality suspect. It is no more than an aspect of its commodity character; the comparison of aesthetic qualities is a "*concours* down the decades," a sort of musical competitiveness. Following these ideas through to their logical conclusion, Metzger would have to subscribe to a full-blooded aesthetic relativism of the kind that he and the Darmstadt school have every reason to reject. But his argument seems too one-dimensional. It is not vindicated by the abstract contradiction between art and its social reception. Historically, the market doubtless played a role in the formation of musical ideas of quality, but what prevailed in the marketplace was never just exchange value—whose blind supremacy is only now in the process of establishing itself—but always something else as well. In the absence of the market, the ability to distinguish between qualities in general would never have arisen, just as, conversely, that ability only became conscious of itself the moment it freed itself from the market mechanism. Not everything resembles the thing from which it sprang; musical quality, which once may have enabled a composition to prove itself a better commodity than others, has long since objectivized itself and become a definition of the music proper, even though the traces of its commodity nature cannot be entirely eliminated, any more than they can be from any other product of bourgeois society. What Metzger himself perceives in the ends-means relationship in art— namely, the migration into art of a category originally alien to it—holds good for musical quality too. In general, the relationship between means and ends is more complex than he suggests. The word "ends" is equivocal. It means both the subsumption of the work of art under purposes alien to it and its intrinsic meaning, for which the means are a preparation and by which they are brought into focus. By escaping from external ritual or social purposes, and seeking its purpose in itself and in its own truth, the art of the bourgeois era did not eliminate the ends-means tension. Instead that tension grew with the increasing meaninglessness of inappropriate means, and it was this, rather than the mere dominance of the means, that ratified *l'art pour l'art*, which is concerned with the radical domination of means. In the autonomous work of art, every means is justified by the function it has for others and that they all have for the work as a totality. In fact, it is because of that function that it becomes meaningful and something more than a mere existing thing. Where artistic means—and we are not thinking about symbols here—fail to transcend themselves, art regresses to its extreme opposite, philistine tinkering [*Bastelei*]. All of this may well remain invisible to artists; it may well be the case that questions about means conceal answers about ends. But where theory would like to become more than the merely descriptive account of what happens in the conscious and subconscious mind of the artist—something that is fundamentally different from their works—it must not let itself be diverted from the question of an intrinsic purpose, in other words, from an explanation of the purpose of every means in the totality, unless it wishes to stand by and witness the degeneration of literal necessity into the spiritually arbitrary.

To deny the difference between articulation and what is articulated, between representation and what is represented, is both right and wrong. It is right to remind ourselves that the truth content of a work of art, the "artistic idea," is not situated outside the art object, as its "intention." It is wrong because the musical means, the "representation," gain more in significance through their context than by what they are in themselves, and in it they create something that transcends the mere fact of means. The distinction between artistic meaning and artistic means, including those than can be determined by calculation, may be very simply imagined. If in the analysis of a composition the legitimacy of a phrase is questioned, the composer is usually happy to point to the row that led to that phrase, and to other serial reference points and correspondences. In contrast to this, we should insist on the function of the phrase *hic et nunc*: what the phrase achieves where it is, and ways in which information about its origins or its deduction from the basic material in fact gives us no adequate knowledge. In our reply, information about its point of departure as well as the plan of the overall work may play their part, for in music both memory and anticipation are integral elements in the present reality. But in isolation from the question of what is achieved by particular patterns in the here and now, what role they play in a living context, and how such a context can be generated, all "genetic" questions in the broadest sense would be nothing more than questions about means and would be alien to questions of meaning.

～

Musical meaning, when realized in the total work, designates an idea in extreme form. If we were to apply it directly, indiscriminately, to every work, we would be riding roughshod over the implied intentions of countless works, and would violate not only the analysis of the works themselves, but also an aesthetic tact that would like us to take art seriously, but not deadly seriously. As a corrective, the concept of aesthetic level [*Formniveau*] may be of assistance—even though it is compromised by the name of Ludwig Klages, who introduced it into graphology—and at the same time it may do away with the error that the task of the ear is at an end once it has tested each work from the standpoint of technical consistency. The present confusion of musical judgment is rooted not just in the loss of the tradition and in a specialization that only permits an understanding of music among ever decreasing numbers, even among experts; it also springs from the fact that in the present chaos of the music business works are compared and contrasted with each other without any inquiry into their aesthetic level. In the process, works on a lower aesthetic level, in which everything functions with relative speed and ease, are more accessible than those on a higher level, which pose far greater difficulties because of their demands for more radical articulation. Needless to say, the concept of aesthetic level must be liberated from psychology; in other words, it must be separated from the composer and his intentions and pursued instead in the objective progress of the works themselves. It would be defined by the problem that every composition sets itself; the weight of the problems thus posed is what distinguishes between the different aesthetic levels. Accordingly, a completely resolved, unproblematic piece of either the motor-rhythmic or monothematic type that disarms all criticism can be inferior to a badly fractured "failure" that demands more from itself from the outset and whose fractures are themselves meaningful; in important works, indeed, the measure of failure itself becomes the measure of significance. Works of art are all the more profound, the more purely they bear the stamp of the contradictions that are implicit in their point of departure, their own possibilities. However, the concept of aesthetic level itself requires caution. The mundane fugue of a composer from the conservatory complete with stretti does not rank more highly than a casually, but brilliantly, written piece of Rossini's simply because of its preartistic, and in any case highly overestimated, difficulty. What we may think of as the intrinsic problem in a piece cannot easily be reduced to the distinction between complicated and primitive, although nowadays, when the simple is no longer simple, but for the most part a resentment-laden reaction to the complicated, that equation may suffice only as a first approximation. In Mozart, however, and also in Beethoven, who is in many ways highly economical and who constantly presses forward to a greater simplicity, the aesthetic level is indicated in the complex and subtle relationship of essentially simple musical characteristics to one another; or else in the totality that generates a dynamic from an almost nonexistent individual motive. The very essence of Viennese classicism consists in the creation of the very highest aesthetic level even as simplicity is carefully preserved, and its brief moment lay in the paradoxical emergence of both elements. In new music the distinction between aesthetic levels could most strikingly be shown in compositions comparable in their simplicity, pieces such as "Kranker Mond" from Schoenberg's *Pierrot lunaire* and "Nachtstück" from Hindemith's Donaueschingen *Kammermusik*. The difference in the aesthetic level of the two pieces is not brought about by the complex textures, abundance of harmonic progressions, and ingenious architecture, but simply by the fact that Schoenberg's work, an unaccompanied monody, is infinitely more flexible, more richly patterned, and hence more expressive in its single voice than Hindemith's, for all its polyphony. The latter does indeed derive its effect from the repetition of its basic motive, but consisting as it does merely in repetitions, and hence far too facile, it is soon exhausted and succumbs to monotony instead of shaping it.

It is a mistake to set up a blunt opposition between the complex and the primitive, as is common in a hackneyed sociology with a collectivist outlook. Such a sociology tends all too easily to defer to a well-worn stereotype that accuses modern art of excessive complexity and unnaturalness, and looks to simplicity as a source of renewal. We do better to point out that the primitive, rejection of ornament, and reduction to the functionally necessary were all elements of specifically new music, in a manner analogous to painting since Cézanne, Gauguin, and Van Gogh. But this simplification, which in Schoenberg, too, contains an undertone of skepticism toward cultivation and taste, a fauvist element, is directed merely against what is superfluous according to the yardstick of immanent construction. Economical composition, however, from Schoenberg's "Mondfleck" [from *Pierrot lunaire*] and Berg's Third Piece for Orchestra down to [Boulez's] *Le marteau sans maître*, has consistently developed in the direction of extreme complexity of tone. At the same time, the fauvist potential, the possibility of a stripped-down, naked "*aridité*," to use Roger Callois's term, must always be present if new music is not to regress to a cultural conformism, the criticism of which has been its driving force. It moves between the extremes in every respect, excluding only the safe middle way. In Webern, for example, extreme subtlety and ascetic frugality come together to the point where they become identical: that inward listening to which in Webern new music owes unprecedented discoveries, leads it also to relinquish all façades and makes suspect as spurious wealth everything that a short while before looked like a paradise of plenitude. Hence even among recent developments we find works consisting of notes scattered pointillistically around the score, as in *Le marteau sans maître* or the Second Piano Sonata of Boulez, who tends in general to try out extreme, unconnected possibilities of the sort ventured hitherto only in avant-garde painting. Primitiveness in new music, at any rate, is only justified as a critical exercise, an extreme mode of demolition and estrangement [*Verfremdung*]. If the primitive acquires a positive value or misinterprets itself as, for example, an authoritative new style, it will already have made its pact with the world. The right to be primitive depends on the aesthetic level, as can be seen from a comparison between *Le sacre du printemps* and any piece of light music. In the former we have the effort, however dubious, to recuperate a past buried in oblivion and yet still wandering about like a ghost; in the latter we have vain and impotent activity, as if simplicity could be obtained on tap—the cliché about the new security turned into music. Such contrasts in the aesthetic level can also be expressed technically. On every page of Stravinsky's *Sacre* we find inscribed the subjective sensitivity and sensibility that conjures up primitiveness, an aspect of the work that the rancorous denounce with terms like "refinement," something absent from light music, whose simplicity merely serves the most comfortable listening habit and the line of least resistance. On the other hand, we cannot ignore the fact that the primitive aspect of all new art—from folklore to the Blauer Reiter's interest in Bavarian peasant painting—had a reactionary potential from the outset. Even the light music of our own day often derives from Stravinsky, with stops off at Hindemith and Orff, despite the former's superiority to the rubbish about one's roots binding one to the community. And this link is doubtless essential, something we shall return to. When archaic impulses and residues are exhumed, they are not just glorified as remembered and luminous; at the same time, something of their spell is broken. With a less extreme adoption of the archaic, however, one that attempts to take over an entire style from the past rather than individual primitive impulses, a composer borrows the illusion of being enclosed that would be destroyed were we to remind ourselves how little music can be confined to the individual subject of bourgeois culture. The term "primitivism" can be applied to the antithetical works of a single composer: the austerity of Webern's works opp. 7–11 stands at the opposite end of the scale from many of his late works.

If technical features are also supratechnical, thanks to their configuration, then the spiritual experience of music may proceed not from the technical but from the supratechnical elements. When Schumann first discovered, in the second piece of the *Kreisleriana* cycle, the gesture in which music recalls something long forgotten rather than simply unfolding it directly, that was no less bold and productive than the strengthening of certain unifying aspects of technique; to say nothing of discoveries like the fragmentary short form, which points questioningly into the infinite, to be found in many of Schumann's *Kinderscenen* pieces and Chopin's Preludes, and without which Schoenberg's op. 19 and Webern's expressionist miniatures could scarcely have been written. Such compositional strata become desiccated through the emphasis on controlling the material of music or, to use the language of *The Dialectic of Enlightenment*, the dominion over nature. This also narrows the scope of music in general, much as the passport control of logical empiricism affects philosophy. Everything threatens to disappear in pure sameness; we now find on the aesthetic plane the same narrowing that had once been brought about in idealist philosophy by the reduction of a qualitative plenitude to the pure cogito. At the moment—and the tempo of change has accelerated in a way that should itself give us pause—everything seems to depend on composers reflecting on the same musical strata and on whether it is at all possible for new musical characters to resist this by no means accidental leveling-out tendency, without its having a negative effect on the structural unity. A work like *Le marteau sans maître*, which admittedly the purists find suspect, is confirmed not only by the density of its texture and the colorful richness of its timbral vision, but also by its power of characterization at the level of detail. It matters little whether the composer was aiming at a looser organization or whether the characters were the product of greater flexibility of structure. Stockhausen's *Gesang der Jünglinge* likewise contains characters that contrast much more strongly than had previously been to the taste of the postwar generation. All these characters are technically interconnected. Even for a whimsical conception like the Schumannesque "It all happened long ago," technical correlatives could be found in the texture, in the sonorities of something that seems to resonate in the distance, in the treatment of appoggiaturas and arpeggios that ambiguate the rhythms beyond their mere existence. The beginnings of such musical knowledge can be found, albeit with an excessive psychological emphasis, in Kurth's *Psychology of Music* and also in his *Romantic Harmony*. In general, however, musical analysis has to this day remained quite backward when confronted by such questions. Even scholars intimately familiar with new music lean toward a merely technical account of the facts and thus pay their tribute to the positivistic spirit of the academic music business.

The preconditions of musical characterization seem to be categories that have been handed down, categories like inspiration or the creative idea [*Einfall*] and originality. Both have rightly fallen into disrepute.[3] They grew into musical norms under the aegis of capitalism and so became tied up with the market, the novelty of the special offer, the trademark of goods for sale. To be sure, the music that was evaluated in terms of its original inspiration also retained an element of bourgeois emancipation, as opposed to stereotyped hierarchical rigidity. But it has long since degenerated into pseudoindividuality, the hit song with the melody that is just like all the others and yet stays in the memory thanks to a minimally distinct innovation, a trick, a "gimmick." Nevertheless, it is a pernicious act of rationalization to reject originality in favor of an objectivity that imagines that its surrender to coercion will free it from a concern for what happens the very first time: and what is pernicious about it is the hatred of individuation itself, the deep desire to drag the individual idea down to the stereotype, the pattern. To secure his own survival the individual subject acquires once again what has been imposed on him from outside. Because there is no longer any space in the machinery for the imagination, those who lack imagination anyway deny it to themselves. Now, in isolation, of course, original ideas do not amount to much, especially the vulgar notion that some people think up melodies that have not occurred to anyone else. It almost inevitably ends up in the stereotype of self-imitation. The development of Kurt Weill, who, as a composer for the theater, is naturally not subject to intrinsic musical criteria, is a very crass instance of this. We can clearly see the limited, one-

---

3. See Theodor W. Adorno, *Dissonanzen. Musik in der verwalteten Welt* (Göttingen, 1956), 92f. [also in *Gesammelte Schriften*, vol. 14 (Frankfurt am Main: Suhrkamp, 1973), 98f.].

sided nature of the kind of music that goes in pursuit of the idol of the memorable idea and that tends to identify individual ideas with the most successful ones, with the consequence that it deprives itself of the very things to which it aspires. Moreover, the composer's subjective originality is of little avail as long as it remains mere gesture and fails to find its way into the structure of the music. But authentic musical characters and their totality, the composer's "tone," which can be heard in every measure of Mahler, Berg, and Webern, share with originality the fact that they are not interchangeable; to drive out such a tone in the name of purism is to forget the best. Aesthetically, too, objectivity cannot simply be achieved by subtraction, by "bracketing out" [*Ausklammerung*] the human subject—to use a term of Husserl's that has become fashionable in Germany today. What is needed now is the formulation of an objective concept of originality, independent of the accidental identity of the composer and of the alien desiderata of the marketplace. This would be comparable to the name that the composition bears wordlessly, unobtrusively, and that circumscribes its configuration. If a composition dispenses with such a secret name, which distinguishes it and contains its universal significance, it becomes bad and preartistic—as often with Reger, whose works so frequently seem to be collections of interchangeable modulations; and particularly nowadays when, relying on a primitive naturalistic idea of musical material and how best to "manipulate" it, people inveigh against the name.

In the tonal system, the question of originality generally referred to themes or motifs, "creative ideas" [*Einfälle*]. The distinction between a genuine creative idea and the mere "material" of composition is so stark that to ignore it would be to throw out the baby with the bathwater. History has witnessed a prolonged phase in which compositional styles, particularly in opera, were dominated by the criterion of inspiration [*Einfall*], and something of this has passed over into new music. Schoenberg's in particular is overflowing with melodic ideas; of the twelve-tone works we might single out the Fourth Quartet: it is known that in general he modeled the row on the primary inspiration, and not the other way around. The question of creative ideas becomes dubious only when they are regarded as the composer's property and composers are evaluated accordingly, or rejected where the echoes of other people's ideas are perceived, even though, as the very term suggests, a composer has hardly any control over them as an individual. This reification of inspiration and its elevation into an absolute value are all of a piece. Great traditional music, in contrast, contains thematic reminiscences everywhere and even very striking melismas that assume quite a different significance in different contexts. The theme of the Scherzo in Schubert's D Minor Quartet becomes the Anvil motive in the *Ring*; the principal theme in Beethoven's C Major Sonata, op. 2 [no. 3], looks on paper as if it is related to the second subject in the introduction to the Seventh Symphony; similarly, the theme in the Finale of Mozart's G Minor Symphony is reminiscent of the Scherzo in Beethoven's Fifth. In all these cases, however, similarities are being reduced, apart from the case of rhythmic analogues, to a category that was not fully developed until the new music—namely, the "row," interval successions that only here still belong to tonality and that are situated on the surface of the music. Then in Mahler the traditional concept of inspiration did a somersault: borrowed, worn-out, or familiar elements now go into a kind of ferment and become vehicles of expression; without them the content would be inconceivable. In the same period, however, composers like Debussy, Richard Strauss, and Reger suspended the category of the creative idea, each in his own way, while Pfitzner, who moved it to the very center of his aesthetics, was unable to live up to it. As early as the text of *Die Meistersinger*, when Wagner transferred the bourgeois concept of property to musical originality, it was no longer possible to measure the latter against the former. Beckmesser's denunciation is something of a projection in a composer whose contemporaries were already criticizing the etiolation of inventiveness that was doubtless to be explained by the exhaustion of tonality. As for new music, finally, what strikes us as original is for the most part little more than the shock of recognition the indolent ear experiences when it encounters a practiced mannerism that gives it the satisfaction of identifying a composer. Mainly, this originality arises through the one-sided tendency to specialize in a single aspect of the musical material—the so-called rhythm, for example, in the limited sense of a consistent beat concurrently with an irregular meter. The more consistent and rich a musical structure is, conversely, the more surface identification marks are reduced. Incidentally, truly advanced music does not suffer from a lack of conventional elements, some of which can be precisely dated. The preference for dissociated notes, whether as expression values or as "points" in the construction, has its roots in m. 15 of "Madonna" in Schoenberg's *Pierrot*, which constituted a break with the pattern rather than a paradigm.

The criterion of originality, without actually disappearing, as objectivist reactionaries would like, has been thoroughly transformed: it has been transferred to the performed totality in all its facets. The nominalist situation of composition,[4] the absence of authoritative musical concepts, endows every composition today with the claim to uniqueness, whether it likes it or not, and this migrates into every detail of the work. The aversion to repetition and repeatability, evident ever since Beethoven dispensed with repetition in the first movement of the *Appassionata*, has long since assumed the character of a norm, like many other initially negative categories: whatever desires only to be itself, and finds no place in any preordained scheme that might require its reappearance, should in fact not reappear. It is all too easy for every repetition to degenerate into the impotent solution to every structural problem. The prohibition on repetition stands behind the principle of total elaboration, the obligation constantly to produce variations, even where balance calls for at least the echo of an identity. Complaints that things were different in other centuries, and the desire to recreate something like a universally binding language of music, are in conflict with the current state of composition, as well as the historical trend of the age in general. The suffering caused by the nominalist point of departure leads constantly to short-circuiting fallacies, which tend increasingly to stand exposed as subjective caprice, the more they indulge in authoritarian gestures. In this respect there is no distinction to be made between Hindemith's hope, of some thirty-five years ago, of creating a new, universally valid style—as if the idea of a general style created by a single composer were not itself a *contradictio in adjecto*—and recent claims from among the camp of serial composers, such as Henri Pousseur's assertion that Webern had created just such a style for music. Neither integral composition nor the formal compliance with psychological conditions of perception can bring about any generally valid norms in a society that is antagonistic both in the minds of its members and in terms of the members' real interests. Even the desire for such norms is open to criticism: it harbors an element of defeatism, the inability to accept the happiness of freedom, including the freedom to express suffering. This is resisted by the "authoritarian" character, who even in the realm of artistic sublimation cries out for the strong man and can-

---

4. Cf. "The Function of Counterpoint in New Music" [p. 144 in this volume— Trans.].

not bear to be autonomous; who praises bonds for their own sake, forgetting that no bonds were ever worth a thing if they were not rooted in the idea of objective truth, and instead postulates universal principles merely from the subjective need for external supports, from the fear of loneliness. In spoken language, social coercion and the sclerotic nature of convention have become so powerful that they inexorably shackle even the insubordinate utterances of the individual. In contrast, the language of music can at least draw strength from its own weakness—its lack of precise definition. In other words, it can derive comfort from the idea that, unlike the language of concepts, it can be meaningful without having either to obey blind dictates or to impose them on others. Where the idea of an authoritative language of music has its truth is in the realization that the individual person and thing are not absolute, even in music, but must be mediated by the universal. However, this insight will fail to do justice to music if it seeks out the universal directly; it will only succeed if it immerses itself in the individual. Compositions that nowadays go under the rubric "*à la manière de . . .*" succeed only in disqualifying themselves; they adopt a language that is not binding on them as if it were both binding and comprehensive, and so end up in a fiction. This is the ugly face of unoriginality today; it has long since ceased to be deficient simply in terms of individual themes or phrases. Seldom nowadays are tangible details, such as themes, simply imitated—in this sense composers have in the meantime become much more adept than major composers ever were—but instead imitation is now a matter of general procedures, patterns, a composer's "tone" (doubtless in analogy to painters). In this respect little has changed over the last thirty years. In the period before 1933 the festivals of the International Society for New Music served up countless concertos in the neoclassical taste, all of them alike as two peas and all of them diluted Stravinsky. In the same way, composers today produce pastiches of such works as Hindemith's piano sonatas, even though it is not possible to say they have copied specific details. This trend is not confined just to the moderates, from neoclassicism to academic music, but can also be found in high-profile composers. From the third generation of the Schoenberg school a string quartet was published that imitated Berg's idiom and technique right down to the most intimate detail. Not a note of Berg's was literally copied, indeed the piece was so carefully constructed that there was not a single echo of the Allegro misterioso from the *Lyric Suite*, which has been copied countless times. Instead the language spoken was Bergish, as if it were possible to steal a man's voice. By an act of conformity, the nonconformist was taken over body and soul and then turned into his opposite. The tendency to make pastiches of Webern has become better known in the meantime, and efforts are now made to prevent it.

However, these pastiches should not be dismissed as harmless, by saying, for example, that less independent minds have always swum with the current, or even with the old philistine saw that the so-called culture of music needs the humus of second-rank composers in order to flourish. For the penchant for stereotypes in new music is by no means just external. Conventions of expression have crystallized even in a language hostile to convention: one symptom of this is the fact that the ideal of absolute singularity is as much of a delusion as that of an immediately binding universality. Even in the purest expression, universal tendencies make themselves felt and cause the windowless monads to resemble one another.[5] Kurt Mautz, the literary historian, has shown that the radical expressionist poetry before the First World War, the poetry of Heym, Trakl, van Hoddis, and others, all contained a highly inflexible color symbolism that was largely independent of the specific contents of individual poems.[6] Looking back today, we can now see that there is an analogous situation in music, where more or less identical compositional gestures come to be linked to more or less identical values of expression, even in the fauvist works of new music. The stock of these gestures is fairly completely assembled in Schoenberg's middle works, from the Three Piano Pieces, op. 11, down to the Four Orchestral Songs, op. 22, and is codified above all in *Erwartung*. It is uncertain whether the expressionist yearning for a form of expression entirely free of conventions is at all possible, or whether the thesis implicit in all expressive music, to the effect that musical configurations express something psychic, does not also contain an element of caprice, of arbitrary agreement, as Nietzsche suspected. Once expression has emancipated itself from the established musical idiom, once it is an

---

5. In this respect, the condition of present-day music does not differ in principle from that of *Jugendstil*. In both cases, the concept of style is without force; it yields no criterion of new music. In both cases, however, individual phenomena press blindly forward toward a collectivity that is not wholly unlike style.

6. Cf. Kurt Mautz, "Die Farbensprache der expressionistischen Lyrik" [Color imagery in expressionist poetry], in *Deutsche Vierteljahrsschrift für Literaturwissenschaft und Geistesgeschichte* 31 (1957): 198ff.

end in itself, it becomes alienated from the dynamics of the music as a totality of which it had been an element. This element is the mimetic, in the sense not so much of a specific reflection of a specific content, as of the impulse to imitate as such. Accordingly, as something fixed and intended, it falls victim to the very reification that expressive art resists. If embedded expression is to be unambiguous, it requires tried and tested gestures and vocabulary. The process of making music more like language—a process that subjectivizes it—also desubjectivizes it through the coining of clichés. These cannot be decreed out of existence or eliminated by any artistic procedure; the paradox lies in the idea of expressionism itself, since it involves the objectification of something inimical to objectification. In general, art translates expression into an image; it is not expression pure and direct. If expression is to "become manifest" [*erscheinen*], the relation between expression and musical form requires something fixed, something that goes beyond the longed-for pure expression and that results in the conventions of expression without any loss of compositional force. As early as *Erwartung*, certain musical gestures recur again and again for impulses such as anxiety, terror, tenseness, outburst, while at the same time the formal law governing the work is that of the coalescence of unique moments in a time span of pure experience. The architecture of Schoenberg's *Die glückliche Hand* confronted this contradiction. But the more such expressive conventions become established historically, the more indifferent they become toward their specific musical realization—to put it crudely, toward the notes from which the expressive gestures have been assembled. In countless contemporary compositions on varying aesthetic levels one finds such things as irregular figures with the very smallest note values to express the abrupt or wild, as opposed to the even and tame. Not only is this expressive gesture so familiar that it scarcely delivers the shock it would like to, but even the question of its precise musical components has itself become a matter of indifference. For the most part, the notes are simply prescribed by the row: what the row wants, it gets. Compositional desiderata such as a feeling for the values of individual intervals in their context, unmistakable in Webern, are neglected. On the subjective side, in the composers' minds we see a kind of second-degree conformism at work: through their expertise in manipulating a limited range of the modernist vocabulary they become qualified to show that they have mastered the new idiom, and for this very reason, they speak it inaccurately. The reactionaries, who speak the language of convention, can then maliciously catch their opponents out using conventional language in their turn. Of course, it is no objection to new music to point out that in the dialectic of the general and the particular it is always bumping up against the limits of the particular. Only, it must have the power to carry this dialectic through to its end.

All of this revolves round the concept of internal musical tension and its enfeeblement, a phenomenon that forces itself on our attention today and yet obstinately resists identification. The process is objectively determined. The concretization of a musical idiom whose whole impulse rebels against concretization is enforced by its languagelike nature, even though it is in conflict with its own underlying ideal. By inscribing its great compositional and expressive discoveries in the material, progressive music has indeed secured a victory. What dominated musical consciousness up to around thirty years ago, to the point where everything different was decried as deviant, has now been eclipsed. Nevertheless, this overall progress has been dearly bought. As soon as the recast material relieves the composer of the need to make an effort—the very thing that gives music the substance—a stylistic modernism starts to make its appearance, negating the whole thrust of the avant-garde manner that it has elevated into the mark of its own style. The blame for this does not lie in the first instance in a waning of the musicians' energies—composers today are as gifted as they were forty years ago, perhaps even more gifted—but in the fact that the material of composition neither contains the critical elements of tension that had once permeated it nor forms such a close fit with the subjective tension, in other words, with the composers' need to express themselves, as had been the case during the crisis of tonality. This preestablished disharmony makes it very hard to create the configurations that transmit tension. The model here lies, above all, in intervals of tension like the major seventh or the minor ninth, which have ceased to be taboo or to induce panic in the citizenry but have driven out the consonant intervals. In the process, however, they sacrificed their own tension, and since they enjoy equal rights with every other interval, they have been neutralized along with them. But if they have ceased to impart any tension, by the same token they no longer allow the composer to impart any tension to them: this loss of tension dates back to the condition of a material that has divested itself of tension. What is true of intervals holds good as well for other elements of composition. This objective loss of tension has its equivalent in the human subjects, who inevitably find them-

selves handing down something that cannot be handed down and dilut-
ing to a jargon something that never aspired to the status of a language.
Their manner reminds us of people who write a book in order to write a
book, in contrast to those who write because they have something to say.
The compulsion to get to grips with the substance gives way to an interest in procedures. The absence of inner tension converges with the loss of
artistic independence; where spontaneity finds itself paralyzed in sheer
obedience to standards once achieved, the work simply accepts solutions
passed on to it from ready-made material, instead of producing them itself. No doubt, all composition is passive, since it is a response to objectively posed problems, but even passivity requires spontaneity of consciousness and the impulses of the imagination, and does not mean ex-
tinguishing the self in favor of would-be scientific tone relationships. The
corrective to this situation, however, is not the reinstatement of a pure
subjectivity, for as something reinstated it forfeits the very possibility of
purity. It is really only in this context that we can fully grasp the rebellion
of the radical young composers against all the traces of the traditional
building blocks of a musical language, and ultimately against musical
meaning itself. What they reject in music is everything that reminds them
of language, and they reject it in order to put an end to the false peace
that is radiated today by everything redolent of language and meaning
and that therefore denies negativity, the agent of tension.

It is undeniable that the progressive advance of standardization reveals
the extent to which composition is subject to external domination. The
rows offer solutions everywhere that are no longer subjectively mediated,
no longer generated from the idea of the work and the specifically heard
needs of its here and now, but instead have simply dropped into its lap,
creating the impression that composing has become easier, much as the
young American thought who in all innocence said that he wrote twelve-
tone music so that he would know where to get the notes from. The international triumph of a musical style that was certainly not foretold at
its birth is by no means free of such infantilism. The punishment for this
attitude is not only the arbitrary nature of such alien necessity, when
viewed from the criterion of autonomy, but quite simply the meaninglessness, and ultimately the monotony, that results from the impossibility of differentiating. Twelve-tone technique as such and its subsequent
development are not the culprits here; its clatter is itself a function of the
withering of the characterizing energies of music, much as the latter have

suffered increasingly under the pressure of the integral mode of composition. The method can never be taken in isolation; it always legitimates itself only by means of the material it is applied to. It is up to the composers to decide whether to make it easy for themselves by relying on the method, or whether they will learn that the method, if it is ever to be anything more, will make it harder for them without their ever being able to evade its demands. Klee's comment that art starts at the point where the system no longer works, a comment which in an artist as methodical as Klee of course presupposes the system, is an insight that has not yet been appropriated by the latest generation of composers.

Schoenberg conceived of the characterizing energies in the notion of the shape [*Gestalt*]. While this overflows into the concept of the theme, as well as that of actual character, it should also be distinguished from both. In line with tradition, we should think of a theme as a "partial whole," a relatively coherent, fixed thing that remains open to its context and creates it from within its own impulse. That is the meaning of the Schoenberg dictum that composition is always the history of a theme. Within a certain spectrum themes are unambiguously formulated and can be worked on to achieve even sharper definition. The changes they undergo are only meaningful with reference to the original formulation. For this reason it is mainly not just the rhythmic relationships, but also the intervallic relations, that are fixed. In contrast, the concept of the musical shape is broader. The absence of ambiguity is not required of shapes; it is enough to have an element by which to identify them and hence recognize them when they recur. Their specific motivic content, and certainly their interval structure, need not be fixed. A feature such as a sixteenth-note movement in which a theme is dissipated may suffice to define a shape, regardless of the notes the figure consists of; the same is true of even just a salient rhythmic passage generated by various row-derivations. A character, after all, is the aspect of those categories that stamps them with meaning: the specific quality by means of which the individual musical detail can be distinguished in its overall context. Expression and "tone" are constitutive features of these characters. They coincide on occasion with shapes and themes, but need not do so; thus a character may be attached to an entire complex of themes that itself consists of a number of themes or shapes. The exposition of Mahler's Fourth Symphony, for all its extraordinary wealth of themes and shapes, contains only three or four characters: the quasi-Mozartian, playful and graceful section at the beginning, the folk song section, and the concluding "reflective" one; we may add the static, meditative section that emerges from a contrapuntal motive of the main thematic complex, before the start of the development. Characters are pointed to, inadequately enough, by performance directions of the kind sought out by modern composers: "with verve" [*schwungvoll*], "leisurely" [*gemächlich*], "erupting" [*ausbrechend*], "driving" [*zufahrend*], "fleeting" [*flüchtig*], "floating" [*schwebend*], and even, in Berg's Violin Concerto, "Viennese" [*Wienerisch*]. In the traditional sonata form and its descendants, the characters frequently correspond to the main subjects. Crucial for the character, however, is its noninterchangeability, that which distinguishes it; the element antithetical to the unity of the work as whole, which is contained within the thematic material. Symphonic music forms a dialectical process between the unifying thematic element and the characters, likewise transmitted through the themes; the unity is achieved only by the configuration of different elements.

In their original meaning, characters are pen strokes. They still are that, but they also represent real music, and this legitimates our use of the name. The articulation of music in terms of characters is what makes possible their principle of individuation. They are the qualitative element, not dissoluble into musical generality. The tendency to rationalization, however, that places Western music in the general movement of Enlightenment is one that moves in the direction of quantification, reducing the individual element to an indistinguishable, interchangeable part of the whole, into which it goes without remainder. The musical principle of individuation is itself subject to a dialectic. As the emancipation from domination by alien powers, it was rationality that made individuality possible. Musical characters had always been held in check, even in Viennese classicism, by the universal principle of tonality, and they only became dominant with Romanticism, particularly with Schubert, in whose works the weight of the individual characters threatens the integral form of Viennese classicism; the formal errors of many of his piano sonatas, evident to every music academician, are the marks of a historical process. The threat the characters posed to musical unity, however, quickly triggered a countervailing movement. The same process of rationalization that was responsible for equal temperament and a fully usable chromaticism was also, on its subjective side, the impetus behind the notion of musical characters and their ultimate dissolution; this was the case as early as *Tris-*

tan, where the universal chromaticism tended to blur the distinction between the individual shapes, and even more powerfully in integral twelve-tone and serial technique. Likewise in late Romanticism we find the characters peculiarly attenuated: in Strauss, where the momentum of the form carries one over the striking triviality of the many motives; in Reger, where vivid melodic characters are thrust aside by modulation as a dominating principle; in Mahler, who does indeed intensify the character principle to an extreme, but in whose music the characters themselves are made into something resembling a quotation, the fully intended, but noncommittal, recollection of something no longer truly present. Because of the progressive reduction of the characters to impotent elements in a totality, however, the integral principle of rationalization ends up by coming into conflict with the requirement of all art that the progressive control over the material should not simply result in the liquidation of the qualitative element in analogy to the natural sciences, but that it should be preserved within the integrating process. This shifts the focus of attention onto the critical reconstruction of the qualitative aspect. We probably have to ask whether characters can at all be desired as such. Among the costs of progress in art we have to count its loss of spontaneity; among its gains, however, is the fact that the spontaneous can be grasped by consciousness, that it can be the object of volition, in line with the cliché routinely uttered by players to the effect that a composer should just come up with something decent. It may well be that spontaneity will always be essential to art, as is the protest of the ruled against their rulers; but as soon as this idea is invoked, and the unconscious consciously set against technical domination, one finds one has made concessions to a bad cause. The revival of the "qualitative" is important precisely because leveling out is not an accidental part of the principle of integration, and because it cannot be reversed at will. What holds good for all dialectic, namely that one cannot simply have the positive while eliminating the negative, holds good for new music too. Whoever is concerned about characters must also take the challenge they represent to the idea of immanent unity in his stride. Keen hearers among the latest generation of composers are well aware of this. They find something anomalous about those works of their own school that make use of characters, seeing it as a concession. It is easy for an avant-garde composer to turn overnight into a salon musician; it would be better to surrender to the extremes than to go in search of a synthesis. Alban Berg anticipated this development. In his teaching he in-

sisted on a rough-and-ready distinction between two types of composition and advised his pupils always to be clear which they were choosing.
He called the one symphonic, and the other, in the language of the nineteenth century, he called the composition of character pieces. This di-
chotomy can be traced back to Bach, in whose English Suites and Partitas
one finds the first type in the first movement, while many of the stylized
dances in the following movements belong to the second. Even in
Schoenberg the distinction is very clear; his chamber music, especially the
two Chamber Symphonies, can be assigned to the symphonic type, while
the George songs and *Pierrot*, for all their considered organization as totalities, belong among the character pieces. In line with this distinction,
the most recent development would be thought of as a one-sided trend
toward the symphonic, while the character piece arouses the same suspicions as the term "genre." Music had to distance itself from the genre
piece as sharply as from the symphonic principle, which becomes mechanical as soon as it fails to arise from its own antithesis and overcome
it. The possibility that integral composition will degenerate into a mere
clattering of the conceptual mill is likewise visible on the horizon today,
as is the opposing trend of the kitsch of merely pictorial characterization.

The psychological concept of the *Gestalt*, as it was introduced by Christian von Ehrenfels and expanded into a full-blown theory by Wertheimer,
Köhler, Gelb, and others, was probably unknown to Schoenberg. Only
more recently, in serial theory, have musical categories been combined
with concepts from Gestalt psychology, especially by Pousseur. What remains problematic in this is whether concepts taken from cognitive psychology can suffice to grasp the nature of musical structures and do justice to their objective dimension. The equation of art and "communication" that is propagated nowadays and that goes back to logical
positivism, that deceptive simulacrum of science, is of dubious worth, for
"no poem is meant for the reader, no picture for the observer, no symphony for the listener."[7] To state the conditions under which works of art
can be apprehended, either favorably or even at all, says nothing about
the merits or demerits of their organization in itself. Aesthetic theories
like those of Hildebrandt and Cornelius ventured decades ago to judge
artistic quality according to the degree to which works were adapted to
the apparatus of human perception. These attempts, however, were for-

---

7. Walter Benjamin, *Schriften* (Frankfurt am Main, 1955), 40.

malistic and left considerable room for pseudoclassical kitsch. Contemporary communication theory can scarcely be mistaken for an aesthetic theory. But in new music the confusion goes far back. Schoenberg's own concept of *Gestalt* shifts between objectivity and psychology. He used it as a vehicle for twelve-tone theory, giving the row in its original form the name "basic set" [*Grundgestalt*]. What is implied is that the basic set preserves its identity, in other words is recognizable as basically the same throughout all its modifications—inversion, retrograde, and retrograde inversion; he used to compare the basic set to a hat that always remained the same hat, regardless of whether you looked at it from the front or the back, from above or below. This psychologizing explanation brings false psychology in its train. The comparison between an essentially dynamic process, not merely in itself but also in reference to other features, and a static thing involves the reification of the aesthetic object, a confusion with the empirical that, as a teacher, Schoenberg had no reason to shy away from. But such comparisons cannot be taken literally; otherwise they result in an intellectual short circuit that the most advanced composers are only now trying to avoid by reflecting on the dimension of time in music. We may point to a work that is not composed according to the twelve-tone system but does feature a retrograde, namely the slow movement in Berg's Chamber Concerto. It is not merely that after the turning point in the middle the individual complexes are played in reverse order, but also that the thematic models that dominate each complex recur as retrogrades. We need only compare the main motive, for example, of the third subject, originally played on the clarinet (mm. 283–86), with its retrograde repetition (mm. 435–38), to see that it achieves its strict mechanical variation at the cost of its "character": an uncommonly vivid, melodically convincing passage is turned into a somewhat forced tone row that somehow eludes memorable definition and at best receives its justification from the recollection, however vague, of its original inspiration and the palpable intention of "denaturing" it. This shows that in the context of twelve-tone or serial music, *Gestalt* is not to be identified with character in any straightforward sense. For this reason a rigorous distinction must be made between the composition and its raw material down to the level of detail. Furthermore, the concept of the shape covers very diverse elements in terms of function. It can just as easily point to a fixed sign—an instance is the beginning of "Heimweh" from *Pierrot*—which functions like a model that has no claim to exist in its own right but acquires its meaning only in relation to what follows or preceded it: thus, too, the principal subject in the *Eroica*, which, instead of ending, remains suspended on a critical note, C#. In it, thanks to the resistance that immediately emerges in the theme itself, the composition receives the impulse for its continuation, namely the need to overcome that resistance and to get going as a symphony. This second type of shape [*Gestalt*] is obviously the one that gained the upper hand with the dominance of the symphonic principle over that of the character; already the principal subject of the *Eroica* was featureless down to that C#. The element that was lost, then, is doubtless the vestige and surplus of a musical present that is not entirely identifiable with its function but somehow survives totality. Unquestionably, this element, that of the nonidentity of the particular in the whole, has been undermined. In this respect Beethoven's procedure is in agreement with that of the later Webern and the most recent serial composers. But now this same universalizing tendency seems to be going into reverse. If the modern "quantified" material—in other words, material that is logically justified, alienated from every pregiven specific quality—no longer contains a shape with which to preserve the surplus of undifferentiated musical essence, if everything exists only for something else, then this will conjure up something of the chaotic monotony that so infuriates the uninitiated listener, and not merely in consequence of his ill will. Above all, it is the universality of elaboration, the resulting liquidation of the sonata, and the compulsion to compose in sections or "fields" that has rendered obsolete the purely dynamic principle of development. It has been replaced by the relation of the fields to one another, and the balance among them. But this means that every section or model can no longer lead naturally into another or emerge from it. Instead, every section would need, if it is to assert its identity against others, to adopt a specific character, like each of the small-scale variations from Schoenberg's Third Piano Piece, op. 23. Such a character can really only be achieved by the radical characterization of the models on which the sections are based. However much we may be concerned about the loss of "characters" in music, that is their inevitable condition at this stage in history. Even in the symphonic music of the high-bourgeois era, the musical models were not simply pure being-for-others, not a mere nothing for themselves, but for the most part—even, or especially, in Beethoven—they were nothing and something at the same time. If music really is the history of a theme, this implies that anything that has a history also "is," as is suggested by the meaning of "theme" as something that has been "stated" [*gesetzt*]. In musical logic, as in Hegel's, the concept of development is not one of absolute dynamism, but it includes as one of its elements—though only as one among others—the existence of whatever is being developed. If Beethoven and Viennese classicism reduced this fixed element in comparison with the dynamic side, this is allowed for by tonality, whose degrees and perspective of modulation suggested the presence of development, even where development was faint and unspecific; for what was developed was itself the cell of that tonality that drove the development forward. But the less tonality relieved the theme of the burden of its continuation, the more the theme had to exist for itself, if it was to be capable of meaningful change. Brahms, who passed Beethoven's idea of integral composition on to modern music, insisted on this with particular force. In Schoenberg, too, this claim was always present; today it is more relevant than ever. What look like the "reactionary" features of Schoenberg's compositions in the eyes of the uninhibited representatives of progress, namely the preservation of traditional musical categories, especially the theme itself, probably originate in his awareness of such a necessity rather than from any lack of resoluteness on his part. If in his last completed work, the Phantasy for Violin and Piano Accompaniment, op. 47, he went over to the emphatic projection of sharply defined groups, it was because no construction will succeed if it ignores the plasticity of the individual components. The more the new musical consciousness of time draws its strength from the configuration of pure present, rather than from memory and anticipation in the old style, the more it needs the undiminished presence of the present, in other words, of characters. Construction must not liquidate what it wishes to unite.

Even after the sonata, however, compositions are only successful if their component shapes and characters convincingly transcend themselves. If the history of subjective bourgeois music, from the Florentine Camerata to our own day, contains any permanent feature, it must be the idea of the moment when the individual becomes form, without being submerged in it and without thereby negating form itself as something lacking in differentiation. The efforts of all recent music to procure for composition the maximum extension in time are intimately bound up with the fact that the distinction between new and traditional music cannot be made absolute: especially since the performer finds himself confronted with the same tasks in either case. It is not possible to make a complete contrast between the two, as the reactionaries would like, with their war cry of "That is no longer music." Of course, neither will it do to deny the distinction and to assert, for instance, that the *ars antiqua* is modern because such devices as isorhythm have been recently revived. At best, we can say with Hegel's terminology that in the older music one can discover everything implicitly [*an sich*] that can be found in new music explicitly [*an und für sich*]: they are both one and different at the same time. At any rate, the task of giving the music its momentum, its "inner flow," as Schoenberg called it, is much more difficult than in music in which the tonal reference system and the surface coherence relieve the composition of the labor of generating its own momentum from within itself. That remains true even though in the meantime this external, automated flow has become suspect even in traditional music; and although even in Beethoven the "inner flow," the immanent relationships of the characters to one another, establishes the form at a deeper level than the superficial movement of pervasive accompaniments or the movement envisaged in the harmonic plan. An inner historicity does not call for an unbroken passage of time, but for the organization of time, for beauty in the sense of the Latin *formosus*, a wealth of forms, internal articulation; this alone, and not the mere pulsing of the beat, is able to reconcile empty time, which threatens the music from without, with that inner time. Berg's mature works, above all the *Lyric Suite*, can probably only be heard aright according to this criterion. Technically, Hindemith, for all his intellectual self-assurance and his fluent skill, still cannot match the music of the epoch that convinces, because he evades that effort and writes as if music can be articulated simply by moving it forward. In contrast, references to the so-called will to style, or to the resolve to simplify in the face of an ostensible threatened complexity, are not convincing at all. Any such resolve would fly in the face of what the language of music requires today; it would be arbitrary, external, intellectual in the bad sense: in other words, the last thing that the objectivists really want. Differentiation and a wealth of figuration are not a matter simply of the composer's psychology; all moralizing about allegedly decadent and fragmenting tendencies is just stuffy sermonizing. The differentiating elements that were historically unleashed by the subjective need for self-expression have long since become part of the logic of the work itself. Of course, like every technical element, the wealth of characters also has its internal side: it is the generous side, the willingness to give of oneself, while any coarse-grained mat-ter-of-factness in music is no more than a deluded faith in architecture and industrial functionality that contains the seeds of its own failure, along with the authoritarian manner of administered vitality.

The demand for differentiated characters is necessarily associated with the call for clarity. What is differentiated resists the classifying order imposed from above. In it the subjugated many protest against the dominating one, and it thereby becomes the spokesman of the chaotic: that means the hatred of all totalitarians. Compositional strength today is the strength that abandons itself to differentiation while retaining control over itself, the ability to preserve a unity. Berg, in whom a death wish was combined with the instinct to differentiate to a degree equaled by few others, was exemplary in the extremes of clarity he demanded from himself. Differentiation and clarity are combined together in specificity. If every part exercises its specific function in context, it must be distinct from everything else, and yet must stand in relationship to everything else, and both must be intelligible. This is why aversion to ornamentation is no mere idiosyncrasy, but is grounded in the requirements of the contemporary technique of composition. To characterize distinctly always means avoiding the blurred and the superfluous. The orchestral picture of the music of *Wozzeck*, which is open to every nuance of feeling, turns out to be surprisingly simple in the score, which by current standards is quite approachable. It consistently looks for the most drastic translations of compositional events into instrumental ones: doublings, fillers, the pedal point as sonority in its own right—all these are absent, and even in visionary passages, like the scene where Wozzeck drowns, the element of vagueness and dissolution is formulated in astonishingly precise terms. Even though *Wozzeck* is so much richer than *Le sacre du printemps* or anything by Strauss, the score seems far sparer, stripped down. There is less on paper than can be heard, whereas in *Ein Heldenleben* much is written that simply fades into the background or cannot be heard at all. At the same time, clarity is not necessarily the same thing as unambiguousness. New music is familiar with ambiguous functional features, and perhaps it is through them that the composition becomes "integral." But even the ambiguities must be clearly realized compositionally. The work will fail where the surface of the music fails to explain its function and to interpret the musical content. Berg's principle of instrumental variation, which is explicit in *Lulu* and has since been elevated to a norm in the most recent music, does not spring from the vague need for coloristic variety, but from the need to make use of timbre to demonstrate the change in function even of identical shapes. In *Lulu* that change in function is still essentially dramatic. Timbre was largely neglected by traditional orchestration. In Brahms, for example, timbre lagged significantly behind structure in its power to clarify. New music provides the answer to a question left open by tradition. And in general its relation to the past is more one of coming to grips with unfinished business than a simple continuation of so-called tradition.

In the general course of the history of music in the West what is decisive, today more than ever before, is the way in which the composition as a whole transcends the individual shape. But if this is so, then alongside reflections on characters and clarity we shall be obliged to think about musical development as well. Details and aspects of form cannot be separated by saying, for instance, that the whole is built up out of its constituent elements, or that the constituent elements are simply determined from above, by the whole: instead each is determined by the other. Ever since Stravinsky, and also in certain phases of the most recent music, there has been recurrent talk of nondeveloping, static music, most immediately in connection with the kaleidoscopic play of tone color and motive. But all so-called static music is mere illusion as long as it is regarded externally and played off dogmatically against the principle of development. In the first place, as a temporal art, music is dynamic in terms of its own material conditions: just as time is irreversible, so all music balks at a manipulation of time that implies its indifference to it. A meaningful musical organization is necessarily one in which meaning and time sequence relate to each other, so that the passage of time proves to be more meaningful rather than more arbitrary vis-à-vis the concrete musical content. Thanks to its integration, great music will undoubtedly deal with the passage of time by making it shorter. Its ability to drive out boredom has, like entire heteronomous musical categories, become an element of the music itself and of its autonomous status. The great, classical symphonic movements of Beethoven, the first movement of the *Eroica* or of the Seventh, can be heard ideally as if they lasted only a moment. If in Beethoven, the profane composer, empty, alienated time fatally oppresses the human subject, if life becomes separated out into a mere sequence of experiences, then in the name of the secular tension between freedom and necessity the sovereign subject will force them together once again into that epiphany that theology once taught as the eternity of the fulfilled moment, the concentration of the mere passage of time into a single instant, καιρός. It is uncertain whether such epiphanies can be attained without illusions, given the present philosophical situation and the state of the language of music. Its alternative would be unsatisfactory—a spatializing treatment of time without actually engaging with it as the synthesis of manifold events. There is no doubt that for Stravinsky, too, time was the problem of music, strictly speaking; that was his greatness. But objectively, his music despairs of being able to annul time through articulation, through the process of what Hegel called statement [*Setzung*] and negation. This is why, in flagrant contradiction to his own New Objective program, he contents himself with a fiction that provides him with a true foundation for his fictive activities and capers: instead of confronting the passage of time and its terrors so as to give it its due, and instead of standing his ground, he manipulates time, as if a temporal succession could be transfixed in a simultaneity; as if motives were interchangeable cubes and surfaces. His music, which is praised for its rhythms, is the opposite of rhythmic. It does not intervene in time; it makes no attempt to shape time by being shaped by it, but instead ignores it. The illusion of time-lessness is installed at the expense of the nonillusory aspect of music, its temporal dialectic. Stravinsky's music expresses the hope that, instead of answering to time, it will deprive time of its curse by taking flight, and the aesthetics of a *musica perennis* is nothing but the ontological enhancement of such weakness, one that coincides with a collective need. Confronted with this need, of course, the mere appeal to development cuts no ice at all, as long as the concept of development is itself in such dire need of repair. It is not enough, as stolid craftsmen would like, for a given point of departure to change into something different by virtue of a series of permutations. The change must itself be meaningful: the variation must do justice to the passage of time. What happens first and what happens next must not be left to chance or whim. Transformations must justify themselves by articulating the passage of time; this is not achieved automatically. Mere change is not development. It is hard to distinguish this from the concept of "exposition," the idea that what comes sooner in terms of inner form becomes the later, and that what comes later is "caused" by what comes sooner, and presupposes it as the basis of its own meaning. The paradigm for this concept is the structure of the first subject from Schoenberg's Violin Concerto, which begins with an unprepossessing motive, but then grows into a statement of extreme power. But even though development cannot be said to arise merely from shuffling groups of notes around, no more does the mere possession of an abstract rule guarantee what is development and what is not. It is by no means always the case that the more or less coherent exposition of a theme should be followed by its resolution, or conversely, that small motivic units should gradually crystallize into a theme or some larger complex. The diversity of what is meaningfully possible is infinite; but judgments about their success in reality can only be made from case to case. Nevertheless, even today a typology of developmental categories can be envisaged. In systematically athematic music all types become transformed, without simply disappearing; even in such athematic music the relations between Now and Then must not be arbitrary, and must be legitimated in the course of time, not simply by virtue of the static mathematical identity of its constituent parts. This is tremendously strengthened if developments are "composed out," in other words, if categories like consequentiality, antithesis, fresh attack, transition, and resolution become graspable, take shape; the radicality with which a piece of music presents the various stations along its path from the earliest to the latest coincides in great measure with its development.

As the meaningful transition to something nonidentical, development always implies a tension between different elements. It remains an open question whether the easing of that tension, the reestablishment of equilibrium, the identity of the nonidentical in the whole, is the ideal of every advanced, dialectical composition. In traditional music the easing of tension was achieved externally, through formal strategies. Beethoven alone legitimated this ritual once again from inside, through the intrinsic autonomous logic of the composition. But in emancipated music the possibility and legitimacy of equilibrium have become problematic. Schoenberg himself composed his music strictly within the framework of tension and resolution, and even called for it in theory. Nowhere is he closer to Karl Kraus than here, even though in general Kraus's conservative attitude to language was at the opposite pole from Schoenberg's revolutionary musical stance. For Schoenberg, too, "the origin is the goal." If Schoenberg did away with traditional harmony, the hegemony and ultimately the very concept of consonance, this only means that the concept of harmony has shifted to the work as a whole: every detail is tension, but the totality must be resolved in harmony. Only here do we discover his traditionalist limits, but these are not a matter of his attitudes so much as a historical limitation that he could not have gone beyond given his own resources. His achievement as a composer has often been compared, rightly or wrongly, with that of Einstein's in physics. Tonality becomes a "special case" for him, much as Euclidean space was for Einstein. But there can be no doubt that his music is as "classical" as relativity theory is classical physics, at least in the eyes of the latest quantum physicists. The universally dissonant shares the harmonious ideal of art of the bourgeois past: with the last note, everything in the aesthetic picture should be reconciled. It is very possible that one day features that stem from the primacy given to the easing of tension will turn out to be affirmative. The ideal, however, is not to be rejected outright; there is no reason simply to insist on the naked representation of tension rather than its resolution. The organization of the musical work of art, its "rationality"—something that Max Weber regarded as the key to Western music in general—is at its core an exchange relation, a tit for tat, a constant give-and-take. At the heart of the morality of the work of art, the determination not to remain in anyone's debt, is a concern to honor the bill of exchange that is underwritten by the very first beat. A general equilibrium becomes the goal of an immanent aesthetic economy. Analogous would be a society freed from exchange, one that also satisfied the idea of exchange by ceasing to withhold anything from the weaker partner. An exchange thus freed from deception would be exchange no longer. If music were to renounce such an idea of fair play as an ideological fraud, it would become amorphous, would abandon logic and inner coherence and entrust itself to mere chance, a bad irrationality. Even the critical work of art that denounces the semblance of reconciliation clings critically to the idea of its reality. But conversely, nowadays, such reconciliation radically resists incorporation into the aesthetic image. That is the inescapable antinomy of all contemporary art. As long as it prevails, a technical easing of tension cannot simply be equated with overall harmonizing tendencies. The substantial meaning that arises from the work of art thanks to such a resolution may, as determinate negation, actually stand in opposition to the harmoniousness of existence. Nor are negation and contradiction to be regarded as absolutes. They entail the idea of unity, just as the concept of unity entails that of contradiction.

Behind all of this lies concealed the question of the relation of advanced new music to reality. By way of apologia we could say that in the

face of the horror of recent events and the continuing fear of total catastrophe, art that ignores such realities is worthless. In fact, this element is
an essential part of the truth content of new music, as of all art today, and
art that imagines it is all right to play it safe instead of going to extremes
is a lost cause. The more zealously the infernal totality is denied, the more
every human being and every impulse will find itself more deeply en-
meshed in it. Positive gestures that are artificially willed simply strengthen
the feeling of impotence. The furious listener who wrote to his radio sta-
tion after hearing a performance of Stockhausen's *Gesang der Jünglinge*
saying that the piece had reminded him of atom bombs, whereas what he
wanted from art was relaxation, exaltation, and edification, understood
more in his subaltern repressiveness than the sophisticated connoisseur
who simply takes note of such music and weighs up its merits in comparison to those of other products. In general, there is more to be learned
from sullen reactionaries than from moderate progressives who do not allow anything that is not moderate to get anywhere near them. But the insight here matches all too well the verdict that advanced music has no
other truth than that it is as full of atrocities as the world in which it is
written. This leads logically to the thesis that art is not needed simply to
duplicate these atrocities. The content of such reasoning is worthy of its
intention. Even if new music were nothing but the expression of that despair, it would still be something more, since it does give it expression. In
the aesthetics of the Dynamically Sublime, Kant reserves exclusively for
the beauty of nature the happiness that arises from our standing our
ground, a happiness in which the completely impotent human being discovers power and hope. Almost two hundred years later, this claim retains
its validity, and this time it is above all the prerogative of art, in a human
world that has hardened into a second nature and is threatened with society's own "natural" catastrophes: "Bold, overhanging, and, as it were,
threatening rocks, thunderclouds piled up the vault of heaven, borne
along with flashes and peals, volcanoes in all their violence of destruction,
hurricanes leaving desolation in their track, the boundless ocean rising
with rebellious force, the high waterfall of some mighty river, and the
like, make our power of resistance of trifling moment in comparison with
their might. But . . . their aspect is all the more attractive for its fearful-
ness; and we readily call these objects sublime because they raise the forces
of the soul above the height of vulgar commonplace, and discover within
us a power of resistance of quite another kind, which gives us courage to

be able to measure ourselves against the seeming omnipotence of nature. . . . In this way external nature is not estimated in our aesthetic judgment as sublime so far as exciting fear, but rather because it challenges our power (one not of nature) to regard as small those things of which we are wont to be solicitous (worldly goods, health, and life) and hence to regard its might (to which in these matters we are no doubt subject) as exercising over us and our personality no such rude dominion that we should bow down before it." Only now, this happiness, when compared to the Kantian triumph of the free, sovereign spirit, has shrunk to the point where its only resource is the ability to express the terrible, without the illusion that some absolute value is guaranteed by our standing our ground; thus it is objective, devoid of any subjective "feeling of the sublime." At the end of the bourgeois epoch spirit recalls the mimesis of prehistorical times, the reflexlike imitation, the futile impulse from which the spirit, the thing that was different from existing reality, once arose. Overwhelmed by the power of the world of things, it took refuge in the rudimentary minimum to which the world of things had forced it to regress. This precarious happiness, however, is as fully present as despair in advanced new music. If the talk about the many-layered complexity of art is to be any more than a phrase to ward off theoretical reflection, then it must refer to this. Those dissonant chords that once so enraged the normal consciousness which was so complicit with catastrophe, and that today, if left to themselves, would spread sterility all around, were the vehicles not just of pain, but also of pleasure. Provincial critics who once fumed about the sadism of new music have grasped this better than the well-intentioned who betray the cause through their general inoffensiveness. The sonorities consisting of a multiplicity of notes do not just displease; in their cutting dissonance they were always beautiful as well. The threshold that separates the advanced composer from the stifling atmosphere of the so-called intact world is crossed when he commits himself to this beauty without reservation, just as he did a century ago, when *Fleurs du mal* was written. What a child feels when it leaves a footprint in freshly fallen snow is one of the most powerful aesthetic impulses. Anyone who has not experienced the yearning, as Berg did, one day to hear a chord consisting of eight different notes on eight brass instruments playing fortissimo, at a time when *Die glückliche Hand* had not yet been performed, knows as little of the riddle of new music as the person who shudders at the din. And its truth is that it states these elements in a synthesis of its own, one truer to experience than the harsh, unambiguous language of concepts, with its decrees. Such happiness, however, is vouchsafed by every discovery of new music, with the force of a constantly rejuvenating immediacy. The less these discoveries are to be found in the individual sound and sonority, the more such happiness permeates the totality that absorbs diffuse and centrifugal musical impulses without doing them violence. Through all the injustice of the totality, new music legitimates itself by ensuring that the individuals oppressed by that totality cannot be reconciled except by virtue of the totality itself. By negating both the general and the particular, new music presses forward to absolute identity, and in so doing, it aspires to be the voice of the nonidentical—of everything that refuses to be submerged.

§ Music and Technique

The Greek meaning of the word "technique" points to its unity with art. If the latter is the external representation of an internal phenomenon, a complex of meaning made manifest, then the concept of technique embraces everything that refers to the making real of that inner phenomenon. In music that means both the spiritual content of the notes and the sensuously reproduced sounds: in other words, both production and reproduction. The sum of all musical means is musical technique; it is both the organization of the content and its translation into an outward manifestation. The word "technique" points to the human agency in that creation of meaning; it reminds us of the human subject, however that may be constituted. It reminds us, too, of the element of know-how, success, function, at which the organization of a musical structure is directed. It is ultimately sublimated into a state of objectivity, a law-governed reality that moves beyond the realm of subjective effort and endows it with the aspect of a being that exists in itself. The work of art becomes a complex of meaning by virtue of its technical organization; it contains nothing that lacks technical legitimation. All talk of mere technique is alien to art.

Content and technique are both identical and nonidentical. They are nonidentical because a work of art acquires its life in the tension between inner and outer; because it is a work of art only if its manifest appearance points to something beyond itself. The work of art without content, the epitome of a mere sensuous presence, would be nothing more than a slice of empirical reality, the opposite of which would be a work of art consisting of mere rationality devoid of all enchantment. The unmediated identity of content and appearance would annul the idea of art. For all that, the two are also identical. For in composition, that which has been made real is all that counts. Only philistines can entertain the notion of a ready-made and self-contained artistic content that is then projected into the external world with the aid of a technique conceived of in similarly thinglike terms. Inner experience and outer form are created by a reciprocal process of interaction. It is by no means the case that the outer husk is simply determined from within, as in the saying about the mind that builds the body for itself. Music is familiar with creation in the opposite direction. The spirit of Debussy and Ravel, the creaturely sadness of sensuous happiness, would not be art were it not in thrall to the delights, however intermittent, of emerging sounds. And this holds too for the relationship of technique to content in general. The sense of darkly mysterious sounds never before heard that Schumann introduced into music derives not just from the discoveries he made in fingering technique; rather, as a novel dimension of spiritual musical experience, it was essentially tied to composing for the piano. He himself said on one occasion that the difference between his earlier and later works lay in the fact that in the former he had specifically tried to give the instrument its due, while in the latter the claims of the piano had become a matter of indifference. This account may be true enough, but the quality of the compositions provides evidence that the path he took was the wrong one. His music was inspired where he let himself be inspired by the piano. And this analogy holds true progressively for music as a whole.

The idea that content and technique in music are at once identical and nonidentical means nothing less than that the concept of technique contains its own dialectic. This can be seen from the fact that the term "compositional technique," however ancient the reality to which it refers, is of modern origin and was scarcely in use before the nineteenth century. It comes into being only with the tendency to artistic reflexivity in composition, the increasing control exercised over the sound-material by the composer's intentions, the growing freedom with which the musical means are manipulated, means which as a consequence become increasingly independent. This advance is accomplished, like any process of rationalization, with the aid of a progressive division of labor. That is to say, new territories are conquered and become separated off as special fields before being reintegrated into new aesthetic totalities. These new sectors emerge initially outside the realm of actual composition. In Bach, for example, there is still a fairly loose, arbitrary relationship between orchestration and composition. Techniques in the narrower sense tended to thrive alongside the process of composition, amounting to additional effects like those which Berlioz praises in Gluck and Weber in his *Traité de l'instrumentation*. This outward-looking, as it were, communicative element of music then penetrates to the very core of the formal laws that govern it. What is henceforth given shape is no longer just the musical meaning, but its musical reproduction as well. Ever since Berlioz musical performance has been virtually surrendered to the composer, thus diminishing the tension between text and performance. This achievement has, however, the negative implication that performance, the means, attains primacy over the thing it is supposed to serve, the composition. Thus the technique of composition became a reflection on means that are initially distinct from ends, that in all probability were identical originally with the treatment of the instrumental parameters as a specific skill deriving from the sphere of performance. But this view of technique did not settle down as an integral part of composition until the second half of the nineteenth century. The technification of the work of art matures along with the inclusion of techniques that had developed outside music in the course of the general growth of technology. Hence the valve horn, the crucial precondition of Wagner's orchestral art, had been in existence long before its hour struck as a suitable instrument for composition—to say nothing of the saxophone. The concept of musical technique grew in complexity in a way comparable to the development of film. Means that did not flow from composition in the first instance were adopted and helped to enlarge its scope, but at the same time, they advanced their own claims such that a nonaesthetic element became the norm within the aesthetic realm. The unity of the age, and ultimately the general social tendency as a whole, asserted its rights in works of art, but, as it were, behind their backs. That is the dialectical law governing the technification of the work of art, one of increasing integration and self-alienation: integration because technification permits the incorporation into the aesthetic form of more and more domains that had formerly lain adjacent to but outside it; self-alienation because such a totality measures itself against a specialized unity, against objectivized means that have been split off from content and oppose themselves to the very subjectivity without which aesthetic meaning is inconceivable. The more completely the ends subjugate the means, the more threatening becomes the rule of the means over the ends: this is the aesthetic dialectic of master and servant. Every process of integration is accompanied, falsely, by a process of disintegration. It causes every part to disappear in the whole, even though it can contribute to the creation of a whole only if it is preserved. Prototypical for all this was Berlioz, the *Urphänomen* of modernity in music, the first composer in whom the continuity of tradition as well as of musical structure was shattered. He created compositional technique as the self-conscious manipulation of a material stratum, namely that of orchestration, that until then had been left to instinct. At the same time, he was the first major composer—setting aside Gluck—with an inadequate grasp of compositional technique, of the ability to create unified, coherent, fully organized structures. His is the earliest instance in modern times of a composer in whose music meaning and meaningful structure seem dubious. The first technician of music was the first composer who was no longer a good musician: instrumental organization and compositional disorganization are mutually complementary in him. This is the source of his modernity. The explosion of meaning in his manipulation of effects is shocking—this is what defines the content of his music. The negation of meaning becomes its meaning, just as in positivism the negation of philosophy becomes philosophy. The fact that his program music aimed to depict an opium trance is no quirk of Romanticism, rather it tells the truth about the incipient crisis of musical logic. That crisis finds its continuation not in Wagner, but in Richard Strauss, in whom technification goes together with the technique of surprise, in other words, the permanent suspension of musical structure, of musical logic. Ever since music has been emphatically involved in progress—that is to say, in industrial progress—ever since the *Symphonie fantastique*, in short, it has had to pay the price of progress—like industrial society as a whole.

If all appearances do not deceive, this development has now reached an extreme. The separation of technique and composition that made its provocative, but innocent, appearance in Berlioz, Liszt, and Strauss has been abolished. All musical domains have become compositional elements by virtue of being subject to rational control and are mutually related: ever since twelve-tone technique this has been the transparent goal of composition. So influenced, the integral organization of the musical text has increasingly restricted the scope for interpretation and has become an implicit threat to the very existence of interpretation. Given scores in which every note, every structural quality, tends toward unambiguous definition, the desire to interpret is becoming obsolete. In the face of such music, indeed, silent reading, precision of the imagination, emerges as the true interpretative ideal. The integrally composed work, designated as integral, is its own complete realization. Conversely, advances in mechanical reproduction that make it possible to fix music, like the plastic arts, independently of ephemeral performances with their arbitrary features, bring reproduction decisively closer to production. Technical developments outside music in the first instance, and then as supervised by the composer's intentions, converge with those internal to music. If works become their own reproductions, the time when reproductions will become the works cannot be all that far away. With the absolute realization in sound of a composition by electronic means, perhaps even in a perfect recording on tape or wire, doubts arise about writing the music down in note form: it is as if the music could be produced as directly as a picture can be painted, omitting the intermediate signifying stage of writing it down as a mere ornamental inconvenience. This necessarily diminishes the tension between technique and content. The less musical representation is the representation of something, the more the sum of the means seems to merge with what is represented. Attempts to reserve a special space for representation, spirit, or meaning separate from technification are doomed to impotence. Spirit, cultivated apologetically as a special sphere alongside that of technique, falls victim to the very mechanisms it mistakenly thinks it is resisting. It therefore negates itself. To preach about spirit in music today is roughly as reactionary as if someone had tried fifty years ago to praise sensuous pleasure in the face of Kandinsky's *The Spiritual in Art*. Spirit, and culture in general, are lost as soon as an explicit appeal is made to them.

But the work of art as the totality of means is not better placed, is no less at risk, than it is as the totality of conserved spirit. The legitimate demand that justice be done to the material, a demand that takes the work of art very seriously, ascribing nothing to it that cannot be guaranteed by its own form, and that finally implements the old ban on surplus allegorical meaning, ends up turning against the idea of inner structural coherence, its own idol. The structure that consists of nothing but relationships that one can pin down ceases to be a structure, but rather breaks down into the elements that it had impotently, abstractly subsumed within itself. Elevating verifiable correctness in a composition to the status of an absolute works to the detriment of a truth content that may not be sought outside the musical structure, but that evaporates the moment that structure becomes coterminous with its immanent existence. It is like a community where the administration informs every activity; the various elements are all interrelated and each one functions smoothly, but no one knows any longer what the overall purpose is. Just as no single element receives back that part of its nonidentical nature that it yielded up under the compulsion of a universal identity of everything with everything else, in the same way individual impulses receive nothing back from the process that drove them toward a totality. But since a work of art as a totality derives its energy from its interaction with the parts, once that interaction ceases owing to the preemptive decision in favor of the totality, the machine just idles in neutral. The unprotesting acquiescence in technical possibilities results in the liquidation of the very thing for which that acquiescence was sought, namely the survival of the composition. Musical technique and musical content, once in each other's power, devour each other just like the two lions in the old comic. Extramusical technique is no longer present to act as a corrective but becomes instead the exclusive authority. The whole official musical culture is moving in the direction of the fetishizing of means, and it is even celebrating a triumph among its enemies in the avant-garde. The integration of technique and content at its peak becomes a reprise of that rigid dualism. The appearance of objectivity regained is a delusion. The expulsion of the subjective factor from a thinglike, objective construction that, not immediately graspable, is able to prove its worth only in terms of abstract correspondences is no act of objectification. Precisely through its elimination, subjectivity is unconsciously taken to an extreme, a project designed to conquer nature that ends up worshiping the fossilized result of its manipulations as if it were being in itself. We thus have the paradox of a musical language whose sense of its own power leads it to proclaim itself authoritative, and it is proud to achieve what tonality once achieved. But instead of simply taking pleasure in the fact that it has at long last liberated itself from the superannuated universality of tonality, it comes close to the gibberish of an arbitrary whim no longer held in check by any authoritative convention. This spells the reinstatement of a magical hocus-pocus as the sound of creation.

The tendency of an integral music to disintegrate is not to be judged according to criteria external to it; it does not represent the loss of sacred treasures that should not be sold off at any price. The fact that all musical elements and dimensions are reduced to a common denominator in order to promote a total structure of meaning, liberated from any foreign, externally imposed element, has the paradoxical effect of undermining the very idea of meaningful structure. It is a feature of every musical phenomenon, which must end up destroying it; for a disposition of the material that rides roughshod over the material itself, with which it is by no means identical, does away with the very element that binds it all together. From a compositional point of view, too, atomization is complementary to integration; here, too, a virtue is made of the victory of thought over being that no longer resists and has already ceased to exist. The absolute necessity that weaves a note cluster here and now from these specific notes, this rhythm, these pitch levels, volumes, colors, and perhaps even modes of playing—a successful subsumption—confers something of an arbitrary character on the individual phenomenon, without which music explicit in time cannot survive. The less it can be anything other than it is, the more it sounds as though it could be different. It is this, and not any ideological loss of extramusical content, that defines the crisis of meaning in which the integration of meaning with technique becomes conscious of itself.

All of this can be grasped technically. The ideal of absolute identity that inspires the technological work of art is that of the unity of a deductive system, in a literal sense that leaves almost no space for metaphorical overtones. Everything that occurs in such music is to be inferred from a basic premise reduced to the minimum, and to the exclusion, so far as is possible, of every element of chance. The ideal once formulated was that in a consistent serial composition the entire piece should be predetermined down to the very last accent by the initial choice of material. But this assumes that all musical parameters can be reduced to a single common denominator—in other words, to that basic material. It is indeed indisputable that everything is related to everything else, and that the isolated treatment of any one dimension of the music not only represents a regression to an earlier stage of music, but even does an injustice to each individual dimension, since each one becomes what it is only through its relationship with others: in this respect contemporary composers have finally succeeded in overthrowing the academic tradition of dividing music up into specializations. The most drastic expression of this change is the way in which it has become possible to substitute one parameter for another. Decades ago Ernest Newman remarked that methods of orchestration could be used to make complex harmonies more easily grasped.

Schoenberg tested this possibility of substitution during his expressionist phase with his use of *Klangfarbenmelodie*, in the Orchestral Piece op. 16, no. 3, for example, and later, in the identification of the vertical and horizontal dimensions, of harmony and melody in the twelve-tone technique, something that, admittedly, could succeed only as the function of a third parameter, that of counterpoint. Most recent practice has elevated this tendency into a principle and a comprehensive, all-inclusive norm. That forces the composer to consider the question of the absolute identity of the parameters, a question tackled theoretically by Stockhausen with an energy that tests it to its limits. His intentions may perhaps be reduced to the formula that the parameters of simultaneity and color, though seemingly timeless, can be identified as temporal in nature. But to identify these parameters in temporal terms remains abstract; they, too, are both identical and nonidentical. The vertical dimension can be said to occur in time, but within time it functions as a quasi-spatial counterforce. Over and above that, however, the most advanced among the younger composers recognize that there is no unambiguous, visible link between musical intervals and real-time relations, from the length of the notes and pauses right up to entire formal structures; just as, conversely, there is no unbroken continuity between tone colors and the other parameters. A distinction has to be made between the objective physical phenomena, including the "psychology of sound"—to use Ernst Kurth's old-fashioned term—and the specific features of music that Kurth misleadingly thought of as the "psychology of music." This includes the subjective mediation of musical phenomena, something that is no more to be equated with physical processes than a percept is to be confused with the events in the brain that gave rise to it. The technical work of art becomes meaningless, or even false, whenever it ignores this nonidentity, and treats unlike things alike, multiplying oranges and typewriters. Mere analogies in the treatment of the parameters of a composition are mistaken for genuine aspects of a strict unity that guarantees a necessary unfolding of events. Illusion, which has been proscribed, creeps back in. Analogy as the means of aesthetic unity could be legitimate where that unity is not given literally, but only as an illusion—as, for example, in the relationship between tone color and harmony in Wagner. But when the claims of integration are rigorously followed through, the demands of unity are intensified so much that when the phenomenon violates that unity, it offends against its own principle and becomes arbitrary, sacrificing rightness along with meaning. An abstract, mathematical necessity that imposes itself on the musical phenomenon from outside, without subjective mediation, has some affinity with absolute chance. It is not impossible that this is precisely what is proclaimed by the recent experiments in "aleatory" composition. In open disintegration, the process of integral composition achieves the state of productive self-knowledge. By denying musical meaning, it denies its own raison d'être. *Summum ius summa iniuria.*

Unless you wish to stand by helplessly as the eulogist of the past anxious to turn the clock back, or to embrace the absurd, a condition that loses its justification as soon as it ceases to be provocative and instead sets itself up as a positive standard, you must reflect on the factors that determine whether we must acquiesce in this entire development as fully as its dictatorial manner implies, a manner that awakens doubts about the actual authority that lies behind it. That authority, however, is the musical text. It is based today on the positivistic notion—one strangely incompatible, incidentally, with the intellectual climate of recent music—that it is a set of game rules, or perhaps a system of signals concerned with communication and "information." This is linked to the unmediated unity of composition and realization, the axiom of the absolute identity of musical parameters, and ultimately, the idea of the straightforward integration of the work of art. This view of the musical text has arisen from the process in which what used to be the mere representation of music has been taken in hand by composers, and by the convergence of musical and extra-musical technology that has promoted the sound engineer and the electrician to the status of composer. Once the latter have acquired the position in the realm of music that they enjoy in industry, the composers hasten to emulate them. All of this is in thrall to that ambivalent progress that measures itself against what are supposed to be the literal facts and hence can act as the guarantors of the irrefutable, but at the expense of what is possible. This idea of progress sinks its teeth into whatever is the case and hence secretly falls into line with a regression that is shared by late industrial society as a whole.

But if, originally, musical notation was not a set of game rules, not a prescription, but a mnemonic, a way of ensuring the survival of a tradition, of objectivizing an imagined, spiritual reality, it can still be said to have retained something of all that. In musical writing, as in verbal script, the graphic element, which has ultimately been secularized into communication, is combined with the element of copying, the resemblance to the object of representation. Musical script not only constitutes the basis of performance, but is also something independent of performance, just as reading to ourselves something that has been written enables us to objectify an intellectual content regardless of whether it is transmitted to others. If this element of autonomy in the musical text is eliminated, the tension between composition, script, and sound collapses in favor of something more primitive that emerges all the more crassly through the complexity of the means that are intended to compensate for it. The best part, one that risks being forgotten and that cannot be rescued in isolation, can be rediscovered only when the composer's energy is directed at the score conceived as the objectification of the human subject, instead of clinging to an extramusical subject or a manipulated objectivity. The leveling down, the reduction of the composition to its manifest appearance, could only be reversed by conceiving of the composition as something that stands in a tense relationship to performance, is not collapsed into it and perhaps thinks no more of it than Beethoven thought of that "wretched fiddle." For then the internal compositional means would cease to exercise blind domination—a domination that is itself the rule of mere appearances. At the same time, such a corrective would draw out the complete sociological implications of the situation of music, which utters the truth about society only if it refuses to comply with the dominant social norms, that mode of being in which everything goes with everything else—a mode of being that simply conceals the will of those who control production. Immanent criticism alone can be the medium of this new quality. The lesson to be learned is that the positivist commitment to positive data does not grant access to the concrete relationship of music to human beings. This lesson can be learned from the experience that to place one's faith in technical communicability as the supreme norm is to end up with a failure in social communication; it can be learned from the discovery that even the formal inclusion of psychological laws of artistic reception in the composition itself (if this were possible) would not be able to win over listeners for advanced music today. The chances of communicating the truth would only lie with a type of music that, instead of going in search of communication, distances itself from manifest reality and overwhelms, through its very refusal to be reconciled, all those to whom it must remain alien as long as it remains at their beck and call.

The progressive intertwining of art and technique need not simply be accepted as irrevocable. It contains the potential for something better. If art is to come to the help of a nature mutilated by the spirit of domination, and to move in the direction of freedom, this can only be achieved by liberating it from the heteronomy of nature. Nevertheless, the falseness implicit in the technocratic practices of the modern age cannot be passed over in silence. Nor is it possible to evade the diabolical difficulty of practicing criticism without constant recourse to the vain gesture of Thus Far and No Further. What is obvious here is the inadequacy of the mediation and synthesis practiced by many middle-aged composers who enrich their works with some of the achievements of a radical process of technical innovation as a kind of prophylactic against their own increasing age, without however taking technology to its logical conclusion. But even those who are able to distinguish between what they are for and what they are against at the strategic level find it desperately hard to put it into words convincingly, and this reveals that the contradiction is objective in nature. For it is a simple tautology to say that senseless composition is senseless. Meaning, however, meaningful composition, is not something that is simply added to an unavoidably integral process. The only help here perhaps would be for meaning to emerge from the objective subject matter as a consequence of ruthless reflection on itself, in other words, for a technical reflection on technique, even at those points where, to the self-critical ear, it seems to present a blank wall without cracks or crannies to give a hold. If it is indeed time for a renewed turn toward subjectivity in music, this cannot be expected to come from subjective intentions. Mediation by the subject will succeed only as an objective mediation, an internal technical critique, and not in terms of what an individual may think, feel, or even what he imaginatively hears while listening in solitary reverie. Musical understanding is improved as much through experience of musical form and its objective tendency as the musical form is improved by the subjective imagination. The aging of modern music cannot be fought by regressing to an older phase, but only through determinate negation: aging must become conscious of itself and so rise above the controversy. The loci of such a process are the authentic works themselves. The theory calls for modesty; only a rogue gives more than he has.

~

For all that, the theory is not utterly helpless in its confrontation with practice; after all, it arises out of the reflection on the latter's experience. Let us make a note of a number of rough-and-ready rules, which at the same time might supply a model of the way in which the composer may apply them in his own work.

1. What is absolutely indispensable in the economy of the technical work of art is the need to keep the relation between input and result in mind. I am constantly being sent compositions by partly or wholly dilettante composers together with letters in which they are lauded for having created some allegedly new serial structures or relationships, which as music turn out to be impoverished in the extreme. Mostly, a single glance is enough to reveal the source of the trouble: a tendency to compose rigidly from one bar line to the next without the overall movement, even the internal movement, being able to disguise this fact. A further giveaway is that after a more or less well-defined idea at the start, the ability to sustain it quickly fades, often after only a few measures. It is then continued in a shapeless, mechanical manner. But in every case, what characterizes such exercises is that the musical substance is incomparably less complex than the row-combinations these youths are so proud of: on occasion they are so primitive that the context would be comprehensible even if no rows had been used at all. There is an extensive reliance on rhythmic symmetries that do not really go well with the asymmetrical interval patterns. Or else, the measures or groups of measures have been duly counted off, but no spirit informs the piece as a whole, and this is unaffected by the tone rows. Nevertheless, such lesser products do throw some light on more accomplished pieces. We might heretically object to a movement like the finale in Webern's Chamber Concerto [for Nine Instruments, op. 24] by asking what purpose his entire serial artistry serves if nothing more than a Goodnight March comes out of it. All the more so in many of his successors, considering the inordinate efforts made to include all the parameters in the piece and create a sort of unity by just splashing down unconnected note clusters; the result is often crassly monotonous over huge stretches of time, and it is hard even for the sympathetic listener to avoid the impression that vast energy is being expended in order to lift rubber dumbbells. For advanced composition, as indeed for radicality of every kind, a measure of common sense is required, if it is going to do more than run on automatic pilot. For those who discover this too late, there is always the risk that they will become renegades and repudiate what they once embraced too naively. No responsible composer can afford to pursue the means so doggedly while failing to keep an eye on the music generated thereby—and on whether its structure, weighti-

ness, and tension justify their use, whether it stands in need of them and none other.

2. If the composer becomes the supervisor of his own work, his supervision must not confine itself to the question of construction, but should extend to asking whether the construction finds its way into the core of the experienced music. This is more easily said than done, for there exists no abstract norm that can determine success or failure. What is at stake here is not whether all the structural features in a composition can be perceived by the listener—in other words, whether they are as obvious as the repeat of a theme. Beethoven himself was aware, as Schenker has shown, of relationships that lie at a deeper level than the motivic-thematic work and that create a deeper, more authoritative unity the less obvious they are. And especially in Schoenberg's case, it was never his intention to make the rows as such audible—whether as themes, or as something comparable to a key or mode. Instead, they were supposed to create a latent organization that proved their worth as a kind of "cement," above all in the extended works of the later Schoenberg. But the presence of such latent features is no license to split them off from every possible link to the actual musical sound. It is a question of judgment. The harder it is to describe in general terms which principles of construction are made real in the experienced music, however indirectly, and which degenerate into arid routine, the more important this supervisory task of the composer becomes. So if parameters like those of interval and length are set apart from the musical identity but nevertheless are treated consistently in the construction, any possibility of sensing the construction in the experienced music will be ruled out from the start and all the labor will have been in vain. Furthermore, it is not possible to grasp, even at an unconscious level, temporal parallels between individual pauses or note values that are very far apart, unless they are highlighted by more obvious means, such as striking analogies of tone color or rhythm. There is need for objective supervision of such matters if the construction is not to remain stuck at a precompositional level and fail to assert its authority over the music. Such supervision, however, can be carried out only by the living subject. Objectivity itself calls for the return of the subject into the composition itself.

3. The test of the relationship between construction and experienced music is the living idea. Now, ever since music escaped from the bonds of tonality, there has been a stream of anecdotes—mainly from orchestra

players—designed to brand modern composers as frauds for not having noticed various crude mistakes that have arisen, intentionally or otherwise, during the performance of their works. These stories are for the most part apocryphal. Furthermore, a keen ear, though an invaluable asset for a composer, is by no means identical with a talent for composition. I have known very major composers whose hearing is anything but reliable. But only schoolmasters could formulate valid assertions about how musicians compose, whether it is on the basis of a precise imagination, or whether the composer starts off from a set of possibilities that are not quite unambiguous and precise, and then goes through a process of listening, testing, comparing—acting, in short, as his own critic—and ends up by selecting the best ideas. Haydn composed at the piano, as did more recently Stravinsky, who certainly cannot be accused of failing to locate his music precisely in its sensuous material. Mozart and Schoenberg spurned such methods. But such things cannot simply be transmitted from the older generation to the younger. In music that claims that even its smallest units are strictly predetermined by its methods of construction, the precision of the original conception acquires a completely different significance vis-à-vis music where the score is understood simply as an approximation to the living music and allows a certain latitude for variation in the idea. If there really is no freedom in a serial composition and if every deviation from the constructed score threatens its inner coherence, then the composer has to realize each note with all its performance marks exactly as it is; otherwise he will negate his own principle. As early as the later Webern it was striking how far he sometimes departed as performer from what was written down on paper. It was indeed thanks to the flexibility he showed in performing his Mondrianesque pieces that they acquired a musical meaning, and we might be tempted to ask whether he did not smuggle it into his austere lines illicitly, even though he had made no direct claim as to their being absolutely predetermined. Nevertheless, if in a spontaneous performance of the latter part of the last movement of the Variations for Piano, op. 27, the notes entering on weak beats cannot be grasped as such, so that the structure of an entire variation is no longer visible in the way in which it was written down, the construction principle itself necessarily raises doubts. Should it prove to be the case that a major composer of the most complex serial music operates high-handedly with the text, especially with respect to rhythm—and even the most experienced will scarcely be able to judge simply from reading the score—this would suggest that he will one day break free from the principles of integral composition and simply follow his ear. The next step would be for him to notate not in the spirit of integral composition, but following the manner in which he hears and plays. At any rate, every composer who does not wish to become the victim of thinglike alienated construction should make every effort to compare the score with his own imagination. Such a comparison might easily undermine the principle of total composition.

4. The new principles of construction were originally designed to cope with a state of profusion—the product, essentially, of Schoenberg's unprecedented combinatorial powers—which, following the elimination of the tonal supports, threatened to collapse in chaos unless it could be restrained internally, by the limits of its own material conditions. But what happens where there is no chaos, nothing to restrain, and where the triumph of certain principles has been laid down in advance—principles that become meaningful only in conflict with their opposite, the unruly, diffuse wellsprings of music? Where, in that case, should Nietzsche's "dancing star" come from? Technically, this question points to a situation that reveals itself as the loss of internal tension. Webern's shudders do not refute the suspicions aroused by highly constructed music that is stripped down but lacks a concentrated quintessential core. Nowadays, every composer would have to ask himself what subject matter is attached to his construct, and what withers away in consequence of the constructive process. This would not in itself suffice to create music with an inner tension, but it would forestall many superfluous diagrams. The contrast between theme and elaboration is obsolete—but the proper inference from this would be a full three-dimensionality; everything should be thematic, rather than equally nonthematic and shapeless. The way to organize complex material is through a thoroughly elaborated polyphony—but such polyphony ceases to be so polyphonous once the sheer extent of implied canonic writing reduces it to monody. The risk is that the actual substance of the composition will wither away in favor of the principles that stand behind it; the devaluation of what is determined as opposed to the determining factors seems particularly flagrant in the case of electronic music. In its conception this involves the unleashing of all the means of creating sound and color, as well as their mediation through each other, whereas hitherto these had been tied more or less arbitrarily to the various media of sound and had been separated from each other by the pe-

culiarities of those media. However, most of the electronic music I have
heard, even such a shocking and powerful piece as Stockhausen's *Gesang
der Jünglinge*, seems to consist of the transposition and extension of piano ideas to the new material, and has shown itself to be strangely untouched by what might be expected from the color continuum, from the
potential of a polyphony that might be able to create a truly new musical space. Only by exploiting the multiplicity of voices straining away
from each other and against each other—rather than reducing one to the
other—might a new constructive synthesis come into its own.

5. Voices have rightly called for the integration of instrumentation into
the process of composition, that it should become a "parameter" of composition. But what is the meaning of functional instrumentation? It can
hardly be the case that orchestral coloring should change according to
specific formulas, that timbres should be shaken around and recur as in
a kaleidoscope, not even if connections could be established between
those formulas and those governing intervallic and temporal relations. On
the contrary, structural instrumentation would be to use every timbre and
above all the mode of orchestration to make real all the structural elements that are indispensable to the articulation of the musical meaning: a
procedure, then, that does not cloak music in orchestral garb, as the critics would say, but that translates its own articulation into that of sound.
The principle of structural instrumentation is not one of a color calculus,
but of compositional clarity. In this respect the orchestral settings of the
far-from-dead Schoenberg remain unsurpassed; Webern provides an object lesson in his orchestration of the six-part ricercar from the *Musical
Offering*. Instead of treating the instrumentation as one parameter among
others to which it is only abstractly related, the composition should develop the instrumentation from the meaning of the musical events. In
that way it would become an authentic parameter, a concrete function of
the music. The music would be the beneficiary of this treatment of instrumentation, since it would be one of the means of objectification music has needed ever since it ceased to lie cocooned inside the traditional
formal scheme. In order to create this structural orchestration, it is of
course necessary to be able to orchestrate in the first place. But every
other treatment of the orchestral palette is just playing around.

6. In that the idea of total predetermination is an illusion—because it
is not possible to create an absolutely unambiguous structure, nor would
such a structure coincide with the music as it manifests itself—composers

ought to conclude that they should renounce illusion entirely. By the same token, the constructive principles wrested from the material should be further developed. This contradiction can probably only be resolved by expecting composers to turn their attention to the relationship between structure and manifest music, to use their artistic rationality to close the gap between rational determination and sensuous presence. Schoenberg was aware of this when he categorically insisted on deriving the row from the thematic idea and not the other way around: the primary musical impulse should always generate the structuring principle. How justified this was can be seen wherever the process of construction prevents it from being done, but instead forces the composer to generate the phenomenal shapes [*die Gestalten*] from the row: every reasonably perceptive teacher of composition could put his finger on the spot where that happens and point to the overcalculated, awkward, and arbitrary nature of such secondary shapes. We might claim without much exaggeration that all integral music consists entirely of such secondary shapes. That is their weakness, and the ineluctable task today is the rediscovery of primary shapes, the generation of immediate impulses in the process of universal mediation. The fact is, there is no mediation without an unmediated primary impulse, just as, conversely, great music tolerates no unmediated primary impulse without mediation. The construction, therefore, must be preceded by an idea of the whole, to which it must be subordinated, and it must propose, athematically if needs be, freely generated structural cells, musical nuclei of whatever parameter, even before the process of construction begins. Since these nuclei cannot be thought of a priori as subordinate to the principles of construction, it is impossible to prescribe specific norms for them—not even their dodecaphonic nature. In this respect the first four piano pieces in Schoenberg's op. 23 are still exemplary even today: they work with basic shapes and are through-constructed; the shapes themselves, however, are "free," and that gives them a concreteness and flexibility that, if lost, cannot be compensated for by the strict twelve-tone pattern of the basic shape of later years, for all its advantages. The task is to import the predetermined into free creativity. The unfolding of music in time, the essence of which is to generate something new, something that has never yet existed, contradicts the notion of predetermination. The latter would blast music out of its native element, time. Totally predetermined music would cease to be a developing thing and would sink to the level of mere existence, while its aspect of becoming in time would degenerate into illusion, absolute un-reality. Asked about total predetermination in the course of a conversa-tion, Stockhausen modified the notion by saying it contained an un-avoidable element of "indeterminacy," a term borrowed from physics. However, this indeterminacy is no concession wrested by the irrational imperfection of the musical material from the idea of the musical domi-nation of nature, but gives a name to the actual underlying substratum of musical construction. It is well known that in the first movement of the Violin Concerto, one of the most magnificent works of Schoenberg's ma-ture phase, the composer made a mistake in his treatment of the row whose aftereffects were felt for quite a long time. The upshot was that the movement was "false" in terms of twelve-tone technique. Michael Gielen performed the experiment of correcting the passage by inserting the right notes and reported, plausibly enough, that it was impossible. However, this does not amount to a refutation of the serial form to which the piece owes its compelling structure. Nor does the "mistake" mean that the mu-sic is less logical, but only that the "mistake" represents the breakthrough of the substance to be structured, the point where it encounters the struc-turing process and but for which the latter could not be legitimated.

Translator's Notes

Translator's Notes

NOTE: Foot-of-page notes within the main body of the text are Adorno's; notes in this section are Rick Graebner's or mine. Notes here are keyed to the page, line, and phrase to which they refer.—R.L.

Some Ideas on the Sociology of Music

1, 8 *"frame of reference"*: In English in the original.

5, 20 *it can now be found as an appendix . . .* : See Max Weber, *The Rational and Sociological Foundations of Music*, trans. and ed. Don Martindale, Johannes Riedel, and Gertrude Neuwirth (London: Feffer & Simons, 1958). This is the English edition of *Die rationalen und soziologischen Grundlagen der Musik*, which was first published on its own in Munich in 1921 and subsequently as an appendix to the second edition of *Wirtschaft und Gesellschaft* (1925).

12, 29 *administered world*: Adorno's term for the growth of a faceless bureaucracy and the growing impersonality and anonymity that characterizes modern capitalist societies.

12, 38 *what fashion had strictly separated*: A quotation from Schiller's "Ode to Joy" in the final movement of Beethoven's Ninth Symphony.

Bourgeois Opera

15, 4 *since the time of the great economic crisis*: Adorno wrote this essay in 1955 and so must have had the inflation of the early 1920s in mind.

16, 11 *green wagon*: The vehicle used by troupes of itinerant actors in Germany in the sixteenth century.

16, 14 *why Goethe subjects it to irony*: The reference is to Goethe's *Faust, Part*

One, which begins with a conversation between the Director, the Poet, and a Clown. The following quotation contains the gist of the Director's views:

> "My toil,
> Indeed my pleasure, is to please the mob;
> And they're a tolerant public, I'll admit.
> The posts and board are up, and it's our job
> To give them a merry time of it.
> They're in their seats, relaxed, eyes opened wide,
> Waiting already to be mystified.
>
> "And let's have action above all!
> They come to look, they want a spectacle.
> Let many things unfold before their eyes,
> Let the crowd stare and be amazed, for then
> You'll win their hearts and that's to win the prize."

J. W. von Goethe, *Faust, Part One*, trans. David Luke (Oxford: Oxford University Press, 1987), pp. 4–5.

16, 22 *'Spieloper'*: A type of light comic opera in which musical numbers are interspersed with dialogue. Examples are Friedrich Flotow's *Martha* (1847) and Albert Lortzing's *Der Wildschütz* (1842).

18, 29 *In his study "Egoism and Freedom Movements"*: Max Horkheimer, "Egoismus and Freiheitsbewegung," *Zeitschrift für Sozialforschung* 5, no. 2 (1936): 161–234; published in English as "Egoism and Freedom Movements: On the Anthropology of the Bourgeois Era," in Horkheimer, *Between Philosophy and Social Science: Selected Early Writings*, trans. C. Frederick Hunter, Matthew S. Kramer, and John Torpey (Cambridge, Mass.: MIT Press, 1993), 49–110.

19, 21 *but he is not Hagen*: In *Das Nibelungenlied*, an epic poem written anonymously between 1200 and 1210, the plot focuses on the Burgundian court at Worms. Hagen is the evil genius who kills Siegfried and makes off with the Nibelungen treasure, which he throws into the Rhine. In the last part of the work, when the Burgundians go to Hungary, where Kriemhild, Siegfried's widow, has married Attila the Hun (Etzel), one of Hagen's boldest companions is Volker, a nobleman, who is finally killed in the course of the bloody battles between the Huns and the Burgundians.

19, 29 *literati*: See Hanns Gutman, "Literaten haben die Oper erfunden!" *Musikblätter des Anbruch* 2 (June 1929): 256–60. The Florentine circle is usually known as the Camerata. Its leaders were Giovanni Bardi and Jacopo Corsi, and it included such composers as Vincenzo Galilei and Jacopo Peri, whose *Dafne* of 1597 is often credited with being the first opera.

19, 34 *Monteverdi, Cavalli, Cesti*: Francesco Cavalli (1602–76) was a student of Claudio Monteverdi's and his successor as music director at St. Mark's Cathedral in Venice. He wrote more than forty operas. Antonio Cesti (1623–69), who was also associated with Venice, wrote eight operas.

19, 36 *Reinhard Keiser*: Keiser (1674–1739) was the most prolific composer of German baroque opera. Some seventeen works survive of more than sixty that he is known to have written.

20, 20 *already an "adaptation"*: Friedrich Kind's libretto for Carl Maria Weber's *Der Freischütz* was based on the *Gespensterbuch*, a collection of ghost stories published between 1810 and 1817 by Johann August Apel and Friedrich Laun (the pseudonym of Friedrich August Schulze).

20, 23 *"happy ending"*: In English in the original.

21, 23 *realm of the Mothers*: Adorno is referring to the Mothers in Goethe's *Faust, Part Two*, act 1, *Finstere Galerie*, ll. 6215ff. Swathed in mystery, they seem to be the ultimate symbols of Nature's creativity, the source of all primeval knowledge.

22, 27 *Thoas*: The barbarian king in Goethe's drama *Iphigenie auf Tauris*. In the play Thoas hopes to marry Iphigenie, the high priestess abandoned on the inhospitable shores of Tauris. He feels betrayed when she helps her fellow Greeks, Orestes and Pylades, to escape, though he finally relents and allows them to return to Greece in peace.

22, 30 *'La dame aux camélias' in Verdi's version*: The reference is to *La traviata*.

22, 37 *"everything is according to its kind"*: See *Siegfried*, act 2, scene 1. Having failed to persuade the dragon Fafner to give him the Ring, Alberich is advised by Wotan to turn to Mime, whose "kind" he will understand better.

24, 10 *the definition Lukács offered*: See Georg Lukács, *The Theory of the Novel: A Historico-Philosophical Essay on the Forms of Great Epic Literature*, trans. Anna Bostock (London: Merlin Press, 1971).

25, 15 *in the words of the forest bird*: In *Siegfried*, once Siegfried has been covered in the blood of the dragon Fafner, he is able to understand the Woodbird's song. The bird tells him first about the gold of the Nibelungs in Fafner's cave and then about the helmet of invisibility and, the greatest treasure of all, the ring (act 2, scene 2). Subsequently it warns him not to trust Mime, and after Mime's death it tells him about Brünnhilde (act 2, scene 3). The verses telling him about Brünnhilde contain the lines "Delighting in sorrow / I sing of love; / blissful I weave / my lay of woe: / lovers alone can know its meaning!" (*Wagner's "Ring of the Nibelung": A Companion*, trans. Stewart Spencer [London: Thames & Hudson, 1993], 253).

New Music, Interpretation, Audience

29, 11 *archenemy of new music*: The reference here is to Julius K. Korngold (1860–1945), the music critic of the *Neue Freie Presse* and father of the composer Erich Korngold.

33, 24 *Sanzogno*: Nino Sanzogno (1911–83) was a conductor and composer. After studying with Malipiero and Scherchen he played violin in the Guarnieri

Quartet. Subsequently he became conductor at La Fenice in Venice and at La Scala, Milan.

37, 2 *Third Program*: BBC Radio established the Third Program in September 1946. Explicitly designed to appeal to minority tastes, it became in effect the preserve of classical music aimed at a highbrow audience.

The Mastery of the Maestro

40, 2 *guest performance*: This was in the summer of 1929.

40, 20 *'Neue Sachlichkeit'*: Often translated as the New Sobriety or New Objectivity, this movement, chiefly in the plastic arts, emerged in the latter half of the 1920s, in reaction especially to expressionism. It is associated with Max Beckmann, Otto Dix, Christian Schad, Georg Grosz, but also with the Bauhaus. In music the relevant names are Paul Hindemith, Igor Stravinsky, Ernst Krenek, and Kurt Weill.

40, 23 *a Settembrini of music*: Settembrini appears in Thomas Mann's *The Magic Mountain*, where he embodies the beliefs of rational humanism and Enlightenment.

41, 1 *taking up the cudgels on behalf of rational humanity*: In 1933 Toscanini turned down an invitation to conduct *Parsifal* and *Die Meistersinger* in the Bayreuth Festival because of the Nazi discrimination against Jewish musicians.

41, 11 *streamlining*: In English in the original.

46, 6 *an extraordinarily lyrical eight-bar passage*: Adorno is most likely referring to mm. 87–94.—R.G.

46, 31 *a moment of unforgettable color is lifted out*: See m. 469.—R.G.

48, 29 *The exposition of Beethoven's Ninth contains a passage*: See mm. 132–37.—R.G.

50, 13 *Reinhardt-like*: Max Reinhardt (1873–1943) was the director of the Deutsches Theater in Berlin and the leading producer of his day. He was known for his innovative productions of contemporary dramatists like Gorky, Ibsen, Wedekind, and Hofmannsthal, introducing such devices as the revolving stage, in sharp contrast to the naturalistic productions of his predecessors. He was known also for the extreme demands he made on his actors. After a spell in Vienna he returned to Berlin, but left again in 1933. He emigrated to the United States in 1938 and died in New York.

51, 25 *Wagner's . . . essay on conducting*: Richard Wagner, "On Conducting," in *Collected Prose Works*, trans. William Ashton Ellis (New York: Broude Bros., 1966), 5:289–364.

52, 16 *Riehl*: Wilhelm Riehl (1823–97) was a journalist, politician, and finally a professor of politics in Munich (1854–92). As a writer he made his name as a cultural historian with such works as *Die Naturgeschichte des Volkes* (The natural history of the nation), of which *Die bürgerliche Gesellschaft* (Civil society) and *Die Familie* (The family) were published separately in the 1850s. He was conservative in outlook and blind to the approaching problems of industrial society, but provided vivid accounts of the society of his day, as well as ideas that stimulated a wide variety of thinkers and sociologists of the next generation.

The Prehistory of Serial Music

55, 13 *certificate of its ancestry*: An allusion to the Nazi certificates of racial purity.

57, 32 *sword-forging scene*: See *Siegfried*, act 1, scene 3.

60, 20 '*Style and Idea*': *Style and Idea*, ed. Leonard Stein (London: Faber, 1975).

62, 37 *the George songs*: Schoenberg set poems from Stefan George's *Das Buch der hängenden Gärten* (The book of the hanging gardens) in op. 15.

63, 3 *Schoenberg essay*: Anton Webern, "Schönbergs Musik," in *Arnold Schönberg*, ed. Karl Linke (Munich: Piper, 1912), 22–48.

66, 11 "*three-times-seven melodramas*": *Pierrot lunaire*, op. 21, is subtitled "Mélodrames: Trois fois sept poèmes de Albert Giraud."

66, 27 *Maeterlinck's 'Herzgewächse'*: The title of the poem on which *Herzgewächse* is based is "Feuillage du coeur." It comes from Maeterlinck's collection entitled *Serres chaudes*.

68, 17 *Leverkühn*: Adrian Leverkühn is the fictional composer and Faustian hero of Thomas Mann's novel *Dr. Faustus*. The musical adviser Mann chose for the novel was Adorno himself.

Alban Berg

70, 32 "*Monoritmica*": See *Lulu*, act 1, scene 2, m. 669, "Du hast eine halbe Million geheiratet." "Monoritmica" is a five-part rhythmic canon, the second half of which reverses the tempo sequence of the first half. According to Robert Morgan, there are only two strict retrogrades in *Lulu*, and the "Monoritmica" is not one of them; see David Gable and Robert P. Morgan, *Alban Berg: Historical and Analytical Perspectives* (Oxford: Clarendon Press, 1991), p. 124. According to Douglas Jarman, the "Monoritmica" makes clear the connection between the *Hauptrhythmus* and its retrograde; see *The Music of Alban Berg* (London: Faber & Faber, 1979), pp. 104–5.—R.G.

70, 37 '*Sing- und Spielbewegung*': A movement that grew out of the turn-of-the-century Youth Movement, which promoted a healthy, back-to-the land ideology, encouraging hiking and camping as a way of countering the unhealthy life of the new industrial towns. It was naturally associated with music and began with a cult of folk songs, often played on the guitar. Subsequently, educators like Fritz Jöde and Hermann Reichenbach urged the young to put their guitars aside and turn to Bach instead. They were also responsible for a revival of Bach's predecessors. After 1933 the movement was integrated into Nazi organizations. Attempts were made to revive it after 1945.

71, 22 *Brahms's words*: It is said that when Brahms was told that the finale of the First Symphony resembled the "Ode to Joy" he retorted that "any jackass may discover a resemblance to Beethoven's Ninth Symphony." See David Brodbeck, *Brahms: Symphony No. 1* (Cambridge: Cambridge University Press, 1997), 65; his source is Max Kalbeck, *Brahms*, 4 vols. in 8 (Berlin, 1915–21; repr. Tutzing, 1976), 3:109.

71, 30 *Willi Reich's biography*: Willi Reich, *The Life and Work of Alban Berg*, trans. C. Cardew (London: Thames & Hudson, 1965).

71, 32 *Altenberg*: Peter Altenberg (1859–1919) was a well-known figure of Viennese café life at the turn of the century. As a writer he specialized in short forms—essays, impressionist sketches, and autobiographical pieces. He was on friendly terms with some of the major figures of the period, such as Karl Kraus and Arthur Schnitzler, and is often thought to embody the aestheticist and bohemian values of the day.

71, 33 *Schreker*: Franz Schreker achieved instant success with his three-act opera *Der ferne Klang* (The distant sound), which was first performed in 1912. The hero of the opera, Fritz, sets out in search of the "distant sound," which will make him famous and enable him to win his beloved Grete and make her his bride. She runs away, though, and becomes a prostitute, whereupon Fritz spurns her. They experience an ecstatic reconciliation on his deathbed, and he recognizes that the "distant sound" he had looked for is in reality enduring love. Schreker was seen as a leading modernist at the time, but his career was destroyed by the Nazis. Interest in his works has been gradually reviving with some notable performances and recordings.

72, 9 *the contemporary climate of restoration*: Adorno is referring here to the conservative tendencies that gained ground in West Germany under Adenauer in the 1950s and 1960s. Related to that is Adorno's scathing attack on the influence of Martin Heidegger's brand of existentialism, which appeared in 1964 under the title *Jargon der Eigentlichkeit*; translated as *The Jargon of Authenticity* by Knut Tarnowski and Frederic Will (London: Routledge & Kegan Paul, 1973).

74, 7 *'durchbrochene Arbeit'*: often translated as "filigree open work," this term is frequently used by Adorno in these essays and generally. It refers to the division of voice function among different voices. According to the *Riemann Musik-Lexikon, Sachteil* (Mainz: B. Schott, 1967), 246 (s.v. "durchbrochene Arbeit"), it occurs in the late Beethoven, in Brahms, and in Mahler and culminates in the *Klangfarbenmelodie* of Schoenberg's op. 16, no. 3.—R.G.

76, 14 *"blessed in itself"*: The reference is to Eduard Mörike's poem "Auf eine Lampe" (On a lamp), which ends with the words "Ein Kunstgebild der echten

Art. Wer achtet sein? / Was aber schön ist, selig scheint es in ihm selbst" (A work of art of the genuine kind. Who heeds it? / But whatever is beautiful appears blessed in itself). This poem has been much commented on by philosophers, including Heidegger, as well as by Adorno. The last lines are often taken to be a rendering of Hegel's definition of beauty in the *Aesthetics*.

77, 5 *the Mahler whose marches* . . . : Presumably a reference to such songs as "Der Tambourg'sell" and "Zu Straßburg auf der Schanz" that Mahler set in the *Des Knaben Wunderhorn* collection and elsewhere.

79, 1 *Wedekind and Kraus*: The libretto of Berg's *Lulu* was a conflation of two plays by Frank Wedekind, *Erdgeist* (Earth spirit, 1895) and *Die Büchse der Pandora* (Pandora's box, 1904). Karl Kraus, the Viennese satirist, was a great defender of Wedekind, who was constantly in trouble with the censorship of the day. The essay Adorno refers to is "Die Büchse der Pandora," which appeared in Kraus's magazine *Die Fackel*, no. 182 (9 June 1905). At the play's premiere, Kraus read his essay aloud as a kind of preface and also acted the part of one of Lulu's more exotic clients in the last scenes, where she is reduced to prostitution.

The Orchestration of Berg's Early Songs

82, 15 *'Erwartung'*: Schoenberg's *Erwartung* (composed in 1912, but not performed until 1925) is based on a nightmarish scenario of infidelity, betrayal, and death, centering on the rather amorphous story of a woman going in search of her unfaithful lover and finding his bloodstained corpse. It may contain echoes of Schoenberg's own marriage: his wife Mathilde had left him for the painter Richard Gerstl, and when he persuaded Mathilde to return, Gerstl took his own life. A monodrama, the opera has just the one character and dramatizes her consciousness—her terrors and longings and incipient insanity. Musically, the work is a turning point for Schoenberg as he follows through the implications of his rejection of tonality.

84, 6 *Reger's 'Romantic Suite'*: Max Reger's *Eine Romantische Suite nach Eichendorff*, op. 125, of 1912.—R.G.

87, 25 *all adagiettos since Bizet*: The score, however, is not actually marked "Adagietto."—R.G.

87, 31 *"Wie Melodien"*: Brahms, "Wie Melodien zieht es mir leise durch den Sinn" [Like melodies there passes gently through my mind . . .], op. 105, no. 1.

Anton von Webern

91, 13 *after a stray bullet brutally destroyed* . . . : Webern was deliberately shot by an American soldier. However, his death was an accident in the sense that it occurred as the result of a tragic misunderstanding, perhaps one of mistaken identity.—R.G.

91, 17 *'Schoenberg est mort'*: The title of Boulez's article memorializing Schoenberg. First published in English, under the title "Schoenberg Is Dead," in *The Score* 6 (February 1952): 18–22, it is now available in Pierre Boulez, *Stocktakings from an Apprenticeship* (Oxford: Clarendon Press, 1991), 209–14.

94, 13 *"fury of disappearance"*: This is the literal meaning of the phrase *die Furie des Verschwindens*, which, usually translated as "the fury of destruction," is used by Hegel to describe the Reign of Terror during the French Revolution. See Hegel's *Phenomenology of Spirit*, trans. A. V. Miller (Oxford: Oxford University Press, 1977), p. 359.

95, 21 *Webern begins with the Passacaglia, op. 1*: Adorno ignores the fact, or perhaps was unaware, that Webern had written a number of pre-opus pieces of a fully conventional and unremarkable nature.—R.G.

96, 14 *the last song*: The last poem, "Kahl reckt der baum" (The bare tree stretches), evokes the image of a tree stripped of its leaves but stretching out its branches. Its hope of spring is used to justify the poet dreaming of an end to suffering. The poem ends with the thought that the spring will put an end to the winter ice. In Webern's setting this seems to have suggested to Adorno the spring sun rising up over the wintry landscape.

98, 21 *Heym and Trakl*: Georg Heym (1887–1912) and Georg Trakl (1887–1914) were expressionist poets whose writings in some ways anticipated the First World War. Heym drowned while skating on the River Havel in Berlin in 1912 and so had no direct experience of the war, but his poem "Der Krieg" (War) is considered one of the major prophetic statements of his generation. Trakl, an Austrian from Salzburg, served in the medical corps on the eastern front but was driven to distraction by the need to care for shell-shocked soldiers without adequate medical facilities. He died of an overdose of cocaine that may have been intentional. His unfinished poem "Grodek," after the battle of Grodek in Galicia in 1914, together with other poems, expresses a searing reaction to war that is very different from that of the English war poets of the day.

99, 18 *Cello Pieces of 1914*: These are the *Drei kleine Stücke für Violoncello und Klavier*, op. 11.

99, 31 *one from 'The Chinese Flute,' the other from Strindberg's 'Ghost Sonata'*: *The Chinese Flute* was a collection of poems translated from the Chinese by Hans Bethge. The poem set by Webern in op. 12 is the second poem, "An einem Abend, da die Blumen dufteten" (One evening when the scent of the flowers arose). He also set translations by Bethge in op. 13. The song based on Strindberg is "Schien mir's, als ich sah die Sonne" (I thought I saw the sun).

105, 20 *Of course, you don't ask him . . .* : My translation. For the whole text, see Franz Kafka, "The Cares of a Family Man," in *The Collected Short Stories of Franz Kafka*, trans. Willa Muir and Edwin Muir (Harmondsworth, Eng.: Penguin Books, 1988), p. 428.

Classicism, Romanticism, New Music

106, 3 *parodied by Schoenberg in the 'Satires'*: The reference is to *Three Satires* for chorus, op. 28 (1925).

106, 12 *Makart*: Hans Makart (1840–84) was an Austrian society painter who made his reputation with vast historical and allegorical canvases. His name became a byword for empty monumentality.

108, 35 *Borchardt*: Rudolf Borchardt (1877–1945) was a writer associated with the circle around Stefan George. He also had a close friendship with Hugo von Hofmannsthal. His writings cover a wide range of genres, but what survive today are mainly his translations—particularly of Dante—and his essays. He believed passionately in the educative value of artistic experience and campaigned eloquently to gain support for his opinions. Adorno is probably thinking of his 1929 essay "Die Aufgaben der Zeit gegenüber der Literatur" (Literature and its challenge to our age), in Borchardt, *Gesammelte Werke in Einzelbänden*, vol. 1: *Reden* (Stuttgart: Ernst Klett, n.d.), 345–96.

111, 32 *'Davidsbündler'*: The Davidsbund (Band of David) was a fictitious society of musicans invented by Schumann and based in part on himself and perhaps other real people. The name was intended to signal the war to be conducted against the Philistines. The *Bund* made its appearance in the 1830s in Schumann's articles on music in the *Neue Zeitschrift für Musik* in the form of supposed conversations between the friends, a literary form popularized in the writings of Jean Paul (Richter). The passionate defense of Beethoven was a cardinal tenet of the *Davidsbündler*.

113, 37 *from Tieck on . . .*: Adorno is referring here to some of the leading representatives of German literary Romanticism. Ludwig Tieck (1773–1853), a prolific writer, published many collections of long-forgotten folktales and poems. He also wrote original works in the folk manner, of which *Der blonde Eckbert* (Blond Eckbert) is perhaps the best known. He was responsible for publishing the works of contemporaries like Kleist. In 1797 he published the *Herzensergießungen eines kunstliebenden Klosterbruders* (Heartfelt outpourings of an art-loving monk) together with Wilhelm Heinrich Wackenroder, a boyhood friend who died the following year. This collection of essays was a major document of early Romanticism, establishing such themes as reverence for artistic genius, the importance of old German art (in an essay on Dürer), and the pivotal role of music in the fictional account of the life of the musician (*Tonkünstler*) Joseph Berglinger. Jean Paul was the pseudonym of Johann Paul Friedrich Richter (1763–1825), an extremely popular novelist in the tradition of fantastic and learned humor going back to Laurence Sterne.

116, 37 *Novalis*: Novalis was the pseudonym of Friedrich von Hardenberg (1772–1801), one of the leading poets of early German Romanticism. His essay

"Die Christenheit oder Europa" (Christendom or Europe), written in 1799 but not published until 1826, is the classic statement of the Romantic nostalgia for the Middle Ages as a time when Europe was united by a single religion.

The Function of Counterpoint in New Music

123, epigraph *Just as the speculative eye* . . . : Søren Kierkegaard, *Either/Or*, vol. 1, trans. Howard V. Hong and Edna H. Hong (Princeton: Princeton University Press, 1987), p. 122n. Kierkegaard argues that in order to understand Donna Elvira's aria "Ah, chi mi dice mai" in act 1 of *Don Giovanni*, we must be aware that Giovanni's "unparalleled irony" lurks concealed inside Elvira's "substantial passion." In other words, to understand her love-hate we must hear Giovanni's mockery, which inflames it, as part of her passion.

128, 11 *spectacle basses*: *Brillenbaß* was a derisive nickname for figures in eighths or sixteenths. See *Riemann Musiklexikon*, 11th ed., vol. 1 (Berlin, 1928), p. 231.—R.G.

128, 17 *. . . as an independent countersubject*: See the earlier, more detailed discussion in "The Prehistory of Serial Music," p. 62 in this volume.—R.G.

129, 35 *'Aufhebung'*: From *aufheben*, meaning (1) to annul, abolish, negate; (2) to preserve; (3) to raise to a higher level. For Hegel its multiple meanings encapsulate the essence of dialectic. A child, for example, may be regarded as the *Aufhebung* of its parents.

139, 6 *not a 'punctum contra punctum,' but a 'lucus a non lucendo'*: *Punctum contra punctum* means "note against note" and refers to things sharply opposed to each other. A passage in Quintilian reflects on the origins of words: "But are we also to admit the derivation of certain words from their opposites and accept *lucus a non lucendo* [a clearing from not being clear], since a grove is dark with shade, *ludus* in the sense of school as being so-called because it is quite the reverse of play . . . ?" (Quintilian, *Institutio oratoria*, trans. H. E. Butler, The Loeb Classical Library, [London: William Heinemann; New York: G. P. Putnam, 1921], 126–27). The point here is that the word *lucus*, a grove or clearing, means something "dark with shade," although it derives from *lucere*, to shine. Here, then, the idea enshrines a notion of counterpoint in which one thing arises from its opposite.

143, 5 *A good man, in his dark bewildered stress* . . . : A quotation from Goethe's *Faust, Part One*, Prologue in Heaven, where God is describing Faust himself. See J. W. von Goethe, *Faust, Part One*, trans. David Luke (Oxford: Oxford University Press, 1987), p. 12.

Criteria of New Music

146, 6 *the middle Scheler*: Max Scheler (1874–1928) was a moral philosopher who established a system of ethics based on the possibility of intuiting values.

This enabled him to criticize Kantian formalism as well as Marx's materialism and Nietzsche's relativism. On the basis of the traditional dualism of mind and body, he established an ethics consisting of ideal and real factors. The latter—which include the need to satisfy the drive for reproduction, food, and power—are given the task of selecting those elements of the timeless, ideal factors that can be incorporated into given societies. After a Roman Catholic phase (which is what Adorno seems to be thinking of) Scheler turned in around 1921, the start of his last period, to a personal metaphysics of a pantheistic kind; this is what Adorno seems to have had in mind.

147, 8 *up to date*: In English in the original.

148, 14 *"necessity"*: A notion stemming from Kant's distinction between the agreeable and the beautiful (*Critique of Judgment*, §§1–22). While one person may find a violet color "soft and lovely," another will think it "dull and jaded." This is the realm of the agreeable: "If it [e.g., a building] merely pleases him, he must not call it beautiful." To call a thing beautiful, however, is to demand that everyone find it so. It is in this demand that the necessity lies. The demand is the expression of a "universal voice"; it cannot be rooted in a concept ("for then it would be the good"), but in what Kant calls a "common sense."

148, 30 *Goethe's chapel*: The reference here is unclear, although it suggests a reverential attitude. It may allude to the scene in Goethe's novel *Elective Affinities* (Harmondsworth, Eng.: Penguin Books, 1982), which, concerned with marriage and adultery, is set in a country estate belonging to Eduard and Charlotte. Eduard falls in love with his niece Ottilie, who returns his love but who is also morally disturbed by the relationship. At one point (book 2, chap. 3) she discovers a chapel on the estate that has fallen into disrepair and lovingly undertakes its restoration.

149, 26 *"cultural lag"*: In English in the original.

150, 4 *laid waste by the ethos of community*: Adorno is thinking here of the Nazi racial community, and perhaps also of the collective values of the recently founded German Democratic Republic.

150, 15 *'Der neue Klassizismus'*: "The New Classicism" is one of the *Three Satires*, op. 28.

150, 21 *Croce's aesthetic nominalism*: Benedetto Croce (1866–1952) was the leading aesthetic philosopher of modern Italy, though his influence extended well beyond the frontiers of his native land. He maintained that aesthetic knowledge was quite distinct from the forms of logical and practical thought created by the intellect. Art for him was an independent mode of knowledge based on "intuition," in which the artist gives direct, unique expression to his own individual insight. The task of the critic is to empathize with the individual work. According to Croce, divisions into literature and the visual arts, or, within literature, into novels, plays, and poems, were artificial and arbitrary—mere names that contained no real substance. Hence the "nominalist" label.

153, 16 *"Historical consciousness of the finiteness of every historical phenomenon . . .* : A quotation from Wilhelm Dilthey, *Der Aufbau der geschichtlichen Welt in den Geisteswissenschaften* (1910); my translation. Dilthey (1833–1911) was a philosopher known for his attempt to provide a rationale for the arts and historical sciences (*Geisteswissenschaften*) that would be valid in its own right, but distinct from the natural sciences. It was based on the idea of sympathetic understanding as opposed to conceptual rigor. Max Weber took up this distinction between *Verstehen* and *Begreifen* and developed it further.

157, 11 *pseudo-ten-part stretto*: Adorno may have been thinking here of mm. 95–100, which contain at least ten stretto entries of the first and third subjects, including suggestions of the second subject in the continuations, so that individual voices are assigned multiple thematic functions that overlap and intersect.—R.G.

163, 12 *ruse of reason*: *Die List der Vernunft*, the ruse or cunning of reason, is the phrase Hegel uses in *The Philosophy of History* to describe the process by which the goal of reason is achieved through the efforts and sacrifices of individuals who, however, never reach their own goals. See G. W. F. Hegel, *Vorlesungen über die Philosophie der Geschichte* (Frankfurt am Main: Suhrkamp, 1970), 12:49.

164, 38 *'Verlust der Mitte'*: Adorno often refers to the Austrian art historian Hans Sedlmayr, whose *Verlust der Mitte* (Loss of the center, 1948) bemoaned the contemporary decline in values.

168, 4 *Klages*: Ludwig Klages (1872–1956) was a philosopher and psychologist in the tradition of German irrationalism. In his main work, *Der Geist als Widersacher der Seele* (Mind as the enemy of the soul), he defended the idea that the original unity of body and soul was disrupted by the intervention of the intellect. Ideas like this formed the basis of his work on handwriting, to which he owes much of his reputation. He had a considerable influence on the Nazis, but also, and for different reasons, on Walter Benjamin.

170, 12 *'Verfremdung'*: A term taken from Brechtian theory. It was formerly translated as "alienation," but this overlapped too much with the Marxist concept of *Entfremdung*, used to describe the capitalist exploitation of the worker and his consequent alienation from himself. Brecht's term is now normally rendered as "estrangement" or "distancing," connoting the use of artistic devices to prevent empathy.

171, 26 *character*: All the technical components—melody, rhythm, orchestration, register, density, tempo, meter—combine to give a span of music a "character" (*Charakter*); this might be identified as a recognized topic, such as a march character, within the given musical idiom, or it could be the stamp of a few works or a particular work.—R.G.

171, 37 *"It all happened long ago"*: Cf. the reference to the second *Kreisleriana* piece above.—R.G.

172, 20 *"gimmick"*: In English in the original.

172, 25 *pattern*: In English in the original.

174, 23 *Beckmesser's denunciation*: Sixtus Beckmesser is the carping critic in *Die Meistersinger*, modeled on the contemporary critic Eduard Hanslick. His head is so full of rules for writing songs that he is unable to write one himself, or even to sing one that he has obtained in an underhanded way. His pedantry and envy of true creativity lead him to denounce the trial song produced by Walther von Stolzing, a young Franconian knight seeking to gain entry to the mastersingers' guild. Throughout the opera Beckmesser's sterility is contrasted with the creativity of both Walther and the down-to-earth popular art of Hans Sachs.

194, 30 *Bold, overhanging, and, as it were, threatening rocks*: Immanuel Kant, *The Critique of Judgment*, trans. James Creed Meredith (Oxford: Oxford University Press, 1973), part I, pp. 110–11.

Music and Technique

197, 1 *"technique"*: The Greek word *technē* means "art" or "skill." In this essay, and more generally in the volume as a whole, Adorno uses the word *Technik* to mean "technique." However, he frequently plays on the fact that it also means "technology" and sometimes uses its derivatives *technisch* and *technologisch* more or less interchangeably.

198, 7 *the saying about the mind that builds the body for itself*: "Es ist der Geist, der stets den Körper baut" (It is the mind that always builds the body) is a line from Friedrich Schiller, *Wallensteins Tod*, act 3, scene 13.

204, 22 *the "psychology of sound"*: The question of Kurth's "psychological aesthetics" is discussed by Lee A. Rothfarb in his introduction to his edition and translation of Ernst Kurth, *Selected Writings* (Cambridge: Cambridge University Press, 1990), 19.

205, 7 *'Summum ius summa iniuria'*: "The greatest justice is [often] the greatest injustice" (Cicero, *De officiis* 1.10.33).

211, 18 *Nietzsche's "dancing star"*: "I tell you: one must have chaos in one, to give birth to a dancing star. I tell you: you still have chaos in you" (Friedrich Nietzsche, *Thus Spoke Zarathustra*, trans. R. J. Hollingdale [Harmondsworth, Eng.: Penguin Books, 1978], 46). The quotation comes in the passage contrasting the Superman with the Ultimate Man, who is incapable of transcendence: "'What is love? What is creation? What is longing? What is a star?' thus asks the Ultimate Man and blinks." But men with chaos in them, and a dancing star, will be able to go beyond that myopic state.

MERIDIAN

Crossing Aesthetics

Alexander García Düttmann, *At Odds with AIDS: Thinking and Talking About a Virus*

Maurice Blanchot, *Friendship*

Jean-Luc Nancy, *The Muses*

Massimo Cacciari, *Posthumous People: Vienna at the Turning Point*

David E. Wellbery, *The Specular Moment: Goethe's Early Lyric and the Beginnings of Romanticism*

Edmond Jabès, *The Little Book of Unsuspected Subversion*

Hans-Jost Frey, *Studies in Poetic Discourse: Mallarmé, Baudelaire, Rimbaud, Hölderlin*

Pierre Bourdieu, *The Rules of Art: Genesis and Structure of the Literary Field*

Nicolas Abraham, *Rhythms: On the Work, Translation, and Psychoanalysis*

Jacques Derrida, *On the Name*

David Wills, *Prosthesis*

Maurice Blanchot, *The Work of Fire*

Jacques Derrida, *Points ... : Interviews, 1974–1994*

J. Hillis Miller, *Topographies*

Philippe Lacoue-Labarthe, *Musica Ficta (Figures of Wagner)*

Jacques Derrida, *Aporias*

Emmanuel Levinas, *Outside the Subject*

Jean-François Lyotard, *Lessons on the Analytic of the Sublime*

Peter Fenves, *"Chatter": Language and History in Kierkegaard*

Jean-Luc Nancy, *The Experience of Freedom*

Jean-Joseph Goux, *Oedipus, Philosopher*

Haun Saussy, *The Problem of a Chinese Aesthetic*

Jean-Luc Nancy, *The Birth to Presence*

Library of Congress Cataloging-in-Publication Data

Adorno, Theodor W.
[Klangfiguren. English]
Sound figures / Theodor W. Adorno ;
translated by Rodney Livingstone.
p.   cm. — (Meridian)
Translation of: Klangfiguren.
ISBN 0-8047-3557-3 (cloth)
ISBN 0-8047-3558-1 (pbk.)
1. Music—20th century—History and criticism.
I. Title   II. Series: Meridian (Stanford, Calif.)
ML60.A26513   1999
780—dc21
98-33460
CIP
MN

Original printing 1999
Last figure below indicates year of this printing:
08   07   06   05   04   03   02   01   00   99